24 Hours with
24 Lawyers

*Profiles of Traditional and
Non-Traditional Careers*

Jasper Kim

ASPATORE

ISBN 978-0-314-27631-5

For corrections, updates, comments, or any other inquiries, please e-mail
TLR.AspatoreEditorial@thomson.com.

First Printing, 2011
10 9 8 7 6 5 4 3 2 1

Mat #41164947

ASPATORE

Aspatore Books, a Thomson Reuters business, exclusively publishes C-Level executives (CEO, CFO, CTO, CMO, Partner) from the world's most respected companies and law firms. C-Level Business Intelligence™, as conceptualized and developed by Aspatore Books, provides professionals of all levels with proven business intelligence from industry insiders—direct and unfiltered insight from those who know it best—as opposed to third-party accounts offered by unknown authors and analysts. Aspatore Books is committed to publishing an innovative line of business and legal books, those which lay forth principles and offer insights that, when employed, can have a direct financial impact on the reader's business objectives, whatever they may be. In essence, Aspatore publishes critical tools for all business professionals.

Acknowledgements

I would first like to thank all those who contributed their twenty-four-hour career profile for this book. Each was truly dedicated, enthusiastic, and willing to contribute to a cause greater than all of us in terms of the legal education process and what it means from a career standpoint. Each contributor's submitted profile was also a pro bono, voluntary effort, which is truly admirable, given each of their extremely hectic and demanding work and family schedules (as you will see in specific detail from their twenty-four-hour career profiles). Without their selfless efforts and informative insights related to their respective professions, this book would not have been possible. I also appreciate the efforts of Yulan Kim and Sung Yeon Michelle Lee for their research contributions. I would also like to sincerely thank Sarah Gagnon, formerly of Aspatore Books, for seeing the value in this book project when I originally submitted the idea to her as well as Kristen Lindeman of Aspatore Books for her truly wonderful editing contributions, which made this very good book that much better. Without their support, this book would not be possible. Last, but not least, I would like to thank my loving and supportive family who have always supported me throughout my years (and various career tracks), including my wonderful late mother (June), wife (Jihye), and sister (Sonya)—I will always love each of you.

CONTENTS

Introduction

The Most Important Twenty-Four Hours You May Ever Experience

So you're thinking of law school or switching legal careers?

Then spend twenty-four hours with twenty-four lawyers through this innovative book—*24 Hours with 24 Lawyers: Profiles of Traditional and Non-Traditional Careers*—arguably the most important twenty-four hours you may ever experience.

Whether you want to be a corporate lawyer or musician after law school, this book gives you an innovatively structured, fast-paced, real-time, hour-by-hour "real world" perspective into the lives of twenty-four professionals working in one of twenty-four legal career "profiles" during a typical twenty-four hour day. The twenty-four-hour format for each of the career profiles is specifically meant to resemble the schedule of a working professional's PDA (or other daily schedule planner) in terms of providing hour-by-hour, minute-by-minute event scenarios, ranging from professional meetings to after-hour sporting events with friends. Each profile covers both the professional as well as personal aspects of each person's specific career field—from the time the person gets up in the morning (to prepare for their workday) to the time that person goes to bed—with meetings, document review, conference calls, and even family or other social responsibilities.

About half of the professionals profiled in this book are lawyers actually practicing law in "traditional" legal careers (namely, working in law firms or as in-house counsel), with the remaining profiled professionals working in a career outside the traditional field of law in "non-traditional careers" (namely, those not working in law firms or as in-house counsel). Traditional legal areas include career profiles as a corporate lawyer, litigator, entertainment and media lawyer, intellectual property (IP) attorney, and technology attorney, to name a few. Non-traditional areas include career profiles as a musician, investment banker, lobbyist, academic, sports news reporter, venture capitalist, UN officer, and elected politician, just to name a few. This book also sweeps across public and private sector career profiles, in both domestic and international arenas, covering civilian, criminal, and military-related matters, in the professional working capacities of law firm attorney, in-house legal counsel, and everything in between.

Despite the amazing array of twenty-four career profiles in this book, the common thread among all profiled professionals—in both traditional and non-traditional career fields—is that they are all law school graduates.

Geographically, this book covers professional career profiles of working individuals in four separate continents—the United States, Europe, Asia, and Australia. Specific cities in which the contributors have based their profiles from include Los Angeles, London, Sydney, Hong Kong, Seoul, Jersey City, Chicago, Dallas, and Salt Lake City, just to name a few.

In terms of academic diversity, although the vast majority of those profiled in this book are US law school graduates (from nearly two dozen different law schools), other law schools are represented, such as from the UK, Australia, Thailand, and Japan. Both private and public universities are represented, from the Ivy League to smaller state schools, in states from the East Coast, Midwest, South, and West Coast, as well as from law schools beyond the United States of various rankings and perceived reputation. This is done purposely to give you a sense of the sheer diversity of law schools that exist and what can be accomplished after attending such institutions.

There are now more than 200 law schools in the United States alone—where the actual number of aspiring law students is thought to outnumber the total number of practitioner attorneys—as well as those thinking of entering law school or considering a post-law school career shift. With that in mind, *24 Hours with 24 Lawyers* will provide keen, unique, and invaluable insight as to what being, for example, a corporate lawyer or litigator really means in terms of more than just the glossy brochures, special one-hour guest lectures, career workshops, or highly edited website descriptions. More importantly and realistically, the reader will see the everyday typical work and lifestyle schedule demands that may very well be expected on a consistent and reoccurring basis day in and day out.

If you're thinking of going to law school, are currently in law school, or are a law school graduate interested or thinking of making a career shift, having access to the professional and personal insights of the twenty-four contributors in this book will prove invaluable for you in terms of developing and strategizing your current and future career aspirations.

For those contemplating law school and before spending hundreds of thousands of dollars—not to mention several often-prime years filled with hard work, sweat, and tears dedicated to law school and a possible legal career—you can first find out what being a lawyer may actually entail through a "sneak peek" and "fly on the wall" twenty-four hour schedule approach that this book innovatively provides. It's like being able to press a career "fast forward" button to see what a particular legal career track may look like for you in the future.

Law school trains people to "think like a lawyer." As part of this, most if not all law schools provide a wide array of courses, from broad to more specific, to train students to reach this objective. But relatively few courses are offered related to law as a career. It's almost as if once you learned what thinking like a lawyer was all about, finding a career that fits you as a person in which to leverage your legal thinking was somehow the easy, self-intuitive part. For me, as I am sure it is with many others, this was far from the truth. In part, this is because, for many, the legal world beyond law school is often fuzzy and unclear, and hard to get a clear sense of apart from, say, intermittent dialogue with mentors and career counselors.

As a law student, I heard many success stories of graduates who went on to became law firm partners, highly paid investment bankers and other leading figures in various fields. But where did they work, how did they get there, and what do they do every day? This I wasn't quite sure of as a law student. After law school, I then discovered—as with many if not most other careers—is that the "inside" view of a particular career can sometimes clash with its "outside" perception. This gave me pause to think, "If only there was a book or resource that could have let me know just how different the inside and outside world in different careers could be in a very specific way by a wide array of people." If others had this type of career "insider information," I thought that this could certainly be very useful to a very large group of people.

When students tell me of their interest in applying to law school, I then often ask, "So what do you imagine your life being after law school?" Sometimes this question elicits some thoughtful silence with a reply like, "I'm not sure, maybe work for the UN or a big law firm, I guess." Other times, it evokes replies like "I want to be a corporate lawyer because it seems powerful and important," or "I want to argue cases in a packed courtroom just like those lawyer shows on TV." Then I ask, "So do you know what this exactly may entail on a day to day basis from the time you get up to the time you go back home and sleep?" Often the reply to this question is met with some thoughtful silence with vague notions of the typical life of a lawyer in characters as personified in TV shows like *Ally McBeal, Boston Legal* and *LA Law* (all very good shows in their own right, please don't get me wrong). However, the portrayals in mass media may not give you a fully clear and accurate picture of the legal career field being represented.

Even assuming that portrayals of lawyers in these types of popular TV shows are in part correct, there are many parts of being a lawyer that is not portrayed in the mass media or entertaining TV shows. So where does one get details and information about this, short of actually tagging along with all sorts of lawyers during their typical twenty-four-hour day? Often, law students enter into summer internships to get a sense of just one specific legal career field over the course of a few, short weeks. This made me realize that I had the unique opportunity to do something about this gap by writing this book. The next step was to decide how to profile such a wide array of lawyers and non-lawyers, with the commonality that each profiled professional would be a law school graduate.

Ultimately, I chose to tell the story of twenty-four lawyers in twenty-four hours based on the unique but honest lens of each individual's specific daily schedule. I had two reasons for taking this approach. First, it provides an accurate and efficient portrayal of what each person does in a typical twenty-four-hour day. Second, it provides a relatively easy and reader-friendly way for each working professional to tell his or her story within the context of his or her day. I also thought this approach would fit the current trend toward highly condensed information in short, bite-sized pieces told in a very personal way relating to twenty-four separate working professionals.

Because this book covers so many different professionals in such a wide variety of career fields, you may find that differences in substance and writing style may exist from profile to profile (including the use of more formal or colloquial writing, narrative style and even profile word length). Unlike a book with a single author or editor, such differences should be viewed as a good thing because—however slight or not—they directly reflect the diversity of the various profiled working professionals and their respective writing styles (which, in turn, reflects the diversity of industries, geographic regions, cultures, and ages profiled in this book). Personally, I believe that it's important to preserve and even highlight such differences since each professional's substance and writing style not only reflects that person's individualistic approach, but often may also reflect the working environment in which each profiled individual is working within, day in and day out. So this should provide another invaluable signal as to whether a particular career field may or may not be a good fit for you.

While other law career strategy books exist, from the more general sole author structure, to the slightly more innovative, such books often tend to fall into one of the more predictable "Top 10," "Careers 101," or "Nontraditional Careers" genre often told from one single, individual person's perspective.

In stark contrast, this book is very different—with its innovative, user-friendly, fast-paced, real-life profiles of both traditional and nontraditional career options (to provide a "360 degree" perspective) for both prospective and former law school graduates—written in a style that is best suited for the twenty-first century generation with writing that is fast, on-demand, and to-the-point.

This book, *24 Hours with 24 Lawyers: Profiles of Traditional and Non-Traditional Careers* is also aimed to a very wide audience—from those thinking of law school to those interested in possibly making the switch from a traditional legal career to a nontraditional alternative career field, or vice versa. Based on this, any person who holds a law degree, or even is merely considering law school as a possible future option, will find this book informative, user-friendly, honest, and at times, hopefully, inspiring.

Although twenty-four career fields represent an extremely broad array of potential career options following one's law school experience, it in no way encapsulates all possible career options. Because a law degree, especially a US graduate law degree, is often viewed as a broad degree that provides extensive skill sets, dozens if not hundreds of potential career options may exist for law school graduates. For this reason, this book should be viewed as a means to take a "fast forward" or "sneak peek" into the lives of some, but not all, career fields following law school.

The individuals who graciously contributed to this book have submitted their profiles based on their respective individual views and perspectives, and not necessarily on behalf of their employer and/or supervising institution. The names, places, scenarios and other related details within each career profile have also been changed for confidentiality. Having said all this, I sincerely hope this book helps you or those you know to navigate successfully through the many career options presented to you after law school.

To conclude, a span of twenty-four hours can often lead to dramatic change.

Whether you are seeking this type of change—or are simply curious what other people in other fields are doing with their law degrees—I truly hope *24 Hours with 24 Lawyers: Profiles of Traditional and Non-Traditional Careers* can be both meaningful and helpful to you and those you know in terms of future traditional and nontraditional career options.

Jasper Kim

1

Profile 1
Kristina: Corporate Transactional Lawyer

Executive Summary

Name:	Kristina
Type of lawyer:	Corporate Transactional Lawyer
Location:	Hong Kong (China)

For people who don't mind frequent and often last-minute business trips and overseas travel for work (even though it may sometimes mean catching only a few short hours of sleep on a red eye flight beforehand) and prefer or can cope with an around-the-clock, non-stop schedule, working for an overseas branch of a large US-based corporate law firm might be a good fit for you. Like Kristina, a considerable number of US lawyers live this career lifestyle. By working in Hong Kong, a lawyer can also gain access to the emerging markets and clientele in Asia, including China (now the world's second largest global economy behind the United States). As more and more American law firms are sending their lawyers to overseas offices, being bilingual is now seen as a critical skill set. As Kristina points out, being bicultural (as well as bilingual) doesn't hurt either since this implies cultural familiarity to the region. Early morning conference calls and late night updates due to time differences are, of course, also frequent. Being a corporate transactional lawyer also means that you must be business savvy in addition to the core legal skill sets such as drafting contracts, disclosure documents, and counseling clients on related issues. Kristina manages to pull all this off with great care and diligence, in which her career as a corporate transactional lawyer, for the Hong Kong branch of a large New York-based law firm, requires working with various clients around the world, around the clock.

Profile

Career Field:	Large Law Firm/International Capital Markets
Current Position:	Senior Associate
Institution:	US-based Global Law Firm
Location:	Hong Kong, China Branch (Main Office: New York)
Education:	JD, University of California at Los Angeles, School of Law
	BA, University of California at Los Angeles (*summa cum laude*)
Licensed (Y/N):	Yes
Jurisdictions:	New York

Schedule

7:00 a.m.	Up and Running
8:20 a.m.	Browse through Media/First Cup of Coffee
8:45 a.m.	Get Dressed/Get on a Taxi to Work
9:00 a.m.	Arrive at the Firm
9:30 a.m.	Attend Internal Biweekly Meeting
10:00 a.m.	Back at Desk/Delegate Tasks
10:30 a.m.	Answer Urgent (as always!) Question from a Client (re: NDR)
10:45 a.m.	Receive Briefings on Tasks/Diligence Issues/To-Do List
11:00 a.m.	Review and Comment on Offering Circular
12:30 p.m.	Lunch Meeting with a Client
1:45 p.m.	Walk Back to the Office
2:00 p.m.	Conference Call with Clients (re: underwriting agreement)
2:30 p.m.	Call Opposing Counsel (re: negotiate underwriting agreement)
3:00 p.m.	Write E-Mail Summarizing the Call with Opposing Counsel
3:25 p.m.	Call with Auditors (re: comfort letter issues)
3:45 p.m.	Return Call to the Client (re: edits on offering circular)
4:00 p.m.	Call London Stock Exchange Representative (re: listing rules)

4:30 p.m.	Attend Weekly Conference Call with Working Group (re: IPO)
5:30 p.m.	Meet with Partner-In-Charge for a Briefing
6:00 p.m.	Cancel Attending Tomorrow's Dinner Event
6:15 p.m.	Review of Publicly Available Corporate Material/Prepare for Meeting
7:30 p.m.	Attend Hip Hop Dance Class
9:00 p.m.	Fill in Diary/Organize Files
9:30 p.m.	Call with New York Office (re: OFAC issues with specialist)
10:30 p.m.	Pack Up/Head to Airport
11:00 p.m.	Check in/Sit Back, Relax, and Prepare for Takeoff
5:00 a.m.	Land at Airport (4:00 a.m. Hong Kong time)
6:00 a.m.	Arrive at Hotel (5:00 a.m. Hong Kong time)
7:00 a.m.	Wake-Up Call (6:00 a.m. Hong Kong time)

24-Hour Schedule

7:00 a.m.   *Up and Running*

I get up and check my BlackBerry for urgent messages. When no messages require an immediate response, I grab my running gear and go for a run on a hiking trail near my home, which is part of the eight distinct stages of the "Hong Kong Trail." You'd be surprised (as I was) to learn that Hong Kong (HK) has some superb hiking trails, including a fifty km (kilometer) trail on HK island itself, which passes through several country parks showcasing the beauty (both rural and urban) of the island. The first stage begins up at The Peak, a famous tourist attraction. I'm proud to say I've finished hiking the fifty km HK Trail—not in one go, you understand, although some dedicated folks do much harder trails (e.g., the one hundred km MacLehose Trail) in one fell swoop each November.

8:20 a.m.   *Browse through Media/First Cup of Coffee*

Once back from running, I take a quick shower, turn on Bloomberg TV, and scan through some of my preferred websites for news while drinking my first cup of coffee of the day (out of many to come during the course of the day).

8:45 a.m.   *Get Dressed/Get on a Taxi to Work*

I'm not a trial lawyer (in fact, I've never been to a court other than traffic court and for jury duty). So I don't wear a suit to work unless there is a client meeting. Today I have a lunch meeting with a client. I pick out a gray suit with a slight shimmer (making it a bit less drab) and a white shirt. With appropriate jewelry, watch, shoes, and purse in place, I walk out the door of my twenty-sixth floor flat in the Midlevels and hail a taxi for the ten-minute ride to the office in the center of the city (appropriately named Central—the main business and financial district of HK).

9:00 a.m.   *Arrive at the Firm*

Today is Monday. Before 9:30 a.m., I have to go through my e-mail because the day kicks off with our biweekly Hong Kong–Beijing offices meeting. As I read through my e-mail, I reply as appropriate, flag some of them for follow-up, and organize them by moving e-mails from the inbox into client-related folders (to help locate relevant messages quickly). I also listen to my voicemail messages left on the answering machine of my office phone, although the preferred method of correspondence nowadays is e-mail or mobile phone (as a result, the number of voicemails I get has been decreasing). I return a few phone calls that are the most important to tackle and must be handled immediately and head over to the boardroom.

9:30 a.m.   *Attend Internal Biweekly Meeting*

The biweekly meeting is held in our boardroom and our Beijing office is connected by teleconference. I grab a bagel and coffee (number two of the day) and sit down as we discuss our current transaction files and give updates by practice groups. We also run over the latest issues and news in the industry. That way, we share our knowledge. As the summer season has come around, we also discuss the summer associates program in the Asia branch offices. We have about half a dozen "summers" rotating through the HK office this year, two of whom are due to start in a week. I make a mental note to assign some meaningful work for the summers and to participate in a few summer events.

10:00 a.m.   Back at Desk/Delegate Tasks

Back at my desk, I assess which concrete tasks arise from my remaining e-mail messages and decide how to distribute the work among my team. On most days, as a corporate transactional lawyer, I come into the office knowing what the day ahead holds and am prepared to attend scheduled conference calls or meetings and delegate tasks—such as legal research or the preparation of legal documents—to the appropriate team members (mid-level associates, junior associates, summer associates, and paralegals). I select the most urgent items and although I am quite up-to-date on most (if not all) of the issues in a particular deal, I call the mid-level and junior associates who have been working on the matters in question into my office to discuss and to confirm the responses to be given before sending them out to the client.

10:30 a.m.   Answer Urgent (as always!) Question from a Client (re: NDR)

Just as I was wrapping up responding to my accrued e-mail (before they pile up again), my cell phone buzzes. An investment bank client advising an issuer in the Korean financial industry on one of the pending transactions wants to know if they can do a "non-deal roadshow" (NDR) to meet some potential investors to test the market prior to the actual deal-related roadshow. An NDR involves meetings or conferences put together for the purpose of meeting potential investors without a specific offering contemplated. In contrast, a deal-related roadshow is conducted after the formal launch of the offering based on the finalized preliminary offering document distributed to the investors. I ask my client a few follow-up questions, and explain the risks relating to an NDR ahead of an offering in the pipeline. From the US securities law perspective, during the period where an offering relying on an exemption from registration with the US Securities and Exchange Commission (SEC) is contemplated (i.e., Rule 144A/Regulation S offering), there should be no "directed selling efforts," which is defined as "any activity undertaken for the purpose of, or that could reasonably be expected to have the effect of, conditioning the market in the United States," as well as no "general solicitation" in the United

States. I explain to the client that it is generally not advisable to do an NDR when there is an offering contemplated in the near future, but if certain safeguards are in place and guidelines are complied with, the risks of undue publicity and potential liability can be minimized. I go through the guidelines with the client, and promise to put them in writing in an e-mail later on.

10:45 a.m.   Receive Briefings on Tasks/Diligence Issues/To-Do List

I receive briefings from the junior and mid-level associates to whom work was previously delegated, and discuss any diligence issues and to-do lists for the day. An important part of our role as international transactional counsel is maintaining control over all key aspects and major developments regarding the deal. The client, whether we are representing the issuer or the underwriter, does not want to have to communicate with a large number of lawyers and other parties to ascertain how each aspect of the transaction is progressing. Accordingly, we (as external legal counsel) must "quarterback" all aspects of the transaction and establish a mechanism whereby all material information resulting from the due diligence process flows to the relevant parties quickly and efficiently. We also closely collaborate with various parties to ensure efficient, cost-effective communication and execution of transaction documents.

In the briefing, a junior associate points out a potential covenant compliance issue relating to financing documents discovered during the course of his documentary due diligence review in connection with an offering by a Korean issuer. He indicates the document in question is in Korean language governed under Korean law. We decide to schedule a conference call with the relevant local counsel to ensure they are up to speed and able to clear the issue prior to the offering. All of the associates in our Korea practice team are either native or fluent speakers of Korean. Language proficiency will very often become an issue in multi-jurisdictional transactions since it is not uncommon for various documents in such transactions to be in other languages in addition to or in place of English. Having lawyers in the office who possess the required language skills is a definite plus if not a must—especially for our firm's Korea practice—in order to maintain and strengthen our market leadership in the region.

We also go through the to-do lists of the day and the week. This includes, among others, drafting of the offering circular, reviewing or drafting the purchase agreement, chasing auditors for comfort letter related matters, checking with listing counsels if relevant (e.g., Singapore counsel in the case of listing of the securities on the Singapore stock exchange), reviewing or drafting the indenture in the case of a bond offering, preparing closing documents when a deal is near pricing or has priced, and so on.

11:00 a.m.   *Review and Comment on Offering Circular*

I review a draft of the offering circular (also known as offering memorandum, prospectus, or listing particulars) that a mid-level associate has prepared for our issuer client in the Korean life insurance business. Preparing the offering circular requires thorough investigation into the business, results of operations, and financial condition of the issuer. In the case of issuers new to the market, the due diligence procedure is more elaborate and the drafting of the offering circular more time-consuming. This is one my favorite parts of the practice—learning about the issuer, its business, and the industry through preparing the offering circular. This is our first insurance company deal out of Korea, as only recently the Korean life insurance industry was deregulated to allow life insurers to access the international capital markets. The challenge of drafting the offering circular about a new business with little precedents makes it all the more interesting and rewarding.

I pay particular attention to the MD&A (Management's Discussion and Analysis of Financial Condition and Results of Operations) section, which requires a thorough understanding of the issuer's business and financial condition. Learning about business in general, and clients and industries in particular, will lead you into non-legal areas. Given the accounting and related financial disclosure scandals in the past, one of those areas is accounting. It is very important for a corporate lawyer today to have a good basic understanding of accounting, which is vital to understanding the issuer's business and its financial statements and drafting the MD&A section, as well as a basic understanding of accounting issues that are in the news today. Through self-study and years of experience reading and studying financial statements, I would like to think that I can hold my own when analyzing financial statements and drafting the MD&A. Nevertheless,

I take time to go through the section thoroughly and provide input to the relevant associate for processing and further revision.

12:30 p.m.   *Lunch Meeting with a Client*

In a client-driven business such as ours, it is important that we build our network extensively. You never know who can introduce you to someone who might bring business to the firm, and a lot of the power of who you are rests in whom you know. When you can leverage your network of contacts to make something happen (e.g., get deals), you can create significant added value for yourself in the firm and further enhance your opportunity for success. This may be easier said than done, since a lot of the time (most of the time, actually), I am working so hard that I only have time for my family (even with only a spouse) and work. However, I try to make a real conscious effort in investing time and getting involved in building my network of mutually beneficial relationships.

Today's lunch is with an in-house counsel at a large US investment bank in HK, who happens to be an ex-colleague and whose company I greatly enjoy. He made the move to go in-house a few years ago and had great success there, as evidenced by his recent promotion to the managing director position. Sitting by a window at a Japanese restaurant overlooking the Victoria Harbor, we discuss the type of transactions he would require our firm to work on. We also discuss a few random topics, including the pending changes in US law affecting the financial industry and its players. Although this is a business lunch, the atmosphere is relaxed and we end the meal with some small talk regarding common interests: golf and running.

1:45 p.m.   *Walk Back to the Office*

While walking back to the office, I go through (in my head) the topics I want to discuss during the upcoming conference call with my clients regarding the mark-up of the draft underwriting agreement we received from the lawyers of the opposing party (i.e., the issuer's counsel). The clients are happy to hear that the opposing party has mostly only made acceptable changes to the draft agreement and that we are therefore moving toward finalizing the document on schedule.

2:00 p.m.   *Conference Call with Clients (re: underwriting agreement)*

I dial in to the scheduled conference call with the in-house counsels of the four lead investment banks to discuss the mark-up of the underwriting agreement. The junior associate also dials in for educational purposes as well as to keep track of the discussion and the revisions to the agreement. Having multiple lead managers is not unusual these days, but it does require additional finesse in our coordinating efforts. After the roll call and confirmation of the relevant parties in attendance, we go through the comments made by the issuer's counsel on the underwriting agreement (also known as a purchase agreement or subscription agreement) containing the formal underwriting obligation to be entered into between the underwriters and the issuer at the time of pricing (or at launch of the offering in certain cases). Most of the comments made by the opposing issuer's counsel are not unexpected and are not too controversial (e.g., whether to include a material adverse effect (MAE) qualifier in the representations and warranties section, whether to give consultation rights to the issuer in the *force majeure* ("superior or greater force") clause if the underwriters decide to terminate the agreement as a result of a *force majeure* event, etc.)—and we discuss which ones are acceptable and which are not at this stage. The hot topics these days in the underwriting agreements in international capital markets transactions include the representations and covenants by the issuer regarding compliance with OFAC (Office of Foreign Assets Control of the US Treasury relating to certain dealings with sanctioned countries), FCPA (US Foreign Corrupt Practices Act dealing with anti-bribery), anti-money laundering, and similar laws and regulations. Our in-house counsel clients do not agree to accept any watering down of these provisions. I make a list of items to discuss and negotiate with the opposing counsel, and promise to revert to our clients afterwards.

2:30 p.m.   *Call Opposing Counsel (re: negotiate underwriting agreement)*

I call the opposing counsel following the call with our clients. In general, most of the time, in contrast to the adversarial nature of trial law, corporate law is team-oriented. The corporate counsels for both sides of a transaction are not strict competitors in that together they seek a common ground for their clients (i.e., a successful closing of the offering). Negotiating the underwriting agreement is one of the few areas adversarial in nature in international securities offerings. Through the negotiation process, we constantly write and revise the legal documents that will bind the parties to the terms related to the transaction. Although I do enjoy this part of the process, it can be lengthy and often results in extremely long hours. And as a deal moves toward its closing, it becomes an exercise in stamina as much as skillful negotiation, which I am hoping will not be the case for this transaction, as I continue to negotiate.

Over the years, I've seen many lawyers who seem only to be trying to win points negotiating a transaction without really taking into account the bigger picture or looking for the win-win approach (i.e., where both clients achieve their objectives). So many times, it's as if they think there's a scoreboard and someone's keeping track of how many points they've won or lost. Unfortunately, I have seen that more and more as the economy has turned downward in the last few years. Transactions are harder and harder to get done—people are focusing on details and worrying about things that they never would have worried about before. Don't get me wrong—some things they should be worrying about. And maybe some of these details were too blasé in the past, especially when the stock market was booming, money was easy to borrow, and companies were issuing their stock at possibly inflated prices. Back then, it wasn't so important to get, say, the best representations and warranties. Now people are more concerned. But the pendulum might have swung too far in the other direction. From a financial point of view, I suppose it's good news for law firms, but not such good news for clients. This is because we have to spend so much more time on every transaction. You can raise issues about every provision in an agreement if you want. But you have to recognize what's important and what's not so important, and how to get to a good result for your client rather than winning points on each provision of the agreement. I am glad to find that the opposing counsel in this case falls into the former rather than the latter category, and we make good progress on the negotiation, leaving only a few outstanding items left to finalize for next time.

3:00 p.m.   *Write E-Mail Summarizing the Call with Opposing Counsel*

After the call with the opposing counsel, I summarize in an e-mail a bullet point list of which items are still outstanding (requesting further input or finalization of the position from our clients, as relevant). In the meantime, I give a mark-up of the agreement to the junior associate so she can start revising the agreement.

I remember the conversation with a client earlier this morning regarding NDRs, and prepare and distribute an e-mail outlining the general guidelines applicable to conducting an NDR.

3:25 p.m.   *Call with Auditors (re: comfort letter issues)*

At the request of the mid-level associate, I call the auditors to iron out the outstanding issues surrounding their comfort letter to be delivered to the underwriters. Comfort letters, as part of the due diligence process, provide the underwriter (among other things) independent assurance that no serious adverse changes have occurred in the financial condition of the issuer during the period since its last financial statements up to closing (of the transaction). It seems increasingly more time is being spent these days by lawyers on negotiating the comfort letters and related agreements (e.g., the "arrangement letter" establishing—or more like limiting—the scope of liability of the auditors in a transaction involving an offering outside the United States—the "Regulation S" portion). We discuss how we can have the auditors increase the scope of their negative assurance statement so that there are no material adverse changes covering more line items in the financial statements. The auditors agree to discuss again internally along with the issuer's accounting department, and then get back to us.

3:45 p.m.   *Return Call to the Client (re: edits on offering circular)*

While I was on the call with the auditors, I receive a voicemail message from an issuer client in Korea regarding the latest edits to the offering circular. I call the client back and discuss the edits with him, a large part of which involved translating certain parts of the offering circular into Korean. The client makes a few suggestions to be incorporated in the offering circular, which I take note of and pass on to the associate in charge of drafting (to be added into the next round of edits).

4:00 p.m.   *Call London Stock Exchange Representative (re: listing rules)*

I get an urgent e-mail from one of the partners currently at an outside meeting regarding a couple of questions on the London Stock Exchange (LSE) listing rules relating to the LSE requirements for voting of a merger and the market cap/market float. These questions seem to have come up during his meeting with the LSE, and although we are not experts in UK law and the listing rules of the London Stock Exchange, our clients direct the inquiry to us since we know how, or who, to contact for answers. As lead counsel on the deals used to managing the transaction, which includes coordinating with third parties, I have compiled a list of contacts in various jurisdictions, including the UK. I make a quick call to my LSE contact stationed in HK who promises to get back to me as soon as possible with answers. At the same time, I request a junior associate to run research regarding the same as a backup. My LSE contact keeps his word and gets back to me with answers within the next half hour. I then pass on the information to the partner who made the inquiry.

I go over to our pantry and pour a fresh cup of coffee for a quick break before the next scheduled call.

4:30 p.m.   *Attend Weekly Conference Call with Working Group (re: IPO)*

I dial in to the scheduled weekly update call for one of the most multi-transactional transactions I've ever been involved in. We are representing the company (domiciled in a country in Europe with operations spread out globally) and the selling shareholder (a holding company domiciled in Europe, which is ultimately owned by a Korean public company), in an initial public offering (IPO) transaction consisting of a public offering and listing in another jurisdiction in Asia and an international offering to institutional investors, including in the United States. It is not uncommon to have weekly update calls in transactions involving numerous parties in multiple jurisdictions such as this transaction, as the number of issues and complexity multiplies. And it's important to get the working group on the same page and get various processes moving forward in an efficient and timely manner.

We are at the fairly early stage of the transaction, and one of the main topics today is the choice of a suitable jurisdiction of incorporation of the listing entity (ListCo), which will form the holding company (HoldCo) of the operating company (OpCo). (It has already been determined that due to certain domestic rules and regulations, it is practically impossible to list the OpCo directly on the relevant stock exchange.) Whenever you cross borders in these manners, tax and other structuring considerations come right to the forefront. The working group discusses the importance of determining the most tax-efficient way to have the money flowing both into the relevant jurisdictions and flowing back out, including potentially critical issues associated with the repatriation of capital. The group also considers other issues such as interest deductibility, withholding taxes, corporate governance requirements, regulatory matters, and the like relating to each jurisdictional option. The issuer resolves to revert with a decision shortly on the choice of legal domicile after due consideration of the advice of counsels, tax advisors, and other working group members.

We go through a list of other items on the agenda, including the schedule for audit procedure and preparation of the financial statements for inclusion in the offering document, various due diligence schedule, drafting of the offering document (and other documentation), and listing requirements focusing on the most immediate matters first.

5:30 p.m.   Meet with Partner-In-Charge for a Briefing

I drop by a partner's office to give a status update on deals in which he is the partner-in-charge. In addition to deal-related advice and guidance, I am very fortunate to have close mentoring relationships with the two lawyers whom I have been mostly working with for the past nine years; they have been great teachers and role models in other respects. The two partners—one who was already a partner when I started with the firm, and the other who became a partner a few years after I started with the firm—took me under their wings and nurtured my career development as a lawyer. They both were well-recognized corporate lawyers in the field who took the time to mentor me. Not only could I learn from watching them in action, but also I could test my tentative judgments against their seasoned experience. At first, we would reach decisions by consensus. As time went on, I gained more confidence in my own decisions. They both have been a big part of the reasons behind my being here today.

Throughout the briefing, the partner asks questions, makes comments, gives instructions, and makes suggestions on various matters, which I take note of for follow-up.

6:00 p.m.   *Cancel Attending Tomorrow's Dinner Event*

I return to my office and note on my calendar an annual event scheduled tomorrow night by a legal publishing house being held to give recognitions to the "leaders in the field" in Asia for law firms and individual lawyers by certain criteria (e.g., jurisdiction, type of practice, etc.). Hong Kong being the financial center of Asia, numerous industry events such as awards nights recognizing investment banks, in-house counsels and outside counsels—as well as deals of the year and the like—are held throughout the year. I wanted to attend this event in particular since it was one of the few (if not the only) prominent legal publications around and my firm as well as a number of individuals within my firm (including myself, which makes me feel very fortunate and honored) are to be recognized this year. I previously RSVP'd to attend this event, but now I unfortunately have to cancel due to a red-eye flight I have to catch later tonight to Korea for a due diligence meeting starting tomorrow. I am a bit disappointed, but certainly not devastated. A big part of "biglaw" (or megafirm) life is canceling plans, and you learn to get pretty good at it and hope that you can make it next time.

6:15 p.m.   *Review of Publicly Available Corporate Material/Prepare for Meeting*

I start preparing for my trip to Seoul, Korea to attend the kickoff/due diligence meeting. The meeting is in connection with a deal involving a convertible bond (CB) offering by a Korean company in the semiconductor industry that is a frequent issuer in the international capital markets. The deal actually started a couple of years ago, but was not completed at that time because the principals decided to postpone the offering until the market conditions became more favorable. I am hoping that the deal will close successfully this time.

As counsel to the underwriters in this transaction, in addition to participating in the meeting for our own due diligence purposes, I am expected to "run" the due diligence session on behalf of the underwriters—meaning basically going through the questions on the due diligence questionnaire, provide translations when necessary, and facilitate the session as the moderator. In preparation, I review once again the tailored due diligence questionnaire that we helped the underwriters prepare. I also review the results of the news run (both the English media as well as the Korean media), and the latest company filings downloaded and forwarded to me by a paralegal.

7:30 p.m.   *Attend Hip Hop Dance Class*

I try my best to set aside an hour each evening either to take various dance (hip hop, jazz, funk) or group exercise classes (yoga, spin, step) or workout at the gym. I look forward to this time set aside hanging out with classmates, trainers, and instructors, listening to the latest music, sweating out the stress, and just having fun away from work. Mondays are my hip-hop dance lesson days, which I particularly enjoy. Despite my flight later in the evening, I decide to hurry over to the class while running through in my head the routine I learned last week.

I am also passionate about a few other hobbies—golf, painting, and piano. Somewhere along with the challenging work hours, frequent business travels, and family duties, I make a real effort to find workable time slots to fit in these activities in my monthly calendar. I believe personal interests are an important part of who you are. And in order to be truly successful at your job, you need to balance out your professional life (since your professional life by itself, no matter who you are or what your title, will never consistently fulfill you) by practicing passions that contribute to your happiness, well-being, and who you are as a person. It also doesn't hurt to be able to chat with clients about my love for golf, which has served as an amazing icebreaker in many of the relationships with my colleagues and clients—if they don't golf, then in most cases they want to learn, or at the very least have followed the careers of Tiger Woods and/or Michelle Wie.

There is a lot of talk about work-life balance at law firms, especially at a biglaw like ours. Most people claim that it is impossible to obtain balance—

when work gets crazy, when you've got endless impossible deadlines, and when your seniors or clients are demanding you stay at work late once again, the first thing to suffer is your personal life, and anything that closely resembles balance goes right out of the window. Throughout my years at the firm, I've seen many colleagues come and go in large part due to the inability to maintain this balance of managing professional and personal lives. I attribute a large part of my being able to stay motivated, stay interested in continuing to learn about and excel in my industry, and realizing all of the other accomplishments I have achieved as a professional, to constantly seeking to maintain a balance between work and my various passions.

After the workout session, I take shower at the gym (conveniently located very close to work), then grab something light and healthy to eat at my desk.

9:00 p.m.   Fill in Diary/Organize Files

After returning to my office, I go through the latest e-mails in my inbox (that have arrived since the last time I checked them). I also organize files and prepare a tentative to-do list for the next day. As there are no pressing items that require my immediate attention, I fill in my "diary" to ensure that my billable hours are up-to-date. We are required to input our hours electronically on a daily basis, but often times, I run a few days to a few weeks behind (in the latter case, I would get an automatic e-mail reminder prompt). I am relieved to see that my diary is currently up-to-date.

9:30 p.m.   Call with New York Office (re: OFAC issues with specialist)

I call an OFAC specialist in our New York head office (my colleagues there should be arriving at their offices from their morning commute right about now) to discuss certain issues that have come up in one of my deals. The opposing counsel to the underwriters has served up an underwriting agreement to our client (issuer and selling shareholders) containing an extensive OFAC-related representation, warranty, and covenant from both the issuer and the selling shareholders. I was hoping to get an insight into the latest market practice in New York since the underwriters in Asia often look to the practices there as guidance. With more than 700 lawyers in our firm globally (mostly in New York), I have access to vast resources and am able to draw upon the knowledge and experience of experts in various specialty law areas including OFAC. One thing I love about my firm is that it has a culture where sharing of knowledge and expertise is important and people aren't reluctant to spend time to help other people. As usually, our expert in New York provides helpful insight and guidance on the issue, and I end the call thanking him and promising to keep him posted on the progress of the negotiation.

10:30 p.m.   *Pack Up/Head to Airport*

Other than the deal-related documents and a few personal items, I do not have many things to pack for my Korea business trip since I keep most of my necessary belongings (including suits, shirts, shoes, makeup, stationery and a pretty respectable collection of prospectuses/offering circulars) at the hotel I usually stay at during my frequent business trips to Seoul (our firm does not have an office in Seoul as the legal market in Korea has not opened up yet). But I remember to pack an extra box of my business cards, which is essential when attending physical meetings in Seoul. I take my suitcase and get in the hired car waiting for me in front of the office building and head directly out to the airport—given the time, there simply isn't enough time to stop by my home if I'm to catch my flight.

11:00 p.m.   *Check in / Sit Back, Relax, and Prepare for Takeoff*

The airport in HK is very efficient, and it takes less than fifteen minutes to check in, pass through the checkpoints, and get to the airline lounge where I sit and grab a few periodicals to browse through before boarding. Once on board the plane, I turn off my BlackBerry and my iPhone, sit back, relax, and quickly doze off to catch a few hours of sleep during the three-hour flight to Korea.

5:00 a.m.   *Land at Airport (4:00 a.m. Hong Kong time)*

The plane makes its scheduled landing at Incheon International Airport. I turn back on my BlackBerry and my Korea mobile phone, proceed out through the arrival hall, and get into the waiting car for the one-hour ride to the hotel located in the heart of downtown Seoul.

6:00 a.m.   *Arrive at Hotel (5:00 a.m. Hong Kong time)*

The car arrives at the hotel and upon entering the hotel room, I try to sneak in a bit more sleep until my wake-up call in about an hour.

7:00 a.m.   *Wake-Up Call (6:00 a.m. Hong Kong time)*

I awake at the sound of the wake-up call, and get ready for the meeting to take place in an hour. Being in attendance at a meeting and simultaneously trying to address urgent matters remotely away from the office using a BlackBerry and mobile phone requires considerable skill and experience. Today's schedule in the life of this corporate lawyer would be quite different from that of the day before, but I save the next exciting twenty-four hours for the sequel—*24/7* perhaps?

Final Thoughts

The area of corporate transactional law is a challenging profession, but one that I really love, even though many joke that the world would be a better place if every lawyer (corporate or otherwise, I assume) were at the bottom of the sea. If you really are an aspiring corporate lawyer or want to find personal satisfaction as a corporate lawyer, I believe you'd need to have a higher purpose than just wanting to make money. You have to believe in what you're doing and believe in the law. It may be old fashioned, but it would help to think of the law as a noble calling, with lawyers providing services that are valuable to society. This may be particularly relevant in recent years where we see a trend toward more and more regulation of corporations in general with all the accounting scandals and bankruptcies of, first, the dot-com companies, and then, the energy trading and telecom companies, followed by financial institutions and the ensuing loss of public confidence. A good step toward the successful answering of such a noble calling, and being happy in doing so, would be to believe in yourself that each day you walk that into your office, you expect you will have the ability to perform exceedingly well in whatever project, assignment, or routine task that lies ahead of you each and every minute of your twenty-four-hour day, and to show up with your best self. Then you will succeed.

2

Profile 2
Walter: Prosecutor

Executive Summary

Name: Walter
Position: Prosecutor
Location: Newark, New Jersey

Working as a prosecutor dealing with criminals, courthouses, and victims can conjure up images reminiscent of TV shows like CSI *and* The Practice. *But underneath the sometimes graphic and violent nature of such criminal minds are the lawyers who represent "The People" or "The State" as prosecutors in the spirit of seeking "justice." But what exactly does this entail? After reading Walter's twenty-four-hour profile, you will find out that it is about handling a barrage of cases and issues at any given moment—from speaking with judges, police, and victims of crimes—to dealing with the constant inflow of new cases while navigating administrative duties to keep the department working smoothly and seamlessly. And, of course, there's also trying to balance work with family. Somehow, remarkably, Walter manages to handle all this with inspiring professionalism. It should not only give you a sense of what the twenty-four-hour cycle of a prosecutor may be, but it should also give you comfort that extremely decent and capable legal professionals like Walter work hard day in and day out to seek justice on behalf of people like you and me.*

Profile

Career Field:	County Prosecutor
Current Position:	Assistant Prosecutor
Institution:	County Prosecutor's Office
Location:	Newark, New Jersey
Education:	JD, Rutgers University, School of Law - Camden
	BA, John Jay College, CUNY (The City University
	of New York)
Licensed (Y/N):	Yes
Jurisdictions:	New Jersey

Schedule

5:00 a.m.	My Alarm Goes Off
6:00 a.m.	Wife's Alarm Goes Off
6:45 a.m.	Get Dressed
7:15 a.m.	Leave for Work
8:20 a.m.	Waiting Outside a Civil Courtroom
8:40 a.m.	Court Doors Open (10 minutes late)
9:00 a.m.	Judge Calls the Calendar
9:10 a.m.	Take Defendants to Prosecutor's Office to Copy Documentation
9:30 a.m.	Contact Newark Police Detective (informing them, "I'm on my way")
9:35 a.m.	An Appointment Shows Up at the Main Office
9:55 a.m.	Arrive at Newark Auto Squad
10:14 a.m.	Call from Public Defender (re: a court case)
10:20 a.m.	Resume Meeting with Newark Detective
10:25 a.m.	Officer Brings Me a Cup of Coffee (Thank You, Officer!)
10:45 a.m.	Conclude the Meeting with the Detective
11:00 a.m.	Arrive at My Office (at the Sex Crimes office)
11:10 a.m.	Contact Defense Attorney (re: one of his clients)
11:15 a.m.	Loan My Car to Sex Crimes Office Detectives/Tell Them, "Fill 'er up"
11:30 a.m.	Speak to My Victim Advocate (re: a recent sexual assault)
11:35 a.m.	Leave a Copy of the Prosecutor's File on My Detective's Desk

11:40 a.m.	Coffee Time
11:45 a.m.	Contact another Assistant Prosecutor to Cover a 1:30 p.m. Motion
12:00 p.m.	Assistant Prosecutor Approaches Me (re: internal staff issue)
12:20 p.m.	Assign New Cases
1:15 p.m.	Coffee Time (Again!)
1:20 p.m.	Call Victim in Case
1:30 p.m.	Assistant Prosecutor Handling Motion Calls for Consultation
1:45 p.m.	Continue Case Review and Assign New Cases
2:00 p.m.	Contact the Lieutenant Officer in the Newark SARA (Sexual Assault Rape Analysis) Unit (re: to discuss recent issues)
2:30 p.m.	Leave Sex Crimes Office/Start Driving to the Forfeiture Unit Office
2:40 p.m.	Get a Call (re: the return of a car)
2:50 p.m.	While Entering the Courthouse, a Judge Pulls Me Aside (re: to inquire about a search warrant we executed the prior Friday)
3:10 p.m.	Accept Paperwork/Arrange for a Detective to Deliver It the Next Morning to the Forfeiture Unit
3:15 p.m.	Inquire with our IT Department (re: quotes to automate the Forfeiture Unit)
3:30 p.m.	Follow-Up with Purchasing Division (re: the automation project, a paycheck issue with one of the staff Assistant Prosecutors and carpeting for the Sex Crimes Unit)
3:50 p.m.	Consult with Detectives Preparing a Search Warrant (re: money seizure)
4:10 p.m.	Drive to the Forfeiture Unit Office
4:30 p.m.	Arrive at the Forfeiture Unit Office/Review Complaints for Filing/Answer Messages Left for Me at that Office/Review Civil Trials Set for Next Monday
5:00 p.m.	Leave for the Day
5:45 p.m.	Arrive Home/Eat Dinner with the Family
6:00 p.m.	Receive a Phone Call from a Victim Advocate
6:30 p.m.	Leave for Vacation
10:00 p.m.	Receive a Call from the On-Call Assistant Prosecutor

2:30 a.m.	Arrive at My Vacation Destination in Maine (after eight hours driving)
2:45 a.m.	Go to Bed
5:00 a.m.	Awakened by the Cell Phone - Another Work Call

24-Hour Schedule

5:00 a.m.   *My Alarm Goes Off*

Some days, I am overly optimistic—and this was one of these days. I had hoped to get up early and get a jump on my day. Today was particularly so since it would be the only day of work for me this week. I'll be taking a short vacation in Maine for the remainder of the week. Despite this, I still hate Mondays.

6:00 a.m.   *Wife's Alarm Goes Off*

This alarm wakes me up. I get up, go in the other room, and wake up my two girls: Grace (age seven), and Meghan (age four). I enjoy waking the kids up. Much of my career choices have centered around quality time with my family.

6:45 a.m.   *Get Dressed*

I wear the suit of a government worker. All my suits are gray or blue and all my shirts are white or blue. I also never wear cufflinks and I do not own an expensive watch. But I always spend money on my shoes. When you spend your days on your feet, good shoes are a must. I toss on a bow tie since this tends to irritate people ever so slightly. But if I'm on trial, I never wear a bow tie (since I don't want to irritate the wrong people in court). In general, I try to dress neat and conservatively.

7:15 a.m.   *Leave for Work*

I currently report to three different locations, the main office located in the courthouse in Newark (New Jersey), the sex crimes office, located in downtown Newark and the forfeiture unit office, located in East Orange (also in New Jersey). It usually takes me about a half an hour to drive from home regardless of which office is my destination.

Today, I'm headed to the civil calendar call at the courthouse for forfeiture trials. Due to budgetary constraints, I am currently the director of the forfeiture unit, the sex crimes unit, and the money-laundering unit. Sex crimes is home for me.

8:20 a.m.   *Waiting Outside a Civil Courtroom*

As a prosecutor, it's always a strange feeling going to the civil courts. It is not a comfortable place. Typically, I would spend most of my Mondays bouncing from judge to judge on my criminal matters. We have fifteen criminal judges and my cases are spread between all of them.

8:40 a.m.   *Court Doors Open (10 minutes late)*

I have grown accustomed to the civil courts running on a tight schedule. When they do, it affords me the ability to conduct my business there and then get to the criminal courts where they start their day at 9:00 a.m. It is becoming painfully clear to me that today is *not* going to go well. I contact my secretary and have her e-mail one of the forfeiture files to my BlackBerry.

9:00 a.m.   *Judge Calls the Calendar*

The judge has put me in the hole by having to wait a half an hour. While I was waiting, I tried to make myself productive. So I reviewed a motion that I have to argue later in the day. The motion is to compel a biological sample from a defendant. This particular defendant was identified as a suspect in a sexual assault through the Combined DNA Index System (CODIS). The CODIS is a federal DNA database that constantly checks DNA from crime scenes against the DNA of known offenders. This defendant was later identified by the victim through a photo array and charged with the sexual assault.

While CODIS is a great tool, I am required to get a confirmatory DNA sample to be analyzed directly against the crime scene evidence before I can use this information against a defendant at trial.

In the end, three of my civil defendants answer the civil call on forfeiture matters and one defendant defaulted. The three who did appear have active criminal cases, so their matters are stayed pending the outcome of the criminal cases. I engage in a short settlement conference with the defendants and they ask me to consider paperwork that they brought with them regarding the legitimate sources of seized funds.

9:10 a.m.   Take Defendants to Prosecutor's Office to Copy Documentation

I walk my civil defendants to my main office so I can copy the documentation of legitimate sources. It takes me a few minutes to make copies. I have a brief conversation with each of them regarding possible settlement of their matters.

9:30 a.m.   Contact Newark Police Detective (informing them, "I'm on my way")

I have an appointment with the Newark Police Department Auto Squad for 9:00 a.m. to discuss the forfeiture implications of a car they had seized several months ago that was outfitted with several stolen auto parts. The criminal defense attorney tells me that her client purchased the parts from Craigslist.com (a commonly used website featuring classified advertisements). I call the detective and tell him, "I'm on my way."

9:35 a.m.   An Appointment Shows Up at the Main Office

While I was on my way to the Auto Squad, I received a phone call from the main office informing me that a woman arrived (in the main office) to see me. I could not turn around the car at this point, as I was already a half hour late for my appointment in Newark. So I enlisted the aid of another assistant prosecutor to handle the appointment. The woman who was looking for me was delivering a check to pay a negotiated civil settlement for her car. I then had my East Orange office fax the settlement forms to the assistant prosecutor who was covering the case.

9:55 a.m.   *Arrive at Newark Auto Squad*

I arrive at the Newark Auto Squad. Initially, I had a short meeting with the lieutenant in charge regarding compliance with applicable attorney general mandates. I then met with the detective handling the case with the stolen car parts. The detective presented a very interesting case involving a stolen car that was later found with several of its body components switched with body components from another car. The other car, recovered about a block from where the stolen car was found, had the missing components from the stolen car

10:14 a.m.   *Call from Public Defender (re: a court case)*

My meeting with the detective was interrupted by a call from a defense attorney who was calling to determine which attorney from my unit was to appear in court on a sexual assault case. I let her know that I would try to ascertain who was assigned to that case. I then make four phone calls, but was unable to ascertain which attorney was assigned to the case. Without sufficient facts to give her an answer, I call the public defender back and suggested that we adjourn the case for a week. The defense attorney agrees and indicates she will call me prior to the new court date to figure out how we would proceed.

10:20 a.m.   *Resume Meeting with Newark Detective*

This job is great for people with ADD (Attention Deficit Disorder). This is because doing six things at once is usually the order (norm) of the day. After the interruption, I continue my meeting with the detective. With the detective present, I call the defense attorney and inform her that her client was not telling her the truth about the source of the parts on the car. Nonetheless, I tell her that the car would be returned to her client without the hood, bumper, fenders, rear bumper, taillights, and side view mirrors.

10:25 a.m.   *Officer Brings Me a Cup of Coffee (Thank You, Officer!)*

Once again, I forgot to eat breakfast this morning. Fortunately, a police officer is kind enough to give me a cup of coffee. To which, I reply, "Thank you, Officer!" I then drink the fine cup of black coffee to fill the empty void in my stomach. I have a habit of not eating when I get a little busy.

10:45 a.m.   *Conclude the Meeting with the Detective*

The detective thanks me for my time and I head out to leave. I drive to the sex crimes office, which is the next item on my list.

11:00 a.m.   *Arrive at My Office (at the Sex Crimes office)*

I park my car and walk into my office. While doing so, I take some time to say "good morning" to my secretary and other staff.

11:10 a.m.   *Contact Defense Attorney (re: one of his clients)*

I called a defense attorney regarding a defendant who had previously been found unfit to stand trial. It was our hope that we could get the defendant into a residential mental health program. Unfortunately, legal counsel was unable to find such a program for the defendant.

The defendant was arrested twice in the past week for various acts of public indecency. I am now seeking to have the defendant evaluated for possible civil commitment. The defense attorney was disappointed in my decision. We agreed to ask the court to schedule the defendant for a court appearance in six weeks. In the interim, he will be transferred to a mental health facility for evaluation.

11:15 a.m.   *Loan My Car to Sex Crimes Office Detectives/Tell Them, "Fill 'er up"*

My detectives borrow my office vehicle to go out in the field. I'm not a big fan of having an office car. Once I no longer have to travel between offices as frequently, I have decided I am going to turn it in.

I jokingly tell the detectives who are borrowing my office car to "fill 'er up" as I toss them the keys (they were kind enough to comply, even though the request was with my tongue firmly planted in cheek).

11:30 a.m.   *Speak to My Victim Advocate (re: a recent sexual assault)*

One of the victim advocates approaches me and indicates that a victim contacted her and asked to arrange to speak to me about her case. As I will be on vacation for the rest of the week, we arrange for the victim to come down.

Victim advocates are a great resource for sex crimes prosecutors. The advocates maintain day-to-day contact with victims, answer questions, and provide services to victims of sexual assault.

11:35 a.m.   *Leave a Copy of the Prosecutor's File on My Detective's Desk*

With the victim coming in for an interview, I have to be sure that my detective and I are prepared. Prior to a victim's arrival, we both review the file and discuss any issues that may come up.

11:40 a.m.   *Coffee Time*

While I usually try to eat lunch, the flow of the day often dictates if and when I eat. I have found that if you drink copious amounts of coffee, you will not feel hungry.

11:45 a.m.   *Contact another Assistant Prosecutor to Cover a 1:30 p.m. Motion*

With the victim scheduled to come into the office at 1:00 p.m. later today, I have to enlist one of my colleagues to argue my motion to compel a DNA sample. I give her the rundown on the case, including a copy of my motion papers.

It is my opinion that the defense attorney opposed the motion to maintain credibility with his client. As the opposition was perfunctory, I was not concerned about asking someone to cover on such short notice.

12:00 p.m.   *Assistant Prosecutor Approaches Me (re: internal staff issue)*

One of the line assistants approached me about a personnel issue involving interactions with outside departments. Dealing with conflicts between our office and outside agencies is always a difficult situation. I try to foster positive relationships with outside agencies to facilitate communication between our office and outside departments. Positive relationships usually minimize conflict. But when there is a personality conflict, I am forced to take action.

This particular situation will necessitate a meeting with the ranking officer of one of our local police departments. I am not looking forward to that unhappy meeting.

12:20 p.m.   *Assign New Cases*

As I move through my day and week, new cases are constantly being placed on my desk for review and assignment. Initially, I read each case, and then assign each case to an assistant prosecutor for further review and possible authorization of charges.

In addition to my managerial duties, I try to maintain a full caseload. Reading each case gives me an idea how our local police departments are complying with the protocol for sexual assault cases promulgated from my office. It also gives me the ability to have meaningful conversations with the assistant prosecutor who is ultimately assigned to the case.

1:15 p.m.   *Coffee Time (Again!)*

Coffee time, again! But I have a good reason—I am trying to maintain mental acuity without getting jittery. Somehow, though, I feel like I'm failing.

1:20 p.m.   *Call Victim in Case*

I call a victim who was originally scheduled to come to my office at 1:00 p.m. today, since by this time, she was twenty minutes late. It is not unusual for a victim who is scheduled for an interview he or she did not request to miss the interview. However, it is rare for them to request such an interview and not show-up.

Once I make contact by phone, the victim apologizes and asks if she could reschedule. Honestly, I really do not have many options at this point. So I offer to reschedule when I return from vacation. On that reassigned day, I will again review the file with my detective in preparation for the interview with the victim.

1:30 p.m. *Assistant Prosecutor Handling Motion Calls for Consultation*

The assistant prosecutor covering my motion calls me to inquire as to my position with regard to the defense attorney being present during the collection of the DNA sample. There is no basis to object to this request, so I inform her that it is fine with me.

Collecting a DNA sample consists of wiping a cotton swab on the inside of the subject's cheek. The swab collects loose skin cells in the mouth and the lab develops a DNA profile from those cells. The process is painless to the donor subject.

1:45 p.m. *Continue Case Review and Assign New Cases*

I continue reviewing the remainder of the cases left on my desk and assign them to the assistant prosecutors in my unit. I take the opportunity to assign a few cases to myself. Hopefully, I can get something to go to trial soon.

2:00 p.m. *Contact the Lieutenant Officer in the Newark SARA (Sexual Assault Rape Analysis) Unit (re: to discuss recent issues)*

The Newark Police Department Special Victims Unit is one of the finest outside agencies that I have the pleasure to work with. One of the attributes that makes Newark so good is the level of communication between this unit and my office.

I call the lieutenant in charge of that unit to address some protocol issues. The lieutenant in charge is a true professional who cares deeply about the subject matter and the quality of her unit's work. These phone calls and regular meetings keep us on the same page and ultimately results in better work product.

Today, we quickly dispatch with our problems and I am confident that they will be corrected. We have a brief conversation about some of our more serious active cases and the lieutenant inquires about charging decisions on those cases. We exchange some pleasantries about the weekend and then hang up.

2:30 p.m.   *Leave Sex Crimes Office/Drive to the Forfeiture Unit Office*

I start the 20-minute drive to the forfeiture unit office in East Orange, New Jersey. During the drive, I usually try to call ahead to the secretaries so they can set up the work that I have to review. Afterwards, I flip on the radio and hope the New York Mets fire their manager soon.

2:40 p.m.   *Get a Call (re: the return of a car)*

I have another unscheduled appointment at the courthouse. I would have been more inclined to tell them to come back tomorrow, but I won't be there since I will be out of the office then (on vacation). I elect to turn around and skip the East Orange office today. I have some other business to tend to in the courthouse.

2:50 p.m.   *While Entering the Courthouse, a Judge Pulls Me Aside (re: to inquire about a search warrant we executed the prior Friday)*

On the previous Friday, we had sought and received an arrest warrant for a suspect and a search warrant for his home. The judge who granted the motion pulls me aside as I enter the courthouse to inquire about the warrant. I was pleased to tell him that the defendant was safely arrested and the gun alleged to have been used in the sexual assault was recovered in the search of the home. I promise the judge that I would follow-up with the executing officers to ensure that the search warrant return was completed in a timely manner.

3:10 p.m.   *Accept Paperwork/Arrange for a Detective to Deliver It the Next Morning to the Forfeiture Unit*

I meet with my unscheduled appointment and have her fill out the proper paperwork for the return of her vehicle. In order to secure the return of her vehicle, I enlist a detective to deliver the original paperwork to the forfeiture unit tomorrow morning.

3:15 p.m.   *Inquire with our IT Department (re: quotes to automate the forfeiture unit)*

Since taking over the forfeiture unit, I have strived to automate its record keeping. Automation will reduce the twenty filing cabinets currently utilized to hold open and recently closed files down to two. Automation will also streamline the unit and ultimately make everyone more productive. But one downside is that automation is expensive!

While in the courthouse, I meet with our information technology (IT) director regarding the quote for scanning our current files into searchable PDF files.

3:30 p.m.   *Follow-Up with Purchasing Division (re: the automation project, a paycheck issue with one of the staff Assistant Prosecutors and carpeting for the Sex Crimes Unit)*

Once I leave the company of our information technology director, I immediately go to our administration/purchasing division to confirm the procedure for procuring the scanning services to complete the automation project.

While I was there, I also check on the status of the new carpeting for the sex crimes unit. I am hopeful that the bidding process will be completed within the next month and we can complete both of these projects within the next two months. While I was in administration, I also correct a paycheck discrepancy for one of the prosecutors I manage. Three fewer things I have to address when I get back from vacation.

3:50 p.m.   *Consult with Detectives Preparing a Search Warrant (re: money seizure)*

I consult with a captain of county detectives regarding a joint investigation with an out-of-state agency. At issue is whether the out-of-state agency will be permitted to take evidence recovered from the warrant back to their home jurisdiction.

While I did not take a position with regard to evidence, I did take a position with regard to any potential money recovered. I inform the captain that if money is recovered, it must be deposited into our trust account and cannot be taken out of our jurisdiction. I'm sure if money is recovered in the warrant, it is going to cause some problems. Fortunately, our state guidelines are very clear with regard to the seizure of money. Anticipating these issues before the warrant is executed cures a lot of trouble later.

4:10 p.m.   *Drive to the Forfeiture Unit Office*

It looks like I will make the forfeiture unit office after all. Unfortunately, I cannot say the same for lunch.

4:30 p.m.   *Arrive at the Forfeiture Unit Office/Review Complaints for Filing / Answer Messages Left for Me at that Office/Review Civil Trials Set for Next Monday*

I have a little time to review and sign about ten civil complaints on my desk. I answer a few calls from various attorneys. I also leave some notes for my secretaries for the remainder of the week when I am away on vacation. Ultimately, though, I end up taking my trial files for next week with me.

5:00 p.m.   *Leave for the Day*

It's now 5:00 p.m. and I prepare to leave for the day. This is earlier than usual for me, since I usually leave for home some time prior to 6:30 p.m. The main reason for leaving early like this today is that I have some loose ends to tie up before I leave for vacation.

5:45 p.m.   *Arrive Home/Eat Dinner with the Family*

I really enjoy getting home before my kids go to bed. My wife has dinner ready for us and we sit together and have some chicken cacciatore for dinner. My wife is a wonderful cook and tonight's great dinner made up for today's missed breakfast and lunch.

6:00 p.m.   *Receive a Phone Call from a Victim Advocate*

A call from the rape care advocate interrupted dinner this evening. The director of our local program has my cell phone number so she can reach me at home. When there is an issue, she calls me directly and we work together to resolve problems quickly.

Typically, in such instances, there is a rape victim in limbo while we resolve the dispute. Fortunately, this evening, the problem is easily solved and everything is resolved in about ten minutes. I then finish my dinner.

6:30 p.m.   *Leave for Vacation*

I expect to be driving for the next seven to eight hours to a small cabin near a lake in Maine. I am looking forward to getting away for a few days.

10:00 p.m.   *Receive a Call from the On-Call Assistant Prosecutor*

The on-call assistant prosecutor calls me for advice on an active sexual assault investigation. I have a brief ten-minute conversation and we wish each other well and hang up.

2:30 a.m.   *Arrive at My Vacation Destination in Maine (after eight hours driving)*

I usually do not like driving eight hours straight. But this time, the end of such driving means the real beginning to a vacation I have been looking forward to for quite a while. I did bring some files with me from work. But hopefully, I can also use this time for some much-needed and anticipated time with my family.

2:45 a.m.   *Go to Bed*

After we arrive, it doesn't take us too long to unload the car and get settled in. We're a tired group. But at long last, we can sleep and wake up the next morning and look forward to some rest and relaxation together as a family.

5:00 a.m.   *Awakened by the Cell Phone - Another Work Call*

It's not long before my vacation is interrupted by an early morning phone call related to work. This time the call is regarding $250,000 that was being deposited in our escrow account. The bank apparently sent us $500,000 by accident.

Why doesn't this ever happen to me?

This is the first of many calls I will take on my vacation. I find it easier to address problems as they happen, rather than wait until I get back to work.

Final Thoughts

My job is a constant barrage of responsibilities covering all sorts of issues pertaining to the general public. But what I find gratifying is that I am doing this not just for myself, but for the protection of our society at large. Prosecutors are charged with seeking justice. Justice is not scored by wins, losses, convictions, or monetary reward. Your quest for justice is ultimately scored by what you think of the person looking back at you in the mirror. As a prosecutor, I have the pleasure of working with many fine and decent people who often find themselves working for little money and making decisions that affect lives far beyond their own. Ultimately, I believe that most of my colleagues are proud of the person who looks back at them in the mirror: I know I am.

3

Profile 3
Douglas: Criminal Defense Attorney

Executive Summary

Name: Douglas
Position: Criminal Defense Attorney
Location: San Diego, California

Defending alleged criminals may raise eyebrows for those not well versed in the US adversarial-based judicial system. Some may ask, "Why defend someone who may be guilty of atrocious crimes?" Like it or not, defending alleged criminal defendants, no matter how seemingly horrific the allegation, is a necessary part of the judicial system based on the spirit that every person is "innocent until proven guilty." In the US adversarial-based judicial system during a criminal (non-civil) trial, a prosecutor (as seen in the earlier career profile) will make the case against the defendant, and on the other side, it is the duty of the criminal defense attorney—like Douglas in the next career profile—to represent the legal rights and interests of the defendant to the best of his or her ability. In fact, failure to do so, under the US system, may lead to severe repercussions of allegations related to ineffective legal counsel. Here, as you read the twenty-four-hour profile of Douglas, a criminal defense attorney based in San Diego, you will step into his shoes during a criminal trial involving the alleged sexual molestation of an underage male victim. By reading this profile, you will see the world from the eyes of a criminal defense lawyer, including the art and science related to putting one's client on the stand as a witness. The pressure is high, and so are the stakes. If defended successfully, the client goes free. If not defended successfully, the client may serve time in prison. So by reading the Douglas's twenty-four-hour profile, you can see the "real world" scenes of a criminal defense attorney fulfilling his legal mandate to represent his client to the best of his ability.

Profile

Career Field:	Criminal Defense (Private Practice)
Current Position:	Sole Practitioner
Institution:	Law Firm
Location:	San Diego, California
Previous Position(s):	Law Professor
Education:	JD, Thomas Jefferson School of Law
	MA, San Diego State University
	BA, San Diego State University
Licenses (Y/N):	Yes
Jurisdiction(s):	California

Schedule

6:45 a.m.	Wake Up (waiting 15 more minutes until getting out of bed)
7:00 a.m.	Think Over Witnesses Taking Stand (in upcoming trial)
7:10 a.m.	Step Out of Shower/Think Over Defendant's Case
7:20 a.m.	Put on Suit/Contemplate Prosecutor's Effectiveness in Ongoing Trial
7:30 a.m.	Thought Process of Having Client (Defendant) Take the Stand
7:45 a.m.	Prepare Briefcase and Other Necessities for Trial
7:50 a.m.	Drop Off Daughters at School
8:00 a.m.	Theoretical (Psychology-Based) Rationale for Positioning of Client Taking the Stand
8:20 a.m.	Arrive at the Office/Review Trial Notes
8:45 a.m.	Leave the Office/Contemplate the Product of Legal Education (and being a lawyer)
9:00 a.m.	Arrive at Courthouse/Meet Client
9:05 a.m.	Judge Enters Courtroom/Direct and Cross-Examination of Witness
10:30 a.m.	Court Reconvenes from Morning Recess/Call Sixth Witness to the Stand
12:00 p.m.	Court Takes Noon Recess/Take Lunch
1:30 p.m.	Court Reconvenes/Resume Examination of Sixth Witness
2:00 p.m.	Call My Client to the Stand

3:00 p.m.	Court Calls for Recess/Discuss Strategy with Client
3:05 p.m.	Continue to Strategize with Client
3:15 p.m.	Court Reconvenes/Client Retakes the Stand
4:30 p.m.	Judge Announces That Case Will Reconvene on Monday
4:35 p.m.	Thought Process Relating to Client's Cross-Examination by Prosecutor
4:50 p.m.	Arrive at Office
5:00 p.m.	Meet Client at Office/Give Instructions for When Trial Reconvenes
5:30 p.m.	Return Phone Calls (to other clients)/Contact Expert Witness (for Monday's trial)
6:30 p.m.	Leave Office to Teach a Business Law Class (at a nearby university)
7:00 p.m.	Begin Business Law Class
9:40 p.m.	Finish Business Law Course/Drive Home
10:00 p.m.	Arrive Home/Tuck in Kids to Sleep
10:30 p.m.	Call Client (to advise on trial proceedings)
11:00 p.m.	Go over Client's Meeting Tomorrow/Watch the News
11:30 p.m.	Finish Watching the News/Go to Bed
6:45 a.m.	Wake Up Again

24-Hour Schedule

6:45 a.m.   *Wake Up (waiting 15 more minutes until getting out of bed)*

Upon realizing that I was awake, I took a quick glance at the clock by my bedside. I decided that I would allow myself another fifteen minutes until the time that I would allow my day to physically and officially begin. The problem for me was that I had been agonizing over for many months about this particular day. .

Today is the day that my client will take the stand as a defendant in a criminal trial to provide his testimony in front of a jury as to what had occurred on an evening some eighteen months earlier. We were entering the third week of a trial that would eventually last a total of four weeks, but would end up being the first of two trials in which two juries would be making a finding as to his guilt or innocence. For the next fifteen minutes, I reflect on the variety of decisions made during the months of preparation for this trial, as well as decisions I made during the course of the trial. I continue to watch the clock until it finally reads 6:59 a.m.

7:00 a.m.   *Think Over Witnesses Taking Stand (in upcoming trial)*

I took one last glance at the bedside clock. The primary thought on my mind was that it was now just two hours before I would be meeting my client in the hallway and walking him into the courtroom, just as we had done for the previous two weeks. As I step into the shower, my mind reviews the witnesses that had already testified. I find myself attempting to envision what surprises might occur during the time my client would be on the stand.

I reflect on the fact that for the previous two weeks, my client had only been a passive observer in his trial proceedings. All my client could do was sit and observe as we spent the first day of trial going through the process known as jury selection. Then he again sat as a passive observer as the prosecution presented each of their witnesses for their case in chief. Afterwards, he again played the role of passive observer, as the initial six witnesses testifying on his behalf (in his case) took the stand and testified in court. Now he was about to shift out of the role of passive observer into the role of key witness in his own case. To say that I was feeling uneasy would be an understatement.

7:10 a.m.   *Step Out of Shower/Think Over Defendant's Case*

I step out of the shower, grab my razor, and prepare to shave. Once again, my mind was not on what I was physically doing at the moment, but on my attempts to envision how my client would do when he took the stand (later today). The client whom I was representing had been falsely accused of sexually molesting a fourteen-year old boy. My uneasiness had nothing to do with my confidence in his innocence. The fact is that I had not the slightest doubt as to his innocence. No doubt whatsoever. But one never knows how a jury will perceive the testimony of a witness.

7:20 a.m.   *Put on Suit/Contemplate Prosecutor's Effectiveness in Ongoing Trial*

I grab the suit that I would be wearing for today's trial. I had set it out the
night. I put it on while continuing to reflect on the testimony the jury had
already heard and that which they would be hearing as the day transpired. It
did not help that for the first two weeks of this trial, it seemed that the
prosecutor in this case had the jury virtually eating out of her hand. Not
only was she bright, but she was attractive and charming, as a prosecutor.
After two weeks of trial, my perception was that she was in the driver's seat
of these proceedings. Obviously, that left me feeling very uneasy.

7:30 a.m.   *Thought Process of Having Client (Defendant) Take the Stand*

I check on my two daughters to make sure that they were getting ready for
school. While I await the time that I would drop them off at school on the
way to the office, I prepare and consume a quick breakfast. Again, I was
somewhat oblivious to what I was physically doing because my mind was
continuing to review decisions made early in this case, specifically, the
decision to have my client (defendant) take the stand. It was not lost on me
that some criminal defense attorneys strictly subscribe to a school of
thought that absolutely prohibits putting a defendant whom they are
representing on the stand. And there are any number of good reasons for
following that particular school of thought.

I, on the other hand, have always subscribed to a policy that hesitates to
take on a case unless I feel comfortable and am prepared to put my client
on the stand. It would be another ten years before I would finally be forced
to ultimately violate what had—up until then—been an unbending strict
policy. Therefore, having early on made the crucial decision in this case to
put my client on the stand, I then struggled over the following months over
the question of how to guide my client through the process of direct and
cross examination—as a witness in his own defense—without having him
irreparably damaging his case.

7:45 a.m.   *Prepare Briefcase and Other Necessities for Trial*

I check to make sure that everything that I could imagine that I might need
for the day's testimony was in my briefcase. This is important, since once I

leave for trial there's no coming back. Afterwards, I then alert the girls (my daughters) that it is time to leave for school.

7:50 a.m.   *Drop Off Daughters at School*

As we step outside the house, I lead the girls into the car and drove them to their respective schools. For the next ten minutes, my mind takes an ever so brief vacation from my ongoing thoughts of the trial. However, once the girls are dropped off, my mind immediately returns to my thoughts of the trial.

8:00 a.m.   *Theoretical (Psychology-Based) Rationale for Positioning of Client Taking the Stand*

I was now on my way to the office. My mind now fully returns to its thoughts of the day's anticipated events. I could not help but reflect on one of the decisions that I had made weeks before. It was based on a concept from the field of psychology. Among a vast array of psychological theories are two parallel concepts known as "primacy" and "recency."

In essence, the concepts suggest that individuals—presented with multiple pieces of information—will be more likely to retain the information presented first and last. As a result, those items presented toward the middle of any trial presentation would make less of an impression and would therefore be less likely to be retained.

Hence, my thinking in this case was that it would be tactically better to bury my client in the middle of the group of witnesses who were being presented. This is because I am hoping that his (my client-defendant's) testimony—if it was going to be as bad as I feared—would make less of an impact. Therefore, I strategically scheduled six of our witnesses ahead of my client's testimony and the other of his six witnesses after his testimony.

8:20 a.m.   *Arrive at the Office/Review Trial Notes*

I arrive at the office building, take the elevator up to my floor, and enter my office. I then grab a cup of coffee, and spend the next twenty-five minutes ensuring that my notes and documents for the morning of testimony are all in appropriate order. My more than twenty years of legal experience has taught me that preparation is critically important for being an effective legal counsel.

8:45 a.m.   *Leave the Office/Contemplate the Product of Legal Education (and being a lawyer)*

I leave the office and head over to the courthouse where the trial will be held in just a few short minutes. As I walk to court, I reflect on the different ways that different attorneys might have handled this particular case.

The fact is that while the curriculum for the study of law in law school is somewhat standardized, the curriculum that *leads up* to entry into law school is not. People enter law school from a variety of backgrounds and fields that is as wide as the imagination will allow. And from that conglomeration of varying backgrounds, law school trains this amorphous mass of individuals to eventually "think and reason like a lawyer."

But in spite of the standardized training that law school provides, the end product of law school graduates is anything but a homogenous mass of robotic thinkers. Different attorneys view cases differently. I wonder if there is anything that I was missing in my approach.

9:00 a.m.   *Arrive at Courthouse/Meet Client*

When I arrive and walk into the courthouse, I notice that my client is already waiting for me by the door to the courtroom. We greet each other cordially and quickly. My client seems nervous, and probably for good reason. Taking the stand is never easy for anyone, guilty or not. I then open the courtroom door and we enter the courtroom.

Although my client appeared prepared for the day's events, I was still apprehensive. This is because when an individual is falsely accused of a crime that he or she did not commit, it can severely alter not only how they perceive the world around them, but more importantly, the demeanor with which they respond.

In my client's case, during the previous six months—regardless of how I tried to question him—his responses were always enveloped by his rage over the situation that he had been placed in. No matter how I tried to coach him, he just came off looking badly.

My agonizing fear was that the jury in his trial would somehow translate his poor presentation into a reason to find him guilty of a crime of which he did not commit. But he would not take the stand until the afternoon session. So for now, I had two witnesses to get through.

9:05 a.m.   *Judge Enters Courtroom/Direct and Cross-Examination of Witness*

The trial gets underway just slightly after 9 a.m. Everyone rises as the judge enters the courtroom. After a few procedural protocols, the ball is now in my court. I then call my fifth witness to the stand. The first step in this process is the direct examination, which I start and finish. The next step is the cross-examination of the same witness, which is in the hands of the prosecutor (the same one I mentioned earlier who was not only smart, but also charming and attractive). This process continues until 10:15 a.m., when the judge calls for the court to take its morning recess.

10:30 a.m.   *Court Reconvenes from Morning Recess/Call Sixth Witness to the Stand*

The court reconvenes and the cross-examination of my fifth witness is concluded. I then call my sixth witness to the stand and initiate my direct examination.

12:00 p.m.   *Court Takes Noon Recess/Take Lunch*

The direct and cross-examination of my sixth witness takes longer than that of my fifth witness. It turns out that this process will be continued in the afternoon, since the presiding judge now calls for the court's noon recess and advises that we reconvene after lunch at 1:30 p.m. I have ninety minutes, so I use this time to strategize over the afternoon's court session over a quick sandwich and a drink.

1:30 p.m.   *Court Reconvenes/Resume Examination of Sixth Witness*

We enter the courtroom again, and shortly thereafter, the presiding judge and jury enter the room. We then begin where he left off before the noon recess. My sixth witness retakes the stand. I then conclude his direct examination and the prosecutor initiates and completes her cross-examination. That sixth witness was the last of the witnesses who I had planned on putting on the stand prior to my client. As the last of the first six witness steps down from the stand, I announce to the court that my next witness was the defendant.

2:00 p.m.   *Call My Client to the Stand*

At long last, the moment I've been anticipating is here—my client takes the stand. I take a deep breath and begin my direct examination.

In the course of the next hour—regardless of how poorly I might have envisioned his testimony going—my worst fears are not only realized, but also exceeded. Specifically, my client's responses to my questions, his body language as he spoke, and his overall presence was all wrong.

Our case was quickly imploding.

3:00 p.m.   *Court Calls for Recess/Discuss Strategy with Client*

After about the first hour into my client's testimony, the judge finally calls for a recess. It was almost as if I was watching a pay-per-view boxing match, in which my client was playing the role of a battered boxer being pounded in the ring by an overbearing opponent for a seemingly eternal round, when finally, the referee signals for a break at the end of the round.

Now that a court recess was called, I have about fifteen much-needed minutes to find some way to turn this thing (i.e., the momentum of the trial against my client) around to his favor.

I watch the jury file out of the courtroom. I then walk my client out into the hall, desperately trying to think of some way to change the direction of the trial in process. If things continue along this path, it will be game over for my client. He is relying on me—and me only—to help get him out of the mess he was in. I need to think of something, anything.

3:05 p.m.   *Continue to Strategize with Client*

At that point, I grasped at an analogy that just came to me at that instant. My client had been a career navy pilot. In fact, he had been a very highly decorated navy pilot during the Vietnam War. Knowing that, I had been searching the recesses of my brain for some analogy within his experience as a pilot to help us in his case. In desperation, I ask him if he could think back and remember the very first time that he had piloted an airplane. He indicates that he did.

I then asked him if remembered how he felt during that first flight. He responds that he was very scared and it did not go so well. I then ask if he remembers the next time he piloted a plane. He again indicates that he did. "How did that second time go," I inquire. His response is, "It went a lot better."

I then explain to him that his previous hour on the stand was like his first time piloting that airplane. But now that he was about to go back again on the stand, it would be much like his second time piloting an airplane. I then assure him that the next session on the stand—much like his second time piloting an airplane—would go better.

I use the remainder of our short time (during the court recess) focusing on some basic, but critical, aspects of his body language for when he retook the witness stand. I attempt to demonstrate to him the messages he was sending with his body language, and how his testimony might be drastically improved by some slight changes in his body language during his testimony. It's times like these that I almost feel like I'm playing the role of an acting (rather than legal) coach. But as defense counsel, these things are intertwined aspects of the job.

3:15 p.m.   *Court Reconvenes/Client Retakes the Stand*

The court reconvened from the recess, and my client and I re-enter the courtroom. Seated back in the courtroom, I watched the jury refill the jury box. The next hour or so before the court recessed for the day was far from great. But relatively speaking, it was nonetheless a tremendous improvement over the previous hour.

At least my client got the message regarding body language when he re-entered the stand. My objective, at that point was defensively postured— just to get him through that last hour or so without doing any more damage to himself. From this perspective—as I couched and promised my client during the previous court recess—things did go better the second time around.

In this sense, it was mission accomplished.

4:30 p.m.   *Judge Announces That Case Will Reconvene on Monday*

More than an hour later from when the court reconvened, the judge announces at 4:30 p.m. that we (the parties to the case) would be in recess until Monday. For the judge, tomorrow (Friday) would be "dark" in his courtroom—this simply means that the trial would not be convening that day.

4:35 p.m.   *Thought Process Relating to Client's Cross-Examination by Prosecutor*

A few minutes following the judge's announcement, I watch the prosecutor leave the courtroom. At this time, I sense what she had to be thinking— namely, that she could not wait for the trial to reconvene on Monday.

The problem before me was this: Most witnesses don't have too much of a problem with direct examination—which merely consists of a friendly lawyer slow pitching soft questions—enabling the telling of the story.

The problem, however, is cross-examination. That is the true test. And seeing how much difficulty my client was having during my direct examination of him, the prosecutor in the case simply just could not wait for the opportunity to virtually destroy him during her cross-examination.

After the prosecutor leaves the courtroom, I walk my client out and instruct him to meet me back at my office at 5:00 p.m.

4:50 p.m.   *Arrive at Office*

I arrive at my office. Since I've been gone for most of the day, I am flooded with messages and things to do. I quickly prioritize which things need to be done right away. I use the ten minutes or so before my client arrives to return a couple of phone calls.

5:00 p.m.   *Meet Client at Office/Give Instructions for When Trial Reconvenes*

My client and his wife arrive at my office and I spend the next half hour giving him instructions for Monday when the trial reconvenes. I tell my client that I would be giving him a phone call at 10:30 p.m. later in the evening, and that it would be a good idea if we meet again tomorrow so I can prep him for Monday. I ask him if that was okay. He tells me it would be.

5:30 p.m.   *Return Phone Calls (to other clients)/Contact Expert Witness (for Monday's trial)*

After my client leaves, I spend the next hour returning phone calls that had come in during the day (when I was away from the office for the trial). I phone the expert witness scheduled to testify on behalf of my client first thing Monday morning (when the trial reconvenes).

6:30 p.m.   *Leave Office to Teach a Business Law Class (at a nearby university)*

I leave the office and head out to San Diego State University to teach a business law class beginning at 7:00 p.m. This class was a part of my teaching assignment for that semester.

7:00 p.m.   *Begin Business Law Class*

It takes me about thirty minutes to get to the university from my law office at this hour. Just before 7:00 p.m., I arrive on campus and walk into the lecture room. The change of pace—from a heavy and serious courtroom setting to an academic setting with young students—is a welcome relief.

For the next two and half hours, my mind again vacations from any thoughts of the trial to teaching basic tenets related to the practice of business law.

One of the shared commonalities between teaching and actually practicing law is that both can involve a potentially captive audience where the subject is being explained using both "art" (i.e., the arguments, the body language, persuasion, and negotiation skills) and "science" (i.e., knowing the black letter law).

9:40 p.m.   *Finish Business Law Course/Drive Home*

During today's lecture, I discuss business law concepts such as contracts and torts to the class. For courses like this, it's always useful to go over case law that relates to the concepts at hand. The students often find these particularly interesting since it involves real world people in real world situations.

At 9:40 p.m., I finish my lecture and the class disperses in different directions to the lecture room's exit doors. I then head to my car and drive home.

10:00 p.m.   *Arrive Home/Tuck in Kids to Sleep*

It takes me about twenty minutes to drive home from the university. Fortunately, at this hour, the traffic is fairly light. I arrive home, and as usual, my older daughter is awaiting my arrival at the top of the stairs.

Seeing her waiting for me literally makes my day. We talk for a short while, and then I put her to bed and turn off the lights in her room so she can sleep.

10:30 p.m.   *Call Client (to advise on trial proceedings)*

As promised, I phone my client and instruct him on what would be transpiring when we meet tomorrow when I prep him for Monday. He sounds tired—as I'm sure he must be—given the course of the trial today. I also realize that he's not the only one who's tired and needs some sleep.

11:00 p.m.   *Go over Client's Meeting Tomorrow/Watch the News*

I feel some relief in the fact that I have three days before my client would take the stand again come Monday. I also feel a sense of hope since I will have the opportunity to meet with my client again tomorrow. The meeting will be not only to strategize with him as to what he might be expecting during Monday's cross-examination, but also to place him under hypnosis. Some may find placing a client under hypnosis unconventional. But for me, with this particular client, my primary purpose is to help relax the client, especially given his performance today, so he can be a more effective witness come Monday when things will become even more intense.

I turn on the TV to watch the news before I go to sleep.

11:30 p.m.   *Finish Watching the News/Go to Bed*

After about thirty minutes of watching the news, I decide to call it a night. I turn off the TV and go to sleep.

6:45 a.m.   *Wake Up Again*

What seemed like just seven minutes must have been seven hours since I went to bed—a stark realization when I hear the sound of my alarm clock. Fortunately, my client's trial is on Monday, not today. But I still have lots of work waiting for me to catch up once I arrive at my law office later this morning.

Final Thoughts

By the following Monday, the trial was in its third week. In the morning, our expert took the stand and was excellent. That afternoon, my client retook the stand and after a very brief completion of my direct examination from the prior Thursday, the prosecutor now had the opportunity that she had been waiting for all weekend—namely, the chance to tear my client to shreds with her cross-examination.

But to her dismay, it did not go as she planned. My client responded perfectly to each question she asked. With each question, the prosecutor became more confused and more frustrated. From that point onwards, the trial took on a completely new direction, which continued throughout the remainder of the trial.

At the end of the fourth week, the jury had the opportunity to hear the attorneys present their closing summations. By this point, it was clear that this case could absolutely go either way.

Regarding the art and science of being a criminal defense lawyer, legal experts will continue to debate the importance of the closing arguments relating to the result in a trial. Some feel it is critical, others would suggest that the jury has made up its mind long before this point in the trial.

Although I had a prepared my closing argument to present at trial, after hearing the prosecutor's argument, I decided to abandon my prepared closing and go off in a completely different direction—a direction that involved using humor to ridicule the prosecutor's just given closing remarks.

As some advice to those interested, based on my twenty years of legal experience, power is an incredibly interesting and fascinating concept. There are various theories that attempt to describe the various sources of power. Without question, the possession of knowledge would make it on the list for sources of power. Humor, on the other hand, might not make every list. But it would certainly make my list. And as risky as it can be to use humor during a criminal trial, I made the decision to invoke a touch of humor in my closing argument in the case at hand.

The jury found my client "not guilty" of all felony counts. But interestingly, the jury was hung on the one misdemeanor charge. The prosecutor refused to dismiss that count and a second trial ensued. The second jury found my client "not guilty" on that remaining charge.

Finally, some may question why a lawyer would defend a potentially guilty client in a court of law. This is a common question many, especially those not familiar with the American legal system, may pose to criminal defense lawyers such as myself. The general answer that most lawyers would give is that the American legal system is based on an "adversarial" system whereby both sides, including the defendant, should be afforded legal representation based on the maxim of "innocent until proven guilty." It's this spirit that I, along with most (if not all) other practicing defense attorneys adhere to, day in and day out, during our twenty-four-hour schedules.

4

Profile 4
Eric: General Practitioner

Executive Summary

Name: Eric
Profile: General Practitioner
Location: Encino, California

Thinking about working with family, rather than other law firms? Or working for smaller law firms that are less demanding than their larger law firm counterparts? If so, you might gain some insight by looking into a typical day for Eric, an attorney who works for his father as a general practitioner in a boutique law firm. One of the advantages to working with family in a law firm practice setting is that you will have more time to spend with loved ones while earning a potentially comfortable amount of money and being able to attain more responsibility and knowledge on chosen cases and clients. Flexible work hours are not what most lawyers can expect from their jobs when joining larger law firm practice. But, as you'll come to find out, this type of flexibility and working environment are some of the many things that Eric enjoys about his career. So if you are okay with a small family-like atmosphere, then you may want to give this career option some serious consideration.

Profile

Career Field:	Attorney (general legal with an emphasis on business litigation and transaction, real estate and estate planning)
Current Position:	Shareholder/Partner
Institution:	Boutique Law Firm (Schreiber & Schreiber Inc.)
Location:	Encino, California (San Fernando Valley in Los Angeles)
Previous Position(s):	None
Education:	JD, Loyola Law School (Los Angeles)
	BA, University of California, San Diego
Licensed (Y/N):	Yes
Jurisdictions:	California

Schedule

7:05 a.m.	Alarm Clock Rings/Time to Wake-Up
7:15 a.m.	Get My Son Ready for School/Prepare Breakfast
8:00 a.m.	Shower and Get Ready/Choose my Coat and Tie for the Day
8:25 a.m.	Court Call (re: status conference)
9:00 a.m.	Take My Daughter to Nursery School
9:15 a.m.	Arrive at the Office
9: 30 a.m.	Check in with My Father (and Partner)/Return Phone Calls and E-Mail
10:30 a.m.	Work on Summary Judgment Motion
12:00 p.m.	Attend My Daughter's Nursery School Play
12:30 p.m.	Lunch
1:30 p.m.	Work on Appellate Brief
2:30 p.m.	Take Call from My Wife
3:30 p.m.	Meeting with New Clients (re: preparation of estate plan)
4:45 p.m.	Conference Call with Client (re: discovery responses)
5:30 p.m.	Talk Over Recent Developments with my Father
6:00 p.m.	More Work on Summary Judgment (including making copies)
6:30 p.m.	Review, Edit, and Copy Billing Sheets
6:40 p.m.	Go Home/Have Dinner with Family/Play with Kids

7:45 p.m.	Play Basketball/Play Wii with Kids
8:45 p.m.	Put Kids to Bed/Take Care of Baby
10:30 p.m.	Put Baby to Bed/Watch TV/Log onto Home Computer
12:00 a.m.	Review E-Mail (to make sure nothing urgent is needed for tomorrow)
12:30 a.m.	Bed Time (or so I hope)
7:05 a.m.	Time to Start Again (for another 24 hours)

24-Hour Schedule

7:05 a.m.   *Alarm Clock Rings/Time to Wake-Up*

Oh, how I hate my alarm clock—I'm not a "morning" person, not now, not ever. Even three kids can't change this. But as school starts at 8:00 a.m. for my son, it would probably be best if he were dressed and had something to eat before he goes. It's nice to have a good friend at the department of Social Services, just in case.

7:15 a.m.   *Get My Son Ready for School/Prepare Breakfast*

Like me, my son is also not an early riser. But if I have to be up, so does he. He gets dressed and I make the lunches for the kids and feed them breakfast. I can't cook. So cereal and frozen pancakes will be at the top of the featured breakfast menu items today, that's for sure. Luckily, my son's school is only a few minutes away from home and my wife gets him out of the door at 7:45 a.m.

8:00 a.m.   *Shower and Get Ready/Choose my Coat and Tie for the Day*

As a member of a small boutique firm, it's absolutely essential I dress professionally. Even though the trend is for attorneys—even in big, prestigious firms—to dress a little more casually, our firm has always had a dress code policy (since its inception more than forty-five years ago) of a coat and tie. And especially for court dates and meetings with important clients, a full suit is a must. Our motto is to provide big firm service and ability at small firm prices. So it's very important to dress professionally every day since I never know when a client may show up unannounced.

Our rates are generally $100 to $300 per hour less than a larger firm, but our attorneys are similarly qualified. Our client base consists primarily of professionals and small- to medium-sized businesses that tend to demand high-end services at affordable prices. Our ability to provide this has kept the firm in business for close to fifty years. So for anyone considering opening a smaller boutique firm and competing with the "big boys," based on our firm's success, I might recommend this blend of competitive pricing mixed with a high value-added services strategic approach.

8:25 a.m.   Court Call (re: status conference)

Court call is perhaps one of the best things to have happened to the practice of law in the last seven to ten years. With a court call, rather than go to court, I can make an appearance by conference call from my office or home office. This is excellent since it really helps me to save time and use my time more productively for my clients. Specifically, by doing this, rather than spending an hour to an hour and a half driving to downtown Los Angeles (and paying $17 for parking, waiting around to speak with a judge for five minutes, and then spending another hour or so driving back to the office), I can instead just make a call to the court five minutes before the scheduled start time, speak with the judge about whatever needs to get done, and afterwards, simply hang up the phone and get right back to work. This service costs only $45 and I can bill my client for about half an hour of my time (as opposed to two to three hours of driving plus parking fees).

Today, I have a routine matter—a simple status conference and order to show cause (re: service). After waiting for my turn for about twenty minutes, I satisfactorily explain to the judge about the case status. He then sets a follow-up status conference date and afterwards I hang up. Total time spent: about thirty-five minutes. I use court call for all routine motions and status conferences. As a result, our firm only goes to court when it is essential or when court call is unavailable. Court call has also made it easier and more affordable for us to represent clients on matters out of the county and even at the far reaches of the state where previous travel costs and time spent would normally have made it too expensive for our clients.

9:00 a.m.   *Take My Daughter to Nursery School*

Luckily, my daughter's school is only a few blocks away from my home. I really consider myself fortunate to be able to take my daughter to school on most days, barring any extremely pressing matters.

9:15 a.m.   *Arrive at the Office*

Another benefit of working in a small firm with my father is that there's almost zero downtime in terms of commuting. My office is less than a half-mile from my home. My father is also less than a mile from the office. This is a real benefit for me since I really can't stand commuting and wasting time driving in a car (especially in Los Angeles, with its notorious traffic congestion). When I arrive at the office, I greet our part-time office manager (we only have one part-time employee since this is all we need), and say "hello" to my brother who is our current law clerk (set to take the bar and join our firm soon afterwards).

9:30 a.m.   *Check in with My Father (and Partner)/Return Phone Calls and E-mail*

The message light is blinking when I arrive at my office—it always is. I listen to all of my voicemail messages and return calls in the order of importance. I also check my e-mail, although my BlackBerry lets me know every time an e-mail arrives. I'll be responding to e-mail all day—it's the easiest, fastest, and least intrusive way to deal with almost every client issue. I then check-in with my father who is also my law partner to see if there is anything critical (as well as seeing how his day is going so far). Since right now there isn't anything immediate or urgent he needs me to do, we take this time to discuss some of the cases we are handling. I then go to work. My father and I both know about every case in the office. We can usually cover for each other whenever a need arises. Generally, one of us will take the primary lead on a case, with the other providing legal support when necessary. Sometimes we both work on a case equally. It all depends on the nature of the matter.

10:30 a.m.   *Work on Summary Judgment Motion*

Currently, I'm working on a summary judgment motion in a case where my client, a corporation, is a defendant in a case. Like most summary judgment motions, this effort has been a massive undertaking. All of my research is done in-house and often online through Westlaw (an online legal research service). While these motions are time-consuming and expensive, they are also often very effective tools in litigation. We will not file such a motion unless we believe we have a good chance of success at knocking out at least a portion of a case. However, such motion is also an effective tool at "poisoning the well" (trying to get my side of the case before a judge in the hopes he or she will sympathize with our position before trial), and to get the other side's best arguments and expert witness testimony out in the open. For this case, I feel strongly about this particular motion and believe we have a solid chance to knock the other side's case out of court. Luckily, it's for a good client that has been with our firm for a number of years who has put a lot of faith and confidence in the firm. Some clients don't tolerate losing motions or cases (which will happen no matter how good the lawyer is). Fortunately, this is not one of them. In this time slot, I often work on either litigation-related matters or drafting agreements or some other sort of transactional matter.

12:00 p.m.   *Attend My Daughter's Nursery School Play*

Although not typical, today my daughter is a knight in her nursery school play, *Boogie Knights*. So my father and I leave to see her. This is one of those benefits that I would never have anywhere else—if I want, I can leave when I choose, and it is up to me by which means to finish the necessary work. And I can do so on my own time, barring a deadline. For me, it's so nice not to have to ask permission to leave work. If I worked far from home, this type of trip would be impossible. This is one of the main reasons I opted to work with my father and close to home versus the other alternatives I had after law school.

12:30 p.m.   *Lunch*

On most days, Dad and I, along with my brother, go out to lunch at a local restaurant. There are several places to eat within walking distance of our office. Today, we choose our once-a-week stop, *Maria's Italian Kitchen*— it's a bit like *Cheers* (the TV comedy show)—everybody knows our name. Lunch is a great time to speak with Dad regarding the status of matters I'm currently working on. And he can keep me in the loop with his cases as well. On average, we'll have lunch with a client about once a week. Sometimes it's a business meeting, other times it's more social (such as when a long-time client, who is more a friend, just wanting to catch up).

1:30 p.m.   *Work on Appellate Brief*

After lunch, I check my phone messages and e-mails to return, and then I'm able to return to work. I'm also working on my absolute favorite type of work—drafting an appellate brief. Some would call me crazy, but this is the most academic and, to me, most interesting part of the job. It is somewhat unusual for a small firm (that is not an appellate boutique) to be involved in so many appellate matters. But I've been able to write and argue numerous appeals, and already have four published opinions to my name— three State Appellate Court and one State Supreme Court opinion. Arguing before the California Supreme Court has been the highlight of my career— and we won the case and negotiated a great settlement afterwards.

2:30 p.m.   *Take Call from My Wife*

I often get calls from my wife, asking a question here or there, or sometimes, the kids just want to say "Hi." It's nice to take a short break sometimes. Then, it's back to work.

3:30 p.m.   *Meeting with New Clients (re: preparation of estate plan)*

I was able to recruit some new business—family friends who would like us to prepare their estate plan. They come in and meet with my father and I, and we explain the process of estate planning to them. This is one of the better parts of the job. There is a litigator's adage that goes along the lines of, "By the time the client comes to see an attorney, something is already wrong." That is, they are either mad enough to sue or have already been sued by someone. Estate planning is different. Usually the clients are not stressed and are happy to be taking care of their affairs. So here, after taking notes and listening to the clients, we provide them with a draft estate plan in about a week. When it's acceptable, they will come in and have it signed and notarized to formalize the procedure.

4:45 p.m.   *Conference Call with Client (re: discovery responses)*

More litigation matters. I recently sent a client proposed discovery responses, and now we have a conference call to go over and edit those responses. Fortunately, most of my clients are efficient and on top of things, which makes my job easier and their bill smaller. After going over everything, the discovery responses are finished, I e-mail the client the responses and a verification form. He signs and PDFs the signature to me. It is then copied and mailed off to opposing counsel. Client cooperation and assistance goes a long way toward winning or resolving cases.

5:30 p.m.   *Talk Over Recent Developments with my Father*

Toward the end of the day, I generally meet with my father and go over everything that happened during the day as well as to exchange case information. Communication and knowledge of all the matters in the office is essential for our firm. This is because if one of us is out or unavailable, the other has to be able to help clients with any pending matter. This is made far easier with e-mail and cell phones. But it's best to know everything going on in the office, and to know if there is anything set for tomorrow.

6:00 p.m.   *More Work on Summary Judgment (including making copies)*

I figure that with our motion filing deadline coming up soon (summary judgment motions have to be filed at least seventy-five days before the hearing date and at least thirty days before trial), it's best I come close to finishing the motion. There is a lot of copying to be done, and since our part-time office manager has gone home for the day, I (by de facto) become the secretary of last resort.

This isn't exactly a big deal. But in a small firm, the attorney has to do a little bit of everything—we simply don't have the budget or space for full-time support staff. So as a result, I do all of my own research and typing. Again, this is the nature of the job, and I have never known any different.

Our office manager is great, and does almost all of the non law-related matters, freeing up the attorneys to do what we do best, the practice of law. But there are times when the attorneys have to do what has to get done. This motion filing is important and it all falls on me if something goes wrong, even if I'm not the one making the mistake. So I often feel more comfortable if I personally oversee each and every step in an important motion like this. And as part of this, I'll review this motion several times for form and content before it is sent with our attorney service for filing in the next few days. It's also nice that the court has a website where I can verify things have been filed, check for case updates, and sometimes, obtain tentative motion rulings in advance. Technological advances like this have made the practice of law more efficient and far less stressful in the past five years.

6:30 p.m.   *Review, Edit, and Copy Billing Sheets*

Billing is the lifeblood of all law firms, big and small. Our firm, for most cases, bills hourly. That is, we keep track of the time we spend on each matter, each day, and then bill in terms of each tenth of an hour increment. Some matters—like estate plans or simple contracts—are billed as a flat fee (one fee for all related services rendered). And we do occasionally take contingency matters, if we believe it is an excellent case or opportunity.

Our firm's primary source of income is hourly billing, but it's nice to have a shot at a big case once in a while. I couldn't live on contingency matters alone—it's simply too risky. Although time is usually kept contemporaneously with the work done, I still review the bills to see if something doesn't look right. Billing is kept by hand and then transferred to our billing program. We do all of our billing in-house. Another nice thing I enjoy at my firm is that there are no mandatory baseline hours or partners looking over my shoulder to make sure I hit the 2,200 billable hours a year that exist in many larger firms. We don't have the massive overhead and a far more reasonable amount of billable hours is sufficient.

6:40 p.m.   *Go Home/Have Dinner with Family/Play with Kids*

One of the main reasons I chose the career path that I have is based on the following simple formula: short commute = more time at home. In other words, by working for the firm that I do, I am afforded many perks such as having dinner and spending quality time with my wife and kids (on a consistent basis at a reasonable hour). I'm not sure if it gets any better than this for me, everything considered.

7:45 p.m.   *Play Basketball / Play Wii with the Kids*

On Wednesdays, I play basketball at the local synagogue with a group of guys similar to me—family men who are working professionals. We aren't all that good, but it's fun and good to get some exercise in like this. On other weeknights, I play Wii (a videogame) with my son, and play and watch TV with my daughters. I don't even think about work during these times.

8:45 p.m.   *Put Kids to Bed/ Take Care of Baby*

I'm lucky tonight—my kids (not the baby) have gone to bed already without much protest (which is rare). When the kids finally go to bed, my wife and I take care of the baby. This is usually a nice time for us.

10:30 p.m.   *Put Baby to Bed/ Watch TV/ Log onto Home Computer*

I'm even more lucky tonight—our baby falls asleep around 10:30 p.m. or so and I have time to myself to watch TV, use the computer, and just relax.

12:00 a.m.   *Review E-Mail (to make sure nothing urgent is needed for tomorrow)*

Before going to sleep, I check my work e-mail, look at the firm website, and review my files just to make sure I don't have anything urgent for the next day. If I have a court call or court appearance, I review my files to make sure I am prepared and don't miss anything. I usually sleep fine (as long as the baby doesn't wake up), unless I have a major matter the next morning. If so, then it's hard to sleep, since I'm concerned and think about what I may have to do with the pending legal matter—it has a way of keeping me awake at night—I just can't help it.

12:30 a.m.   *Bed Time (or so I hope)*

Assuming all is in order, I take a quick check of the house and the kids. And then it's off to sleep.

7:05 a.m.   Time to Start Again (for another 24 hours)

It's time to wake-up once again. And I prepare myself to prepare all the prior steps above, five days a week. While many attorneys put in hours over the weekend, I consider myself fortunate in that I rarely, if ever, have to work on weekends.

Final Thoughts

Overall, I'm very happy with the life and career path that I've chosen and the opportunities I have been given. Unlike many, I have since I was very young (when I first realized I wouldn't be able to make it as a professional athlete) wanted to be an attorney, just like my father. I also quickly realized that while I had the credentials and ability to make a huge, big firm salary, I simply didn't want to put in the weighty-plus billable hours a week and deal with the resulting big firm politics and stresses that go along with it. I know many friends who are partners at large firms and are very happy; it's just not for me. I had the opportunity to choose time and family over money, and gladly took it. I still make a decent salary on which my family and I can live on. I work great with my father and we have not had one argument in more than thirteen years. I think he's happy to pass on his life's work to his son, and maybe one day, I can do the same for my children. I can come and go as I please, I can work at my own pace and schedule, and answer to no one but my father and myself. I believe my JD and law license has afforded me the life I want to live, and would highly recommend the solo/small firm lifestyle to those who have the opportunity and for those who value time over more money.

I also consider myself fortunate to have had options when I graduated from law school. As a student who graduated in the top 5 percent of my class, I had the option to choose from many firms. I was also very fortunate in that I also had the option to work with my father, and his firm, which was established with a client base in place. I know that I'm lucky to have been offered such a choice, when few have had such opportunity. In choosing my career path, my family, my time, and my stress level were far more important to me than a larger salary. While I still work hard, and make a decent salary, had I instead chosen to work for a large firm, it would have been at the cost of time away from my family. While I don't make the massive amount of money some large firm attorneys make, I can come and go as needed, I don't have minimum billing hours to be on the "partnership track," and I work a fairly normal schedule. For me, I would make this choice one hundred times out of one hundred.

5

Profile 5
Samuel: Intellectual Property (IP) Litigator

Executive Summary

Name:	Samuel
Profile:	Intellectual Property (IP) Litigator
Location:	Chicago, Illinois

Although Samuel may admit to the benefits of his status working for a large law firm specializing as an IP litigator, he also candidly describes how there are now no guarantees to long-term prosperity, given the current competitive marketplace, even with his "partner" title. The intense pressure to amass "billable hours" only gives Samuel very few precious hours every day for the bare necessities, like to eat and sleep (lest he should sacrifice his weekends and holidays). As for his work as an intellectual property litigator, which typically requires a background in science and law, it is a position for only a few. Samuel hardly has a peaceful moment during his day, which is often jam-packed with reviewing patent applications, litigation work, meeting with clients, and providing trademark information—all of which must be executed fast and efficiently. Anyone thinking of entering a big law firm practice focusing on innovative and cutting-edge products and design should take a closer look at Samuel's typical day. But pay heed to the rigors of his daily twenty-four-hour day.

Profile

Career Field:	Intellectual Property Litigation
Current Position:	Partner
Institution:	Large International Law Firm
Location:	Chicago, Illinois
Previous Position(s):	Judicial Clerk
Education:	JD, Loyola University, School of Law (Chicago)
	BA, University of Chicago
Licensed (Y/N):	Yes
Jurisdictions:	Illinois/US Patent & Trademark Office (USPTO)

Schedule

5:00 a.m.	Wake-Up Daddy!
5:45 a.m.	Wake-Up (again)/Check my iPhone for Messages
6:15 a.m.	Prepare for the Day
7:00 a.m.	Get Showered/Notice a Few Gray Hairs
7:30 a.m.	Get Dressed
8:00 a.m.	Take the Subway (to the loop for the office)
8:25 a.m.	Arrive at the Firm/Make a List of Things to Do
9:00 a.m.	I Work the Phones/Call Opposing Counsel
10:00 a.m.	Telephone Status Conference (with Judge Smith)
10:30 a.m.	Review Patents/Create Litigation Strategies
11:00 a.m.	Phone Call from My Wife
11:10 a.m.	Interview a Law Student
11:30 a.m.	Crisis #1: Congressional Subpoena
12:30 p.m.	Lunch at My Desk
12:45 a.m.	Phone Call from a Friend (re: possible business development opportunity)
1:15 p.m.	Personal Appointment
2:15 p.m.	Meeting with a Pro Bono Client
2:45 p.m.	Phone Call from Senior Partner
3:00 p.m.	Draft a Trademark Application
4:00 p.m.	Prepare for an Expert Deposition
5:00 p.m.	Review Work Product from Various Associates
6:00 p.m.	Meet Client at Hotel (to go to a Cubs game)
10:00 p.m.	Head Home

10:20 p.m.	Stop in at a Local Bar
11:15 p.m.	Get Home
11:30 p.m.	Do Some Administrative Work (for the firm)
12:00 a.m.	Personal Business/Preparation for the Next Day
1:45 a.m.	Sleep
5:00 a.m.	Wake-Up (to the alarm clock)

24-Hour Schedule

5:00 a.m.   *Wake-Up Daddy!*

Every morning, I wake up from my sleep with the inextricable feeling that I've overslept. Today is no different—I jump out of bed thinking I overslept. In reality, I've only slept two hours and thirty minutes.

My two and a half year old son is having trouble sleeping and is tugging at my arm. "Wake up daddy!" Huh? He usually sleeps until 5:45 a.m. What happened to my extra forty-five minutes of sleep? Does he know that I stayed up until 2:30 a.m. drafting an appellate brief? No, of course not. Does he know his mother is pregnant with his sibling and needs her rest? He doesn't seem to care.

Being a good husband, I let my pregnant wife sleep in and take my baby boy back to his room. I try to coax him into sleeping a little bit more. "See, the sun's still asleep. So that must mean we all need to sleep!"

He wakes up again at 5:45 a.m. "Daddy, daddy! The sun's not asleep anymore!" Curse these early morning sunrises. I have no choice but to really wake-up this time.

5:45 a.m.   *Wake-Up (again)/Check my iPhone for Messages*

I am *not* a morning person. In fact, the opposite is true. So everything I do in the morning is on autopilot. Our son starts his day, every day, with so much energy and enthusiasm. I remember when I used to look forward to my day like that.

The first thing I do, as soon as I wake up, is to check my iPhone. This is automatic. I do this as a habit without even thinking about it. I do it even when I'm on vacation. The only time I went off the clock completely was during my honeymoon. That seems like forever ago now.

Twenty-five e-mail messages. Not bad. Six electronic filing notices I expected, ten news and law summaries, two e-mails from friends, and seven junk e-mails. Some days, I wake up to emergency e-mail from insane senior partners and clients who get to work at 5:00 a.m. I make no mistake on what we do. We're in the service industry. We get paid a lot of money to be available 24/7 for our clients. Luckily, today is not one of those emergency days.

I take our son downstairs for some breakfast and television.

6:15 a.m.   Prepare for the Day

I'm still barely awake and I'm still on autopilot. I make breakfast for our family. My wife lets our dog out to take care of his business. She makes coffee and prepares our dog's breakfast. I turn on *Sesame Street* (a children's educational TV show) for our child. She tells me about a strange dream she had last night. I can't remember the last time I remembered a dream—I'm usually so tired that my brain just shuts down completely when I'm sleeping.

My wife and I are two smart, educated parents. We're both attorneys. Yet, we still use TV as a babysitter for moments like this. We have to. We're too tired to be active stimulating parents when we can barely function ourselves. The important thing is that we're here for our son and spending time with him.

7:00 a.m.   Get Showered/Notice a Few Gray Hairs

I feel better after a couple of cups of coffee. But I'm still not ready to wake-up. I go upstairs to shower while my wife keeps an eye on our son. Then she showers while I keep an eye on him. I remember the days when it was just us (without children). It took us thirty minutes to get ready. We used to have intelligent conversations in the morning. I'm not complaining. But things are a little different now.

I wait until the last possible moment to get dressed, because there's at least a 90 percent chance that my child has gotten his breakfast all over him and will insist on giving me a bear hug. I've ruined too many good shirts and ties that way. Not today.

I look in the mirror and notice more gray hairs. Ugh. It really makes me look older than I want to look. It makes me upset that I'm not getting carded anymore too. Should I get my hair colored? I should if I still want to look young. Or do I? As I'm becoming more and more responsible for client relationships and business development, I'm becoming increasingly more aware of how my youthful appearance is a liability rather than an asset. So I just shrug it off. A little gray is good for someone in my line of work. You want to look *older* rather than *younger*.

7:30 a.m.   *Get Dressed*

What to wear? This is Chicago. Not New York or London. We're Midwesterners. We're sensible. But we're still lawyers. My clothes and accessories are a balance of these things. An off the rack Thomas Pink shirt. A Mont Blanc watch. A tailored suit I picked up during a business trip to Hong Kong. A classic black Tumi computer bag. These things are nice but not ostentatious. It says "trust me" with your invention, life's work, and business, while at the same time, it signals that I'm not here to get rich off your money to buy Rolex watches.

8:00 a.m.   *Take the Subway (to the loop for the office)*

I kiss my wife and son goodbye, and I'm finally out the door at 8:00 a.m. I walk one block to the train station: five minutes flat.

Chicago is one of the worst cities for commuting. But my commute's twenty-five minutes door to door. This is no accident. I spent a lot of money to live exactly where I do because of the short commute. Compared to someone who drives in from the suburbs, I save thirty minutes each way on my commute. That may not sound like much to you, but that's one hour each day on commuting alone. That's 250 hours a year. That can mean the difference between my child knowing who I am versus spending years in therapy with daddy issues.

I wait at the train station: three minutes. There's a train every six minutes, so I rarely wait long. I listen to an NPR (National Public Radio) podcast on my iPhone. It gives my brain a rest from my near-constant thoughts of legal issues and to-do lists.

8:25 a.m.   Arrive at the Firm/Make a List of Things to Do

Travel time on the train: twelve minutes. Walk to the law firm: five minutes. I stop at Starbucks in my building to grab a Venti Café Americano and a sandwich for lunch. After I pick up both, I head to the building lobby, push the button to my firm, and then take the elevator to my office.

I never really notice the view from my office. But I do today. I work in a near corner office with floor to ceiling windows overlooking Lake Michigan. My furniture is dark cherry wood. It looks serious. In fact, our entire office building is designed to intimidate any opposing counsel who visits us. It exudes money, power, and strength.

Sure, my office looks and feels like I've made it. But did I? This is what people think of when they start out in law school. A partner at a large law firm with a view of Lake Michigan—they all think, "Now *that* person has made it!" But I don't notice my view or my office much these days. In fact, I'd rather not be here today. I take things like this for granted, because my job isn't exactly satisfying my creative side. I'd rather be a travel writer or a photographer.

I use my morning time to make a list of what I need to do today. I drink my coffee and get settled for the day. It's going to be a busy day, and I have to hit the ground running. If I don't make a list, I know I'll get sidetracked with problems that come up during the day and forget to do something. I've made that mistake early in my legal career. Not anymore.

9:00 a.m.   I Work the Phones/Call Opposing Counsel

The first thing that I do is to work the phones. I am an IP (intellectual property) litigator, which means I'm a litigator with an IP specialty. That means everything I do is in an adversarial context.

Talking to opposing counsel is never fun, so I try to get it out of the way first. The mornings are the best time to do it. This is because my mind's sharp at this time—I haven't had time to over-think anything—and I know that I can at least catch them in a better mood. I'm direct and to the point. "I'm calling to let you know that my client rejects your settlement offer." "I need to talk to you to set a date for the deposition of Dr. John Smith."

After this and several other calls, I follow up with e-mail. These days, if it's not in writing, it didn't happen. So everything has to be documented. "Per our conversation, Dr. Smith will be produced on (such and such date) at (such and such place) for a deposition."

Having a junior associate send a letter or e-mail would have been easier. But I still prefer to pick up the phone and talk to opposing counsel. They're more reasonable when they're talking to you as a real, live person, than when responding to you via an e-mail or letter.

10:00 a.m.   Telephone Status Conference (with Judge Smith)

By 9:45 a.m., I'm finished with my phone calls and am preparing for a status conference in front of a judge I'll refer to as Judge Smith for one of my cases that's pending in the state of New Jersey. There are four districts—New Jersey, Delaware, Texas, and California—that are the busiest for patent litigation in the United States. I have cases pending in every one of these districts.

Even a few years ago, Judge Smith would have brought us all into court for this conference, which meant that I would be in New Jersey today. That would have sucked. Nothing against New Jersey. But I would have had to fly there yesterday, spend the night at a hotel, appear in court this morning, and fly back this afternoon. I would have missed sleeping in my own bed last night and missed spending the little time I have with my family. These days, judges are much kinder to out-of-town attorneys. So they schedule telephone conferences on routine matters like this.

The call with Judge Smith is mostly to provide a status update on where the parties are on discovery. But, nonetheless, I have to over-prepare for the call. It's because anything can happen. Opposing counsel can complain, for example, that we're refusing to produce relevant documents and prejudicing their rights. So I had an associate put together a chart for me on the dates of our document production, how many documents we've produced, and the efforts we've made to locate all relevant documents.

Today, everything is routine. More often than not, status conferences are just that: routine. The old days of fighting *everything* and *everyone* is, for the most part, over. Even large, institutional clients want me to avoid petty discovery disputes if possible to save on legal costs. In the call, I'm happy to report that the parties have been cooperating for the most part and that the things that we disagree on we're trying to work it out. The judge is pleased. She tells us to try to work things out if possible, and to ask for a conference if there are irreconcilable problems.

10:30 a.m.   *Review Patents/Create Litigation Strategies*

Time to give the phones a break and to do some old fashioned analysis. Yesterday, we got a new case from an existing client who wants to file a declaratory judgment against a company that's threatening to sue them.

Declaratory judgment actions are advantageous because we get to pick the venue (i.e., the location to sue). My client is a Chicago-based company. So, of course, we'll sue them in the Northern District of Illinois (federal court in Chicago) and fight them in our own turf. When you litigate patents, you're either protecting your patents or trying to invalidate someone else's patents. I like being on the side that is on the offensive and tries to invalidate patents. It's more challenging and requires a little bit more creativity than trying to protect a patent from an invalidity challenge.

As a licensed patent attorney, it's usually my responsibility to take the first crack at developing our legal strategies. So what does being a "patent lawyer" mean? It means that I have two things: (1) a science or technical undergraduate degree; and (2) a passing score on a day-long test on patent law given by the US Patent & Trademark Office (USPTO). These sound like silly requirements, but these are the rules. Some attorneys I know can probably pass the test, but they do not have a science or technical degree. Therefore, they are not licensed patent attorneys. Most lawyers recognize that you don't need a science degree to be a patent lawyer, so these are silly requirements. But being a patent lawyer does put me at a somewhat unique position among lawyers. Most lawyers are not scientists and most scientists do not become lawyers. So there are not too many of us.

And not all patent lawyers do the same thing. We don't all write patents. Some of us choose just to litigate. This is, by no means, an "either-or" proposition, because patent prosecutors (i.e., those who write patents) get involved in litigation and vice versa. But almost without exception, experienced patent lawyers do either one or the other. I think it's a specialty thing. Litigation and prosecution require different skill sets and it's hard to do both seamlessly. Litigation is fast-paced and adversarial while prosecution is more deliberate and technical. Generally, patent lawyers tend to gravitate to one or the other. I chose litigation. But some days, I wonder if I should have chosen to prosecute patents instead. I also know some patent lawyers who prosecute patents who would love to litigate patents. I supposed the grass is always greener on the other side.

11:00 a.m.   *Phone Call from My Wife*

My phone's been ringing steadily. But I don't generally answer my calls. The amount of phone calls I get is mind-boggling. Some are legitimate calls from clients or opposing counsel. But some just want to give me financial advice. Some are headhunters. Some offer patent-related services. Most end up wasting my time.

My wife calls. I have to answer this one. She asks what we should do for dinner. I don't know. She asks if I'll be home for dinner. I don't know. For someone who gets paid to make quick well-reasoned decisions, I feel silly saying "I don't know" and "I have no idea." But my schedule is unpredictable. So I honestly don't know. An opposing counsel can file a frivolous motion that requires my immediate attention. A client could call with an emergency. I just don't know. It's for this reason that it's impossible to make plans with friends. This kind of dedication is hard to understand for someone in a "9 to 5" job. I'm on the clock anytime, anywhere. Calls to my office are even forwarded to my cell phone automatically twenty-four hours a day.

My wife also tells me that our son cried when she dropped him off at the daycare today. She feels guilty. I feel guilty too. She's an attorney and even though I make enough money for both of us, she's not ready to give up on her career. I'm not either. And I know my time here is probably limited. Odds are not good. About fifty of us started as first year associates. And of this number, only about five of us made it to the partner level. Chances are, another three or four of us will be gone in less than five years. Being a big firm lawyer is grinding, grueling, relentless work. I don't think I have many more years left in me. I also may get laid off, because the work sometimes dries up. My friend at the firm just got laid off last year. I don't have my own big clients yet. So the future's still unpredictable for me. Like it or not, there's no such thing as loyalty anymore, from both the law firm's perspective and the lawyer's perspective.

11:10 a.m.   *Interview a Law Student*

I hang up the phone with my wife at 11:05 a.m. and have exactly five minutes to review a law student's resume before I interview that person at 11:10 a.m. I've tried to wing it a few times. But there's nothing worse than obviously reading a person's resume for the first time during the actual interview. I'm busy. But that's just rude. I still remember being on the other side of the table. So I try to take my interviews seriously.

The way I approach interviews is simple. If a resume is in front of me, the person's probably well qualified academically. I've never looked at a resume and thought, "How did this person get an interview here?" Our recruiting department does a good job of not wasting my time. This one's no different.

Our interviews are quick and efficient: twenty to thirty minute individual interviews at our offices. Each interviewee will typically meet with six attorneys: four to five associates and one to two partners. I'm often the most senior interviewer. So most interviewees are eager to impress me with their credentials. But that's the wrong approach. I don't want to know about your credentials. You pass on that point if you're in front of me. At this stage, I want to know whether you can hold yourself together, whether you can hold a conversation, and whether you have a decent enough personality to be a future rainmaker or to relate to a jury. Are you observant and can you make small talk? For instance, "Is that a picture of you in front of the Eiffel Tower? Paris is wonderful, isn't it?"

I ask my interviewee how she likes Chicago. She says she likes it. But she doesn't know if she can get used to the weather. She's from Florida and most of her family now lives in California. I don't count this against her. But I wonder to myself if she really sees a future here in Chicago? We're going to invest a lot of money wining and dining her as a summer associate and training her as a junior associate. Do we really want to devote that kind of resources on her if she's just going to leave us after a couple of years? I note my concerns. But ultimately, I recommend that we hire her. She may grow to love Chicago, despite its weather. I did.

11:30 a.m.   *Crisis #1: Congressional Subpoena*

I walk my interviewee to her next interviewer, and I see that I received a message from a senior partner. There is a crisis. One of our biggest clients just received a subpoena from the office of a particular congressperson (who I will refer to as Congressperson Doe).

The subpoena demands all documents related to a patent licensing deal with a competitor. Apparently, some important constituents have complained to Congressperson Doe that the deal violates antitrust laws. The subpoena lists a date of production as one week from now. One week! That's impossible. It will take that long just to get the documents searched, organized, processed, and in our offices ready to be reviewed. Then the documents will need to be reviewed for relevance and privilege.

The client has a million questions. Why are we being investigated? What's going to happen? Will the subpoena be public information? Will this blow up to a full congressional hearing? Will these documents, many of which contain trade secret information, be treated as confidential documents? I've dealt with congressional subpoenas before. So fortunately, I'm in a position to anticipate these questions.

When you're an IP litigator, you have to know something about antitrust laws. Patents are government granted monopolies. Antitrust laws discourage monopolies. Sooner or later, one of your clients will be accused of violating the antitrust laws. So there is definitely tension that exists between patent and antitrust laws, and there are no easy answers to navigate these waters.

I call a senior associate who I know can handle time-sensitive matters like this. She knows what to do. She'll put out request for proposals to several trusted temp agencies and hire contract attorneys to do document review. We don't use first year associates anymore for document review. We outsource that. They're cheaper. I also start a dialogue with the Congressperson's office to work on getting that extension we so badly need.

12:30 p.m.   Lunch at My Desk

I look at the watch and realize it's lunch time already. What's for lunch, you may wonder? Well, it's basically the sandwich I picked up earlier this morning at Starbucks on my way into work. Most lawyers of my generation don't do power lunches. Nobody I know does martini lunches. In fact, most lawyers I know eat quick lunches at their desks. Today is no exception. I reach into my private fridge for a Diet Coke. I used to have a microwave in my office too, until I realized it sent the wrong message to summer associates and my interviewees. It's okay to have a fridge in your office. But if you have a microwave, then you're probably spending too much time at the office. I don't want to scare off potential recruits. At least not yet.

12:45 a.m.   Phone Call from a Friend (re: possible business development opportunity)

I take a call from an old friend. He tells me he has a friend who is interested in starting a clothing design company. His friend has a number of IP-related questions. How does he protect his company's name? How does he protect his designs? How does he steer clear of copyrights of other companies? Do I know any good affordable IP lawyers? Could I help him?

When you're an IP lawyer, you get many of these calls. I usually do whatever I can to help them. I usually don't charge anything for my time. Most entrepreneurs don't have a lot of money to spend on lawyers. Plus, this kind of thing is too small for a law firm of my size. In fact, any client that generates less than $100,000 in fees a year is probably too small for our law firm. Most of my cases have budgets of $1 to $2 million *a year*. But who knows? Maybe this person's company will get big in the future and he'll remember me. Plus, it feels good helping the small guy, at least that's what I tell myself.

1:15 p.m.   *Personal Appointment*

Crap. I'm late for my doctor's appointment. My personal life doesn't stop because I'm a lawyer. I woke up yesterday with welts on my arm and chest. It's probably some allergic reaction. But for safety's sake, I need to get it checked out.

I spend an hour going to the office, waiting, seeing the doctor, and coming back to my office. I think to myself that this is one less billable hour in a day. In order for me to bill 2,000 hours, take weekends and holidays off, and take a one-week vacation, I need to bill 8.33 hours per working day. That means I'll need to work very efficiently for *at least* twelve hours a day, which if you think about it is insane if you have a family. You commute for at least an hour. So if you leave at 8 a.m. every morning, that still means you get home at 9 p.m.—well after dinner time and the time your kid goes to sleep. That's on a good day. Most days, you can't bill all the hours you've worked or you spend time doing business development or non-billable work.

That's why most lawyers I know work on the weekends, on holidays, and at nights. That's why some lawyers start their days at 5 a.m. or work until midnight. You have to. I usually come home early, have dinner with my family, put our son to bed, and then put in a few more hours at home.

2:15 p.m.   *Meeting with a Pro Bono Client*

I meet with a pro bono client (work done voluntarily for no pay in return) who is having a custody dispute with her ex-husband who was abusive to her as well as her child. I'm not a family law attorney. But I feel a strong need to do pro bono work. I feel that it's my payback to the profession of law for being a corporate attorney.

2:45 p.m.   *Phone Call from Senior Partner*

I'm interrupted during my meeting by a senior partner. He just found out that a client is in town. He wants me to take him to the Chicago Cubs baseball game tonight. He has firm seats for me. I really can't say no.

I finish my meeting with the pro bono client and call my wife to tell her I won't be home for dinner. She understands. But I can't help but notice the disappointment in her voice.

3:00 p.m.   *Draft a Trademark Application*

I look at my list and I still have three things to do before I leave for the Cubs game. I have to respond to a USPTO preliminary rejection of a trademark application. The USPTO examiner thinks that my client's proposed trademark is confusingly similar to a trademark that's already been registered by another company. I allot myself exactly one hour to draft an opposition.

My client can't afford to have me spend any more time on this. But that's okay. That's what I do. I can crank out a five-page response in an hour. Law school teaches you to spend hours perfecting journal articles and cite checking everything. In the real world, though, speed and efficiency matters just as much. I get it on file and send a copy to my client. It's a small client, and I sometimes cut my hours so he isn't stuck with a large bill. But I love working for small companies. They're so much more appreciative than the large institutional clients we have.

4:00 p.m.   *Prepare for an Expert Deposition*

I know that my secretary leaves at 4:30 p.m. every day. So I call her to make travel arrangements for my depositions. I need to be in San Francisco in one week for a deposition. I need a conference room, a hotel room, and flights. Our travel department has all of my preferences and information on file, which is why this is all I need to tell her. Quick and efficient, that's the way I like it.

I start to think about what I need to prepare for this deposition. The opposing side's expert has opined that the patent we're challenging is novel and non-obvious, because the results were unexpected and surprising. I disagree, of course. I spend the next hour putting together documents and an outline that will show that this particular PhD scientist working for the other side from a prestigious university is wrong.

5:00 p.m.   *Review Work Product from Various Associates*

Good. I still have an hour. I have time to review memoranda, interrogatory responses, motions, and letters that junior associates have written per my instructions last night. I fly through each one, making quick redline changes and comments. I have to make sure the comments are meaningful enough so that I get a better draft the second time around. I also read an associate's research memorandum and make decisions about our litigation strategy.

6:00 p.m.   *Meet Client at Hotel (to go to a Cubs game)*

I run out the door at 6 p.m. and meet our client at the Peninsula at 6:15 p.m. I suggest that we take the train to the ball game. It's rush hour. So it'll be so much faster than taking a cab. Besides, taking the El (the "elevated" train system) in Chicago is an experience itself. So I don't feel weird taking clients on trains.

Entertaining clients can be exhausting at worst and somewhat fun at best. I usually just think of it as having some fun without any real business objectives. I just try to get them to know me and have a good time. People like to do business with people they know. If you think of it strictly as "business development" and try to talk too much business, it can get pretty painful.

I suppose the best would be to have friends who are clients. I know a number of partners who get business that way. Their frat buddy from college is now the vice president of a large company. My friends are not quite there yet. Someday, maybe.

10:00 p.m.   *Head Home*

Cubs win! The masses of Cubs fans are spilling into the streets of Wrigleyville (the area surrounding Wrigley Field where the Chicago Cubs play baseball games) to celebrate at the numerous bars. I offer to take the client to the *Cubby Bear*—a local post-game favorite—but I secretly hope that he refuses. He does. He has a meeting tomorrow. So he's going to call it a night. I ask him one more time to make sure that he doesn't think I was just being polite. He says he really can't. I later breathe a big sigh of relief. I also should call it a night. I hop in a cab. It's been a long day. Time to head home.

10:20 p.m.   *Stop in at a Local Bar*

On my way home, I change my mind and stop at local pub, located about a block away from my house. I'm an investor at this place. Five years ago, back in the boom days of high bonuses, I invested one of my yearly bonus checks on a start-up bar. It was a silly thing to do then. But it's a tangible reminder that my job does have its side benefits. I stop in, chat with the bartenders, have a complimentary beer, and walk home just slightly buzzed.

11:15 p.m.   *Get Home*

I get home and my dog gives me a big sloppy welcome. I know everyone's asleep. I check in on my kid. He's sound asleep now. But I know he'll be awake soon, sure to be waking me up in less than seven hours. I missed him tonight. That's the fatherly side of me coming out.

11:30 p.m.   *Do Some Administrative Work (for the firm)*

I gather my receipts from tonight to submit for reimbursement. I enter the hours I've worked in six-minute increments into the computer for billing. Clients are demanding increasingly detailed bills these days. This is why I spend my late hours to make sure to account for every (six-minute) aspect of my work. I know that if I don't do this tonight, I'm going to forget what I did today.

The billable hour is the bane of most firm attorneys' existence. At least government and in-house lawyers don't have billable hours. They're so lucky, at least in this respect.

12:00 a.m.   Personal Business/Preparation for the Next Day

I log into my e-mail account once again and respond to more messages awaiting me in my inbox. I e-mail some of the associates on my case-specific tasks I'd like them to do the following day. It's technically considered work. But I can't bill for this time. So it's "non-billable" work. I know some attorneys who do bill for doing this type of admin work. But I've had a few drinks. And I wouldn't feel right.

I check my personal mail and my various financial accounts: banks, credit cards, and 401k. I glance through my magazines: *Wine Spectator, Condé Nast Traveler, Businessweek,* and *People* (yes, even lawyers can be interested in the latest gossip). I don't pay attention to my bills, because nearly every one of them is paid automatically: credit cards, mortgages, electricity, gas, telephone, cable, and even my dog walker.

I check my accounts to check for signs of any fraudulent activities or transactions. Between my business and personal spending, my credit card bill routinely runs up to $10,000 a month from several dozen different places in several different cities. My record is $45,000 in one month. So a fraudulent charge can easily be overlooked if I don't check every so often.

Sure, I have a corporate card issued by the firm, but I don't use it. The reason is simple: it doesn't get me miles. I'm almost at a million miles on my frequent flyer account, which would get me lifetime elite status. I'm no Ryan Bingham (from the movie, *Up in the Air*). But I enjoy my elite status. I'll be leaving my job in the near future. But I can't say that I don't enjoy the perks that have come along with my job. But then again, I've been saying I'm going to leave my job for ten years now.

1:15 a.m.   Sleep

Sleep. I know I have four hours and thirty minutes before our son wakes me up. I know this lifestyle is unsustainable. My body needs seven hours of sleep each night. This lack of sleep will catch up to me some day. It's already having an effect on my body. It'll also shorten my lifespan. But I don't care about that right now. I made it through another twenty-four-hour day without committing malpractice!

5:00 a.m.   *Wake-Up (to the alarm clock)*

After less than four hours of precious sleep, I wake-up again to another filled twenty-four-hour day. How time goes by so quickly, especially when I'm sleeping!

Final Thoughts

Intellectual property (IP) litigators will always be in demand because we live in an information and technology based society. And that's not likely to change anytime soon. And unlike real estate (or so-called *real* property), *intellectual* property that's created by human ingenuity potentially is endless. So if you're thinking of becoming an IP lawyer, you're at least looking in the right direction. But *should* you become an IP lawyer? And more importantly, do you really *want* to become an IP litigator?

First, you have to understand that IP litigators (and patent litigators in particular) are a special breed. You have to have a critical, analytical, and detail-oriented mind of a scientist. At the same time, you have to have good judgment, good instincts, and the sensibilities of a good litigator. These are not things that a law school can teach you.

You also have to ask yourself—do I really have the patience and the innate desire to learn about obscure technologies that I will never, ever hear of again? You may not think this is a big deal until year after year, your friends are litigating cases that deal directly with real world events and people. Meanwhile, you're looking at some rat genome sequence or chip circuitry design that you never even knew existed. But to be fair, you do occasionally get a case that deals with the latest cell phone technology or blockbuster drug that makes it all worthwhile. And you do get to work with some brilliant scientists and leading experts in their field.

Second, when you choose to be an IP litigator, you also have to realize that you're choosing a certain lifestyle as a large firm lawyer. Why? Because IP cases usually are high stakes, and clients demand big international law firms to handle them. And with big law firms comes the high pay, high pressure, and high stress. My life is crazy hectic some days. And if I'm not careful, my life will pass by and I'll be looking back wondering where it's all gone. Because my job pays well and appears prestigious, dozens of lawyers are willing to take my place if I'm not constantly improving myself and polishing my trade. Sure, my student loans will have been paid off and I'll have lived a jet-setting lifestyle, but that gets old fast. Big law firm life as an IP litigator is not for the faint of heart. You have to *really* want to do this, or you'll burn out quickly.

So here's the bottom line. I don't hate my job most of the days. Most days, I don't regret that I've decided to go to law school and pursued a career in IP law. Most IP litigators I know dislike their practice *less* than their big firm peers who practice in other specialty fields. Considering that lawyers are a cynical bunch, these are tall compliments.

6

Profile 6
Eddie: Finance and Banking Lawyer

Executive Summary

Name:	Eddie
Profile:	Finance and Banking Lawyer (In-house Legal and Compliance)
Location:	Jersey City, New Jersey

Eddie sums up his job in a straightforward and direct way, which is what working in the banking industry is like, according to him. As a banking and finance lawyer, he lets people working at his firm know what the law is. In other words, he provides creative and innovative strategies to complex deals or advises on taking (or not taking) certain legal action when faced with a problem, without treading on the law. Eddie represents, validates, and protects the firm on legal issues. This is the case whether it is keeping up with what goes on in his firm's foreign branches or threatening lawsuits to certain counterparties. While having a more predictable schedule is often one benefit of being an in-house legal counsel, the harsh reality of the finance industry still persists. Eddie is not always considered as the "people who actually make the money" in the "front office." This can leave him with less authority sometimes. However, Eddie considers his job very important. And for anyone who sees a future in finance-related legal work, he adds some tips in his twenty-four-hour career profile on how to adapt your skills from law school to the real world.

Profile

Career Field:	Finance/Banking
Current Position:	In-House Legal Counsel
Institution:	US-based Global Financial Services Company
Location:	Jersey City, New Jersey
Previous Position(s):	General Counsel, Asia for major investment bank
Education:	JD, Fordham University, School of Law
	MA, University of Michigan
	BA, Georgetown University
Licensed (Y/N):	Yes
Jurisdictions:	New York/New Jersey

Schedule

5:30 a.m.	Wake-Up (beating the alarm clock by 15 minutes!)
6:25 a.m.	Driving to the Office (War of the Road Warriors)
6:40 a.m.	Board the Train
7:45 a.m.	Transfer from Grand Central Station to Jersey City
8:32 a.m.	Return Urgent Call from Indonesian Legal Counsel
9:25 a.m.	Discuss Possible Candidate for Department
10:00 a.m.	Instructions for Swap Valuations
11:10 a.m.	Meeting with Bank Executive (that mirrors something more akin to a screaming match)
11:40 a.m.	Prepare to Attend Monthly Luncheon
12:00 p.m.	Listen to the Chairman's Luncheon Presentation
1:35 p.m.	Prepare for Firm-Wide Webcast
3:00 p.m.	Meeting with Firm's General Counsel
4:00 p.m.	Call to Counterparty (and threaten lawsuit)
4:50 p.m.	Review Swap Valuations
5:30 p.m.	Attempt to Go Home and Catch Ferry (to Manhattan)
6:25 p.m.	Go to Nippon Club (to attend Japanese tea ceremony)
8:29 p.m.	Head Home (to Upstate New York)
11:05 p.m.	Go to Sleep
5:30 a.m.	Wake-Up Again (for another 24 hours)

24-Hour Schedule

5:30 a.m.   *Wake-Up (beating the alarm clock by 15 minutes!)*

I rub my eyes. "Aha, I beat the alarm by fifteen minutes. If I focus, I can catch the 6:47 am train instead of the 6:57 a.m. and get to my desk fifteen minutes earlier. Even though I'll be the first one there, it'll still make me feel good." So I decide it might be worth it—I figure the hardest part is getting out of bed.

6:25 a.m.   *Driving to the Office (War of the Road Warriors)*

In the car, scrubbed and polished, I bask in self-satisfaction: always in a custom-made suit, Brooks Brothers shirt (French cuffs to show off an extensive cufflink collection) and rubber-soled shoes that give the right impression, but not discomfort. I'm most pleased with the Italian silk tie I picked up for $12 in the subway. I put the key into the car's ignition (a 1990 Buick, chipped and dirty). It starts without a hitch and I'm on my way down the road, take my next left, and then a right. All of the sudden, the car screeches as I hit the brakes, "Gotta stop for the squirrel," I realize in the nick of time. Hardly a moment later, a massive SUV appears in the rear-vision mirror. "An over-testosteroned thirty-year old," I murmur to myself. I know that the only way to protect myself from being rear-ended is to force the guy to slow down. So I gradually reduce the Buick's speed, much to the frustration of the shaved head executive (I presume) in the SUV. As I brake to avoid a pothole, I see the smoke coming out of the SUV's tires. I notice that the driver then honks and looks for a chance to slip over the double yellow lines to pass in the oncoming lane. But alas, a school bus is approaching; out pop the flashers. This means a full stop for all, including the SUV driver—justice exists, I think to myself!

6:40 a.m.   *Board the Train*

I wheel the lumbering Buick onto Route 9A, taking my foot off the accelerator to match the road's incline toward the train station. This lets me coast into the station without braking. My road warrior adversary in the SUV swerves into the passing lane, and barrels down into the arms of the Sleepy Hollow police speed trap. I pull into the parking lot with ninety-two seconds to spare, and after boarding the train, I find a window seat, just as the train leaves the station. I use the commute to polish off *The New York Times*, *Wall Street Journal*, and *Financial Times* before reaching Grand Central Station in Manhattan.

7:45 a.m.   *Transfer from Grand Central Station to Jersey City*

In an effort to beat the rest of the pack for work, I'm the first out of the train at Grand Central Station. I'm hell bent and determined ("Women and children, look out!") to make the 8:00 a.m. boat across the Hudson to Jersey City, New Jersey, where my office is located. The driver deftly negotiates the traffic going west, as I gaze at the often-raucous sights and sounds of New York City below. After this momentary gaze, I take a quick look at my watch—three minutes to spare! So I glide down the gangplank, grab a café latte at the concession stand, and head to the foredeck (jutting my chin forward to pick up the spray from the river on my face).

8:32 a.m.   *Return Urgent Call from Indonesian Legal Counsel*

I am the first in the legal regulatory department at the Jersey City headquarters of a firm I'll simply refer to as "The Brothers," a global financial services institution. "What fun and games are in store for today?" I wonder. I see an urgent e-mail from PH Gartadi, a colleague in Jakarta, Indonesia, which says, "Call my cell number immediately. I can't put what you want in writing." Upon hearing this news, I notice that my hand is trembling as I punch the numbers on the phone to return the call. All the while, I wonder what terror may have emerged from the South Jakarta District Court. Fortunately, I reach Hendra, who then quickly explains, "Judge Rupiah called our legal counsel into his chambers right after the hearing, which, by the way, did not go well for us. Hotbod Shanghai (counsel for the "aggrieved" Indonesian partner) is demanding that The Brothers' investment banking fees be garnished to pay off his spurious damages, allegedly arising from having his collateral seized by The Brothers to offset his owed debt. So Judge Rupiah said that he could 'help' The Brothers case, and that we could express our gratitude to him either before or after his judgment."

I was speechless. The judge was essentially asking for a bribe, clear and simple—something that would be relatively uncommon in the United States, but unfortunately not so uncommon in places such as Indonesia. If The Brothers lost the case, millions of dollars in fees could potentially be lost. But a bribe was out of the question. "We just don't do business that way, PH Hendra. Let the chips fall where they may. I'll brief the general counsel, and get back to you with more details."

9:25 a.m.   *Discuss Possible Candidate for Department*

My right-hand lawyer, Stevie, comes into his office, "I gotta talk to you about this new hire we're looking for. What about asking Scott to transfer from equities prime brokerage? He's bright and great to work with." I respond, "Great idea, Stevie. But what makes you think he'd want to join us here when he's got a real job? Why would he give that up to come to our world?" "It was just an idea," Stevie replies. "Good try, Stevie," I respond, "But we need to get real. Dudley needs to close out the swaps book with OPM (OPM = Other Peoples' Money) Bank. Let's jump on that."

10:00 a.m.   *Instructions for Swap Valuations*

Stevie and I are on the trading floor, briefing Dudley for the third time on the procedure set up by a well-known association related to derivatives issues. The Brothers had declared a default by OPM Bank and elected to terminate all transactions. To do this, each outstanding swap between The Brothers and OPM Bank had to be valued impartially, in determining how much money was owed to which party for each transaction. Then all the amounts owed to each party were aggregated and netted against each other, with one party owing the difference to the other. "Okay, Dudley," I say, "You go to the open market and get four valuations for each swap, drop the highest and lowest, and take the mean of the other two. Got it?" "Sure, no problem," Dudley retorts, fixing his attention to the auction rate trader one row over. "Okay, Dudley, I'll check back with you at market close so we can draft the notice," I retorted.

11:10 a.m.   *Meeting with Bank Executive (that mirrors something more akin to a screaming match)*

My phone rings. It's Cindy, secretary to The Brothers' chief compliance officer, managing director (MD) Chupaculo. "She wants you here, immediately," Cindy warns. "Oh man, what have I done now?" I wonder as I board the elevator for the green granite executive offices—known as the "Emerald Kingdom"—located on the thirtieth floor. I'm ushered into the office. "Hey Eddie, I have a bone to pick with you." MD tells me (she is just over sixty inches in height, but quite a sparkplug nonetheless). "You didn't tell me what's going on." The executive was working herself up into her usual rage. "With the hair and glasses, she looks straight off the $100 bill," I thought. "You Brothers trash, I got reamed in front of Nicky (MD's boss) because you kept me out of the loop." "What is she referring to?" I think to myself (as I desperately review my past actions related to the deal). "You knew that the audit department was checking registrations in the LA office and you didn't tell me. Your name is all over the e-mails!" she wailed.

"But MD, what's unusual about registration statements being audited? It's done every day of the week." "Yeah, but you knew and didn't tell me," she shot back. I reply by saying, "Also, isn't it important that the audit department do what it is supposed to do? Anyway, if that's so important to you, shouldn't you look at the audit department's exam schedule?" The reply from her was fast and furious, "I don't trust you. Now, get out of here," she yelled back (as she slammed her fist on her desk).

11:40 a.m.   *Prepare to Attend Monthly Luncheon*

Shaken, I try to compose myself before I join the compliance and legal monthly luncheon in the executive dining room (located on the building's top floor). Today was particularly important as the chairman and CEO, Rick, was going to address the department on "Doing the Right Thing." I arrive there early, escaping the morning's trauma by glancing dreamily at the city skyline. My friend, Francois, a French equities trader takes a seat next to me, "*Salut,* how's everything?" inquired Francois. "Boy I just got reamed out by MD," I reply. "Oh, I see," said Francois with a smirk.

12:00 p.m.   *Listen to the Chairman's Luncheon Presentation*

The luncheon's main speaker, the firm's chairman, enters the room. All of us quickly take our seats at the tables, as the chairman's time was precious. Twenty minutes later, the chairman finishes with an illustration. "We have to be nimble. We try a business. It doesn't work. You cut your losses, and get out," he explains. I make a mental note of this. And it helps to give me—someone who is there to help support the "business side" (also known as the "front office," which refers to the people who generate the firm's revenues, such as in the trading, sales and investment advisory divisions)—some deeper insight into the mindset of the guys whom I try to support from the legal side of things. After all, I figure, it's because of them, the business side, that the firm exists. And it's also the front office that, in essence, pays us legal and compliance guys at the end of the day (and at the end of the year, come bonus time).

1:35 p.m.   *Prepare for Firm-Wide Webcast*

Following the luncheon, and having returned to my desk, I still recall the stinging conversation I had with the MD before the luncheon. It immediately makes me feel chastised and educated. But this is the nature of the banking industry. It exists for profit, and lots of it. For this reason, it draws the best, brightest (and often the most aggressive) minds together in one place at one time for one thing—make as much money as possible. So one result of this modus operandi is that time is money, and so, people often need to speak directly, which in many instances, requires thick skin. In other words, you can't take things too personally. Still, even after many years in the banking industry, I can't help but feel some sort of damaged emotions from that conversation with the MD.

Before giving the incident any more thought, I quickly regroup myself and try to regain my calm for the filming of my firm-wide webcast later this afternoon. I act as the firm expert in political law, which includes lobbying, ethics, and pay-to-play regulation for dealing with governmental officials. Any underwriting of municipal bonds or advisory contract with a state pension fund brings into play a plethora of often-conflicting laws and rules. Since this was an election year, the general counsel thought it would be a good idea to remind employees of the need to clear dealings with public officials before taking any steps that could prejudice the firm's business. I appear at the film studio and the makeup artist notes "You look just like an attorney today!" That's good, I think to myself, because, after all, I *am* an attorney. The format was to be a dialogue between the interlocutor, a person I'll call Carmen Miranda, and me. I was pumped. "Ladies and gentlemen," Carmen begins as the camera zooms in on me in front of a picture of the Capitol (Washington, DC), "Here we are today in Washington with, Eddie, from The Brothers. So tell us, what can we expect in this election year?" I then go over the various federal lobbying laws as my prepared presentation slides outline campaign contribution limits for each US state flips behind me.

3:00 p.m.   Meeting with Firm's General Counsel

I have a heated meeting with the firm's general counsel regarding the recommended actions a regulatory agency directed toward The Brothers. "Who do they think they are, telling The Brothers what we can do?" the general counsel proclaimed. I reply by stating, "I think we need to keep our eye on the ball. The regulators have the legal authority to close us down if they want. What do we care if we think they're not acting reasonably? Our job is to make sure that The Brothers opens for business on this Monday morning and every other business day, not reform the entire country's regulatory system overnight. We've got to give them something." The general counsel calms down, thinks this over, and finally relents, "Okay, I suppose you're right, but that doesn't mean that I agree with it." Well, that's banking—sometimes to get a little, you have to give a little.

4:00 p.m.   Call to Counterparty (and threaten lawsuit)

My colleague Stevie runs into my office in a panicked state, "A counterparty in one of our deals is refusing to honor the guaranty. We're out $50 million." "Get me their phone number," I snapped. I finally get their CFO on the line. After a brief explanation to him, he replies, "I'm sorry, I really don't have the slightest idea what you're talking about. We never guarantee anything. Besides today is a day of observance in our jurisdiction." At this point, I just lose it. "Listen, today may be a holiday where you are, but the courts in New Jersey are open for business. I'm looking at a guarantee signed three years ago, when you were manager of the New York branch of your respective institution. If you don't honor this, I'll have no other option but to sue you." As you can tell, in the banking industry, we have to cut right to the chase. Sometimes, in conversations like this, it's posturing. But in many instances, it's the real deal. So the thinking is that hopefully the other side blinks first, in a game of strategic chicken.

4:50 p.m.   *Review Swap Valuations*

It's only 4:50 pm, and I'm exhausted. I return to the trading floor to get the swap valuations from Dudley. "Good to see you, and yes, I've got those valuations for you." After I take a look, I quickly notice something's missing, "Dudley, there are just three valuations here. I told you to get four." "Yeah," answers Dudley, "I figured three would do," he replies. "But Dudley, we need four." "Yean, well, I just got three. That should be enough, right?" "You've got to get a fourth valuation for The Brothers to be able to terminate and collect the $15 million from the counterparty bank, one-third of which will be your bonus. Can't you do that?" I shoot back. "Okay, it'll be a bit of a pain. But I guess I can get it if you really need it." Sometimes getting the business guys to do what they need to do is like pulling teeth. Their thinking is, "Who's this legal guy telling me what to do, after all, who makes the money around here?" When this type of thinking rears its ugly head, such as in situations like this, the best line of counter-argument is to let them know that it can affect their bottom line (including their bonus)—if money talks for average folks, it elevates to a piercing scream for traders on the trading floor.

5:30 p.m.   *Attempt to Go Home and Catch Ferry (to Manhattan)*

Most legal and compliance staff working in an in-house capacity generally maintain more reasonable and predictable working schedules than, say, in a law firm. Sometimes it can be a trade-off in terms of money. But many legally trained colleagues I know have jumped to the business side of the bank. For many lawyers, this makes sense since it can be much more lucrative from an economic point of view in the form of higher potential bonuses (since it is the business side that has first dibs into the firm's year-end bonus pool—the remaining portion then goes to the back office personnel). So why would this happen? For the business side, they would want a legal expert on their team since the legal skill sets brought onto the business team will, in their view, more than offset for the possible added headcount cost that could take away from their team's bonus pool. For those like me, I've opted to be a lawyer who actually works in a legal capacity (rather than leverage it toward the business side). For me, I see it as a capacity that I was trained to do, and at the end of the day, this is what I enjoy doing. Being here in the Jersey City location, it also gives me the opportunity to leave the office earlier than my counterparts in law firms. So although it may be early by law firm standards, I take this time to rush for the ferry back to Manhattan.

Prior to working in Jersey City, I worked for seventeen years in the firm's Asia Pacific office located in Tokyo, Japan. Being there, I had the opportunity to use not only my legal skills, but my multilingual skill sets as well—namely, Japanese and Korean (in addition to my native language of English). In my early days, being a US lawyer who could speak multiple languages was a great competitive career advantage. Nowadays, it's almost a necessity to know languages above and beyond English, in addition to being aware of the cultural norms and nuances that exist in offshore jurisdictions (i.e., it's good to be multicultural as well as multilingual).

Living in Japan has its costs and benefits. And for those not familiar with Japan and its unique peculiarities before they get there, it's often enough to do them in. But in my case, it transformed me into a "tea junkie." As a result, I got hooked on the age-old traditions related to a Japanese tea ceremony. To me, I see being part of this as a perfect complement to the lawyer's role of being a shaman of proper corporate behavior.

In preparation for the tea ceremony, the twenty-minute ferry ride from Jersey City to Manhattan gives me enough time to slip into the men's room and change from my otherwise cookie cutter Brooks Brothers gray suit into a custom-made kimono, reflecting centuries of Japanese tradition and culture. The sudden appearance of a white Caucasian male donning a Japanese kimono in the ferry draws a few stares, to say the least. I then jump into a waiting taxi at Pier 47.

From inside the taxi, I think, "Okay, the driver's wearing a turban and I'm wearing a kimono." But on second thought, I then think, "So what's so odd about that?" Zipping through Manhattan traffic to the Nippon Club on 57th

Street, my cell phone rings. A colleague tells me, "The chairman of the firm wants to contribute $2 million to the New York mayoral campaign. Can he do it? The fundraiser is tonight." My first reaction is panic, but after a couple seconds, I do my best to respond in measured tones, "Isn't the chairman a Connecticut resident? If that's the case, Municipal Securities Rulemaking Board Rule G-37 prohibits a municipal finance professional, which he is, by virtue of being CEO, from making any contribution to someone for whom he is not entitled to vote." "How about the $250 de minimis contribution?" he asks, pushing, "Surely he can do that." "No," in an effort to push back, "The de minimis exception is not available to a candidate for whom the contributor is not entitled to vote. Sorry."

Although this may not be the answer he wants to hear, it's the law. And that's what I get paid to do—to let the people working at my firm know what the law is. Whenever possible, in this capacity, I generally try to find solutions to make deals or other issues move forward, so long as no violation of the law exists. In other words, find creative and innovative ways, if necessary, to make a deal happen, then stop a deal from happening. But for this particular issue, there's simply no way around it.

6:25 p.m.   *Go to Nippon Club (to attend Japanese tea ceremony)*

The taxi reaches the front door of the Nippon Club. Even in Manhattan, where it takes a lot to get people's attention, I notice a few eyes stare my way (whether in a good or bad way, who knows!). Clad in my kimono, I find my way to the specially constructed Nippon Club tea room. Tonight I'm only a guest, kneeling before the gurgling kettle in the brazier, but someone has come from Kyoto, Japan (the former ancient capital of Japan) to serve tea to the New York chapter, and so I want to be respectful. "*Otemae chodai itashimasu* ('I gratefully partake in the tea you have prepared')," I murmur, bowing and raising the tea bowl in affirmation of the ceremonial ritual. In part, here as well as in Tokyo, this ceremony is what helped to keep me sane at The Brothers. And although the Japanese tea ceremony may not be for everyone, the point is that it's always a good idea to find some outlet outside of work to let off steam to help enjoy life around you. Life is more than just work.

8:29 p.m.   *Head Home (to Upstate New York)*

After the Japanese tea ceremony, I say a few polite words to the others who also attended. I try to use as much of my Japanese as possible—not only does it fit the occasion, but it also helps me to keep up with my Japanese language skills. As the mantra goes (especially when it comes to second languages), "If you don't use it, you lose it!"

I then jump into a taxi in front of the Nippon Club and tell the driver to go to Grand Central Station. It's night now, and I figure it's high time to head back to my home where my family await me. While riding the Metro-North express returning home from Grand Central, I gaze at the Hudson River—another serene moment before what is sure to be another busy day tomorrow.

11:05 p.m.   *Go to Sleep*

After I return to the station, I get in my car and drive back home. The house is pretty dark since almost everyone is asleep by now. And it won't be long before I do the same. I change clothes (out of the kimono) and kiss my beautiful wife goodnight. I then drift off in a blissful snooze.

5:30 a.m.   *Wake-Up Again (for another 24 hours)*

The alarm clock ringing already? Let another day in the life of a tea junkie lawyer begin!

Final Thoughts

Law school should be thought of as a trade school, although a very sophisticated one. And one useful thing the three-year process of the JD program teaches you is how to approach issues. What I can suggest is that if you are fighting it the whole time (i.e., you don't appreciate what the process is trying to achieve), don't go into private practice. But if you decide to use the JD degree for actual legal practice, either in a law firm or in an in-house counsel capacity relating to financial services, I would highly, highly recommend taking a bankruptcy course. This is because, although the JD curriculum is fairly general in terms of breadth, the more concrete and specific the courses you take, the better off you will be.

7

Profile 7
Mickey: Wall Street Lawyer

Executive Summary

Name: Mickey
Profile: Wall Street Lawyer
Location: London

Mickey can be categorized as a Wall Street lawyer, except he works in the London branch of a New York-based global financial institution. Most of his work of designing and building investment products for Europe is done while also simultaneously connecting and working with his various counterparts in his firm's Asian and New York offices. His job includes disclosing drafts and documents to the investor, making sure the firm's new products are viable based on the investment strategy in the market, and once again, communicating such details seamlessly without mistakes to other offices at a global level. Mickey has no problem working in the rushed and often raucous environment of the financial trading environment. And he manages to keep his schedule balanced to maintain his productivity, as you will see from reading his twenty-four-hour career profile.

Profile

Career Field:	Banking and Finance
Current Position:	Structured Products/Financial Engineering Division
Institution:	Global Financial Institution
Location:	London, UK
Previous Position(s):	Lawyer: Sydney, London (both private practice and in-house)
Education:	BEc/LLB, Macquarie University (Sydney, Australia)
Licensed (Y/N):	Yes
Jurisdictions:	Supreme Court of New South Wales/Supreme Court of England and Wales

Schedule

7:00 a.m.	Alarm Rings
7:30 a.m.	Get Ready for Work
8:15 a.m.	Commute into the Office
9:00 a.m.	Arrive at the Office
9:45 a.m.	European Product Design
10:30 a.m.	Product Structuring Meeting
12:00 p.m.	Investment Meeting
2:00 p.m.	Calls with New York
4:00 p.m.	Documentation Drafting
6:15 p.m.	Hit the Gym
7:30 p.m.	Back in the Office
8:00 p.m.	Journey Home
8:30 p.m.	Dinner
11:00 p.m.	Bed Time
7:00 a.m.	Wake-Up to the Sound of the Alarm Clock Again

24-Hour Schedule

7:00 a.m.   Alarm Rings

The alarm on my BlackBerry is very loud. Notwithstanding the fact that I have chosen a fun, happy tune, it frightens both my wife and I out of our respective sleep. I inevitably hit the snooze button—this gives me another ten minutes of much needed slumber—although it's not out of the ordinary for the snooze button to be hit again. On the rare occasion I wake-up before the alarm rings, I take great pleasure in turning off the alarm so that the cacophony doesn't enter my ears.

7:30 a.m.   *Get Ready for Work*

It's usually breakfast before shower. Breakfast can be anything from cereal to a small tub of yogurt or a piece of fruit. I usually watch a news program (Sky News, BBC News, CNBC, etc.) while I eat—this helps me catch up on things that may have happened overnight. I usually don't think about work while I'm eating. But I do keep an eye on my BlackBerry to see if any queries have come in from one of our Asian offices while I was asleep. Shower time is one of my favorite times of the day. It's a relaxing way to start planning for what I have to do once I get to the office. Our dress code is relaxed, so I tend only to wear a suit with a tie on days when I know I have a meeting with an external client.

8:15 a.m.   *Commute into the Office*

Our office is in the north part of the city of London (UK) near the Moorgate area. Commuting time by the London subway system (otherwise known as the Tube) is approximately forty-five minutes from my apartment in Notting Hill (the same Notting Hill as the movie of the same name featuring a certain well-known British actor). The walk to the subway station is pleasant enough, although on a cold winter's day the walk seems to take an eternity. Today the weather is what you would expect weather in London to be on most days—overcast clouds with temperatures not too warm or cold. I take the Central Line into Liverpool Street station before completing my journey on foot.

The carriages are crammed with other commuters making their journey into work and it's rare that I get a seat. The train ride is crowded and uncomfortable. Any attempt at trying to read the newspaper or a book is futile as usually there is only just enough room to twitch the end of one's nose.

9:00 a.m.   *Arrive at the Office*

With a slight jolt, the train stops, and seemingly thousands of commuters disembark from the subway to get to their respective offices. It's busy, of course, since it's during the peak of rush hour. But as I look around, I'm reminded of the cosmopolitan nature of London. For instance, within a small area around surrounding me, there are people of different colors, races, and ethnicities—quite a melting pot of people here to pursue their dreams and aspirations in one of the largest financial centers in the world. At the same time, despite such a Benetton commercial-type atmosphere, there is an amazing convergence for those in the banking industry in terms of fashion, style, and dress.

After a short walk by foot, I see the tall modern building where my office is located. The lobby area to take the elevators is packed. After waiting for a few seconds, I board the elevator, which is almost as packed as the subway car I was riding in just a few minutes earlier. Despite the high density of people in such a small compartment, it's fairly quiet as the elevator makes its way up the various floors in the building. Finally, I hear the elevator ring for my floor—off I go—and in a few seconds, I'm at my desk. The environment isn't too different from what you would imagine a global financial institution to be—long rows filled with computers, people talking rapidly and furiously on the phone, lots of noise, and so on. The sense of tension, greed, and fear that dominate the markets is definitely palpable in the air as you walk around the trading floor.

The first thing I tend to do when I arrive at work is to scan my e-mail inbox for any matters that need to be dealt with urgently. Usually there are queries that have come in from Hong Kong or our Tokyo office. The queries usually relate to either new products we are in the process of designing for the Asian market or existing products that the Asian offices happen to market already. Depending on what time I get to these, sometimes I can call our Asian offices with answers or responses on the same day. Our Asian colleagues tend to work quite long hours and it's not unusual for them to still be in the office late into the night. This saves them from "losing" another day before they receive their answers (quite important in an environment where "time is money"). Sometimes I'm required to attend to conference calls with Asia. If this is the case, then I need to prepare the night before. Because of my position being a global (rather than country or region-specific) role, my day can quite often be divided up into servicing different geographical regions at different times of the day. London is well placed to do this given that its time zone sits somewhere in the middle between Asia and North America.

In the old days before e-mail, being centrally situated geographically as London is was a distinct advantage in an era when most communication was done primarily by phone. However, with e-mail, along with BlackBerry devices accessing e-mails at all hours of the day and night, time zone differences for phone calls is not as critical as before. But for many instances, it's good to make contact by phone for the personal touch or for very urgent matters. Some junior level analysts or associates may not realize this, instead simply sending lengthy e-mails to various people inside and outside the firm. But because the sheer volume of e-mail traffic is so extraordinarily high these days, just because someone receives an e-mail doesn't mean they have always made the time to read it. However, when a phone call (versus an e-mail) is made, you have the receiver's (mostly) undivided attention, at least for a few minutes anyway. Sometimes, this can make all the difference in the world in terms of finding out information or closing a transaction.

9:45 a.m.   *European Product Design*

Once the work for our Asia office is taken care of, I move onto my core range of work for the day, which is designing and building investment vehicles and strategies using our European investment fund platform. Much of our non-US investor base tends to invest via our European vehicles. And being in London, we spend a large part of our time servicing the needs of European clients. Typically, product ideas come through to me via our institutional sales team or other marketing focused personnel in our firm. Once the ideas are broadly sketched out, it's my responsibility to make sure that we can execute on the ideas to finally create a product via which the client can make an investment. This process usually starts with me commencing discussions with the investment team to make sure that the investment idea is not only financially realistic and/or viable, but that we have the capability to manage the investment on an ongoing basis.

Quite often, I will have meetings with members of the portfolio management team and run through with them in greater detail the likely financial instruments they would look to use as well as the related trading strategies they would utilize. Portfolio managers often do not think as lawyers do and part of the challenge is to disclose correctly how they will manage a product as well as the key risk factors associated with the investment strategy. I have to liaise with external as well as internal legal counsel in order to get feedback on the way the documentation related to the trade needs to be drafted and also to obtain sign off for the final version. All new products go through a rigorous internal sign off process. And the role of the lawyers is important to that process as all disclosure documents must be drafted in the correct way so as to present the product in a fair and reasonable manner. Part of this involves using language that the investor will understand clearly. Often the disclosure documents will be subject to review and comments by the regulator. Therefore, I need to be ready to answer any questions from the regulator before the product is finally approved.

10:30 a.m.   Product Structuring Meeting

The second part of my product design role is related to structuring. We offer a range of investment platforms and vehicles. Each is regulated to differing degrees. The choice of vehicle for a particular investment strategy will be governed by a number of factors including types of financial instruments to be traded, corporate governance, taxation, regulatory constraints, issues affecting distribution, costs, as well as any special needs of the client base. Sometimes if the client is large enough, we may look to design a bespoke (custom tailored) product to cater for their particular needs. This is the exception rather than the rule, as the costs associated with setting up a bespoke product outweighs the benefits for most clients. Instead, I tend to spend most of my time creating investment vehicles where investor funds are pooled.

Another key part of the product structuring process is understanding the operational impacts of designing and running a product. I have to make sure that the middle and back office of the firm can support the investment strategy that we would like to implement. This usually means that from a technology and oversight point of view, the firm is able to process the flow of trading that the product requires. This sometimes means having to follow the process all the way from inputting of the trade right through to settlement of the financial instrument.

Much of the product design ideas and choice of vehicles we use are well known to the market. However, there will be times when the product design may need to be quite novel, especially when designing products to cater for the needs of single clients. It's important to keep abreast of legal, tax, and regulatory developments for this. As part of this, given that developments in the finance and legal industry change so rapidly, I quite often attend seminars and conferences sponsored by city (of London) law firms, accounting firms, or even other banks.

12:00 p.m.   *Investment Meeting*

At least once a week, I will attend a meeting of the portfolio managers to get a market update and gather ideas as to trends in the market. I work on the fixed income (debt product) desk and the core sector areas we focus on at meetings are corporate credit (investment grade or high yield), ABS (asset-backed securities, including the mortgage market and structured products) as well as government bonds and emerging markets. It's interesting to hear from the actual portfolio managers and traders on their particular market views—it provides a useful insight into what type of products may come into demand. It's also important from the perspective of knowing what product opportunities may lay ahead. Both macro and individual trade ideas may be discussed at the meetings.

I usually just eat my lunch at my desk, which will usually consist of a sandwich or a salad. It's rare that I will go out for lunch other than to meet with a business colleague. The exception is if I have organized some gathering with friends. By eating at my desk, I can make more efficient use of my time—check e-mails, gather news, or make/return phone calls. Every minute counts in finance, so that's why I try to stay close to my desk as much as possible. And even in the instance where I grab a quick bite to eat outside the office (albeit lunch or dinner), my BlackBerry is always close at hand to read e-mails during any down time (such as waiting for my food, standing in line, and the like).

2:00 p.m.   *Calls with New York*

I have a global role in relation to new products for my firm. Much like part of my mornings are spent liaising with my colleagues in Asia on new product initiatives, I spend a considerable part of my afternoons on the phone with my colleagues in New York. In the not too distant past, there was a hierarchy in terms of offices. For American firms, the hierarchy was generally (from top to bottom): New York, London, and then Asia (Japan/Hong Kong), mostly based on the yearly profit each would make, but with the rise of emerging economies, this order may soon change. Although the investment strategies for the US products may broadly be in line with what we structure for Europe, there are always differences from a legal, tax, and/or regulatory point of view.

The discussions I have with the New York office are around the launch of new products or changes to the features of existing products. Unlike Europe, most products that originate out of New York are usually designed just for US investors. Obviously the United States is a big market and there are a number of investor groups we can target (e.g., retail, institutional, tax exempts, and endowment funds). Notwithstanding the similar strategies, the US market uses jargon to describe their products that are very different to those used in Asia or Europe. And this is one of the main things I need to watch out for in discussions with the front office (the "front office" is a term to describe the revenue-generating side, such as traders and institutional sales; the "back office" is a term to describe the administrative and booking side; while the "middle office" is a term to describe a team that helps to seamlessly connect the front office to the back office).

4:00 p.m.   *Documentation Drafting*

This is the part of the day where I most feel like a lawyer. Having spent most of the day on conference calls or in meetings, I usually save up my late afternoons for undertaking drafting or reviewing tasks. Documents that I would typically work on include prospectuses, indentures, agreements of all kinds, product specifications, and marketing documentation. Often I will review documents created by counterparties or by external legal counsel. But it's rare now that I will negotiate the documents directly. I usually provide comments to internal or external counsel, who then undertake the bulk of the negotiation on my behalf. Although I don't mind reviewing documents, I find drafting and proofreading a little more tedious than when I was a lawyer in my earlier days of private practice (for a law firm). My preference now is definitely more orientated toward designing or structuring financial products rather than documenting them. And this is a natural career progression for the aspiring so-called Wall Street or finance lawyer—law firm, in-house, and then maybe the business side. Nevertheless, I recognize that the task of reviewing documents is still a necessary evil!

6:15 p.m.   *Hit the Gym*

I try to get out to my local gym at least twice a week. I try to get there a little earlier if I can to avoid the peak periods. Gyms are relatively expensive in London for what you get. But it's really the only means of getting regular exercise when you work in London. Going for a run or walking after work is possible in the summer time. But with the sun going down anytime after three o'clock in the afternoon during the winter months, the gym is about the only place that you can get a decent workout without freezing to death. I usually use the cardio machines and weights and leave the spin classes and aerobics to the more ardent gym junkies. This helps me to not only stay fit (since most of the day I'm sitting at my desk working on deals), but it allows me to release some stress from the day. It also gives me some down time to think about various other matters not related to work—some very precious time indeed! While on the treadmill, I turn on the monitor to watch some BBC and then tune into another station to see what's happening around the world. I look around and I see other people who must be in the same or similar industry as I am. Looks like I'm not the only one in this gym with the same idea.

7:30 p.m.   *Back in the Office*

After my workout at the gym, I come back to the office to tie up things for the end of the day. Often documents will have come in from New York for review while I've been away and this gives me time to have a quick read of these. I will also do a quick e-mail check and make calls to New York, if necessary. It's nice to have time to tie things up when it's a bit quieter around the trading floor. Normally, it's just a whir of noise from all directions. For some lawyers, this creates an environment that makes it very hard to concentrate. But if you're able to concentrate in a fast-paced and noisy environment, then working on or near the trading floor may be a good fit for you. On the other hand, if you're the type who can only concentrate (or study, as in the case of law school) in a quiet environment (like a closed-door office in a law firm, or law school library), then working for a law firm may be a better fit.

8:00 p.m.   *Journey Home*

By this time, most people in London will have made their way home after work. So I quite enjoy the commute home on the Tube where I can sit down and read the paper in peace (usually *The Financial Times* along with maybe a local paper).

8:30 p.m.   *Dinner*

It's pretty late, and I'm quite hungry. So my next task is to think about what to have for dinner. I usually eat out since where I live in London has a number of places to eat around the neighborhood. Italian, Mexican, Greek, Chinese, Indian, and Japanese restaurants are pretty much at my doorstep. So I like to blame it on this for my laziness when it comes to cooking for myself. On the rare occasion I do cook, it's usually a very casual affair with the eating done in front of the television.

I also quite often eat out with my friends who tend to live close to home. I'd typically do this at least once a week, if not more. As for today's dinner, my wife and I go to a nearby place for some Indian curry and rice with some naan (bread) to go.

11:00 p.m.   *Bed Time*

My sleeping patterns are random at best. But I do make an attempt to get to bed before midnight on most weeknights. How successful that is depends on what bar I may have been at earlier in the night or what is showing on my favorite TV networks. For many people fresh out of school or not too long thereafter, a quick recuperation period is all that's necessary, which doesn't have much impact on the work day. But as people get older, the recuperation period from the night before tends to take longer and longer.

So for me to be as productive as possible at this stage in my career, I need at least a decent amount of sleep—which is why it's sleep time for me now.

7:00 a.m.   *Wake-Up to the Sound of the Alarm Clock Again*

I wake-up to the sound of my alarm clock—fighting the urge to press the snooze button for a precious few more minutes of sleep.

Final Thoughts

I think studying both law and economics helped me to adapt better to working in the financial sector. Obviously, there is a difference between the theoretical and the practical, but I believe my studies provided me with good fundamental knowledge for my career. I would encourage any law graduate to look at wider opportunities than just those offered through the legal profession, as legal education forms a sound basis for entering a range of professions.

8

Profile 8
Patrick: Venture Capital Investor

Executive Summary

Name: Patrick
Profile: Venture Capital Investor
Location: Menlo Park, California

After working as a lawyer with entrepreneurs regarding cutting-edge technologies, Patrick has now secured his spot as a venture capital investor in the fast lane—actually one of the fastest lanes of all—Silicon Valley. The biggest appeal of this job is the access to the newest ideas and brightest minds. This is also a classic example of how your experience as a lawyer can take your next career to the next level. As a former lawyer, Patrick has opportunities to network and think in various perspectives while working in Silicon Valley's network-intensive working environment. He also utilizes his legal skills throughout his everyday tasks such as evaluating contracts, term sheets, and documents. For those who dream of working on the next big thing in business, the career profile of a venture capital investor could be the ideal path. Patrick's success in his career change rests in his ability to think critically and to be ready when presented with new opportunities. He understands negotiating deals as a lawyer. Yet he also is simultaneously able to find the blind spots that may be invisible to others, which he gives credit for based on his past training as a lawyer—as you will see in vivid detail in his twenty-four-hour career profile.

Profile

Career Field:	Venture Capital (VC)
Current Position:	Managing Director
Institution:	US-Based Venture Capital Fund
Location:	Menlo Park, California
Previous Position(s):	Large Law Firm
Education:	JD, New York University, School of Law
	AB, University of California, Berkeley
Licensed (Y/N):	Yes
Jurisdictions:	California

Schedule

6:30 a.m.	Alarm Clock Set, Wake-Up Call
7:30 a.m.	Leave the House
7:50 a.m.	Arrive at the Sun Deck
8:00 a.m.	Breakfast with Angel Investor
9:00 a.m.	Head to Office
9:30 a.m.	Negotiation with New Company
10:00 a.m.	Team Meeting
11:30 a.m.	Conference Call with Attorneys (re: ongoing transaction)
12:00 p.m.	Lunch Interview with Potential CEO
2:00 p.m.	Board Meeting with Portfolio Company
4:00 p.m.	Meeting with Potential Investment Opportunity
5:00 p.m.	Conference Call with Potential Co-Investors
6:30 p.m.	Company Pitch Meeting
9:30 p.m.	Prepare Investment Case
11:30 p.m.	Answer E-Mails, Go to Sleep
6:30 a.m.	Gear Up for another 24 Hours in Silicon Valley

24-Hour Schedule

6:30 a.m.   Alarm Clock Set, Wake-Up Call

I like to sleep with my iPhone. It's comforting to have it near me for some reason (I've never treated my other phones that way). I set it for 6:30 a.m.

and when it goes off, I have to hunt for it since it has traveled in the bed somewhere during the night. Once I find it, I hit the snooze bar at least a couple of times. When I finally enter consciousness, I check my e-mail—which really seems to wake me up. I then confirm my calendar for the day and see who I'm going to meet. If I'm meeting someone who I feel is formal, I'll put on a suit (no tie). Otherwise, I'm in jeans and a casual jacket.

7:30 a.m.   Leave the House

I open the garage and jump into the car. Welcome to Silicon Valley where we have to drive everywhere. I leave the house to head off to breakfast with a friend who is an angel investor (a person who provides capital for a business at the very early stages of a company's development—usually before there is a prototype).

The roads are crowded with employees from household names (like Google, Yahoo, Facebook, and Cisco) as well as entrepreneurs. The engineers and software developers are probably still asleep since they were probably coding until late in the evening.

My breakfast will be on Sand Hill Road, the famous street lined with venture capital funds and their billions of dollars, of which my funds represent a small portion.

Just like the California gold rush in the middle of the nineteenth century, people flock to California with their dreams of creating the "next big thing." Everyday there are thousands of business plans circulating around Silicon Valley—from angel investors, lawyers, bankers, accountants, and venture capitalists. Many of these plans have been around so long that they are known to investors before they even show up. In addition, many investors have seen the same company more than once. This gives a sense of the small biosphere that makes Silicon Valley what it is—everybody knows everybody, and word spreads quickly, both good and bad, even among entrepreneurs. The incessant competition for venture capital, along with the competition for strong ideas and the human talent to execute the ideas are some of the driving forces that help spur constant innovation in Silicon Valley.

Due to IPO success stories of the past involving well-known tech firms like Google, Yahoo, eBay, and Microsoft, the average person may get the sense that receiving funding for "the next big thing" may be easier than it actually is. But the cold reality is that the odds of getting funded by venture capital funds are probably less than one in 1,000. What most entrepreneurs fail to understand is that investors will compare each company against other companies under review and look closely at the opportunity to invest from a technology, market, and management team perspective. If any of those factors are weak, then it's easy to turn to the next best opportunity. Sometimes entrepreneurs don't fully understand that they are not just in a competition with others in their market, but also in competition with other entrepreneurs who are trying to raise money. We hear a lot of, "If I just had the money to show you what I can do, I can prove that I have a great business." Unfortunately, for those entrepreneurs who complain, there are great entrepreneurs who can prove their business without getting funded. All VCs want to invest in the great entrepreneurs and compete to invest in them. As one noted VC put it, "I invest in people, not ideas."

7:50 a.m.   *Arrive at the Sun Deck*

I arrive a little early at the Sun Deck, a small café that happens to be in the middle of a famous complex of venture capital funds at the top of Sand Hill Road. The Sun Deck and Buck's Restaurant in Woodside are historical landmarks for the famous companies that received funding from meetings in these restaurants.

8:00 a.m.   *Breakfast with Angel Investor*

There are many angel investors in Silicon Valley. These investors come from a long line of successful companies that have made a lot of money through their stock options in companies like HP, PayPal, eBay, and, of course, Google. As part of the Silicon Valley ecosystem, these are the folks who have made money from their companies and circulate their wealth, knowledge, and network of friends by investing their personal funds to get small companies started.

This tradition of investing by angel investors (on such a large scale) is something that is quite unique to Silicon Valley. These angel investors not only provide capital, but also advice and the network in order to create a larger business. The network includes not just business contacts, but also contacts with other venture capitalists who are prepared to invest more money if the company funded by the angel investor is showing signs of doing well.

My breakfast this morning with a particular angel investor is with someone who was one of the first ten employees of a very, very large Internet company. We exchange pleasantries, catch up on friends and family, and see how things are going in general.

I like meeting with angel investors because they see a lot of really early-stage trends and it's good to compare notes from one angel investor to another. As the mantra goes, "information is power." And no place does this ring true more than in my particular industry.

Angel investors also like to meet with venture capitalists because they can promote some of their fledgling investments in the hope of receiving funding from venture capitalists with deeper pockets. This constant circulation of ideas and companies are really part of the unseen fabric of Silicon Valley.

Today, each of us orders a breakfast of oatmeal and yogurt. This angel investor and I talked about some of the interesting potential investments we are considering and some of our portfolio companies and the different markets they are trying to win. We both recommend other investors that might be interested in looking at our respective investments. We also talk about the recently funded companies that other investors have funded since everybody seems to know who else is putting money in these companies.

9:00 a.m.   Head to Office

After breakfast, I jump back into the car and within a few minutes (just down Sand Hill Road), I'm back at our office. Our location is in the middle of a great many other venture capital funds, which makes impromptu lunches and meetings very easy. When companies come to visit funds, it is fairly easy for them to visit multiple firms at the same time. Many times, a VC will meet with a company from the East Coast, Europe, or Asia, and then quickly refer them to other VCs who also might be interested. Those companies can have impromptu meetings and meet quickly since there isn't far to travel.

Once I get back to the office, I try to answer as many e-mails as I can. It always seems like I'm swimming against the current—too many e-mails, too little time.

9:30 a.m.   *Negotiation with New Company*

We have an outstanding term sheet (a document outlining the key terms regarding the economics of a potential transaction, including how the company will be governed) and we received comments on it. It's time to call the CEO to discuss the open issues on the term sheet. This situation is one of the times in which it is beneficial to being a former lawyer, like myself, who has experience negotiating these types of term sheets.

When looking at any term sheet, it is important to know all the different levers that can be pulled and to understand the ramifications across the entire term sheet. For that reason, we always advise the CEOs to make sure that they have the best legal counsel available to them so that are fully aware of what they are getting and giving up in the term sheet.

One additional reason we want our companies to have good legal counsel (and not the cheapest) is that the better lawyer will often have better judgment. In this case, due to his counsel's advice, the entrepreneur was focused on the wrong issues and skipping over things that were important. It was unfathomable to me that his counsel would keep advising his client to fight over the small issues and not focus on the bigger issues at hand in the term sheet. I make a mental note that we would have to change legal counsel if we invested in the company.

The one thing that lawyers may not quite understand is that time and efficiency are extremely important for us. Arguing endlessly about small issues in a simple financing deal gives me a window into how the company's counsel thinks through issues. If and when the company is solicited to be acquired (the most likely outcome for venture backed companies), I do not want this counsel getting in the way of completing the M&A (merger and acquisition) documents due to endless discussion over nonsensical issues. Just like an investment, an acquirer may change its mind at any time, so it is important to move as quickly as possible to the closing of the deal.

As a result, our negotiations in a venture financing serves as a quasi-interview for the current company counsel. If the lawyer can't show good judgment, can't properly advise the CEO, or demonstrate appropriate behavior, we will lose confidence in him or her, and decide to replace that counsel with one of many other lawyers that are in Silicon Valley who are already proven to be effective counsel. In other words, "Do your job, and do it well, or someone else will do it for you."

10:00 a.m.   *Team Meeting*

It's time for our team meeting with all of the members of the fund in one room. We always start by discussing each portfolio company and updating the team on any interesting developments. For example, some companies may have signed an important customer; others may have attracted new investors; some may have received an offer to be acquired; and others may be in trouble. At all times, we are thinking and discussing ways to help them out.

Next, we discuss companies for which we have a signed term sheet. We talk about some of the deal issues as well as any particular open items that would be good to discuss among the team. We then discuss companies for which the investment committee has approved an investment, but the term sheet has not yet been fully negotiated. For these companies, we talk about the negotiating process (usually valuation issues or issues uncovered during due diligence). We also discuss the timing of when the deals might close.

I think the next part is the most fun: talking about companies that we have recently met and are considering in terms of making an investment in them. We start in alphabetical order and go down the list. At any given time, we usually have thirty to fifty companies under consideration for investments between $250,000 and $5 million. Generally, we have an open discussion among the team members and discuss whether a company has a great management team, great technology, and a large market.

I really wish entrepreneurs had a better sense of how venture capitalists reviewed investment opportunities, although I'm sure how we discuss deals is different compared to similar discussions at other venture capital funds. I remember during my former life when I represented companies as their outside counsel the reasons why a VC would or would not fund were hard to comprehend. However, some people understand that there is a numbers game: we will look at more than one hundred deals and we might be lucky if we even do one deal. Fewer people understand that there is incredible competition for an investment dollar when comparing two companies, side-by-side. In other words, decisions are made on a comparative basis where each company is in effect being compared against the other companies that we have reviewed.

Today, we agree to elevate two companies for deeper discussion for which we will prepare investment memos to present to the investment committee. I always am asked what it takes to get a deal approved by our team. The answer is simple, but elusive: we need one person to be passionate about moving the investment forward.

11:30 a.m.   *Conference Call with Attorneys (re: ongoing transaction)*

It was now time to call our lawyer to get an update on the status of one of our deals. There are still outstanding due diligence issues and issues with the financing documents. In this type of situation, I really appreciate having a long relationship with my lawyer. Since we have worked together for so long, he knows which issues are important to me, which issues require discussion, and which issues he can take care of by himself and don't need my attention, even if we don't discuss them. The level of trust is high and such trust can only be earned over time. So for those reading this, it's important to keep this in mind.

The call goes well—there are no deal-breaking issues so far. Based on the call, I have a list of issues that need discussion with the company.

12:00 p.m.   *Lunch Interview with Potential CEO*

I head to the Rosewood Hotel, located nearby on Sand Hill Road, for lunch to meet a prospective CEO. One of our portfolio companies is ready to take the next step in its evolution and the board of directors (of which I am a member) and the current CEO agree that a new CEO is necessary. The company has hired an executive recruiter and I'm supposed to meet him for lunch to get to know each other.

I walk in and am guided to my table where the prospective CEO is waiting. We sit down and have a nice conversation about background, kids, and so on. A fun side distraction during the lunch was seeing Marc Andreessen, the billionaire founder of Netscape (one of the world's first Internet browsers). While celebrities at the Rosewood Hotel are fairly common—billionaires are still rare—and so it was an unexpected treat. The CEO and I have a good time talking about other celebrity sightings we've had.

Our discussion turns to the vision of the company and hearing his opinion of the company and its prospects. As I'm talking and listening, I'm trying to figure out if this person would fit with the board, the company, the company's employees and customers, and whether he has the big vision to push the company in a new direction, and has the experience of leading the development of the technology. Based on my conversation, he is definitely in the running. If this person is as good as I thought, he would probably be looking at multiple opportunities. I need to inform the board that they should move forward and meet with him ASAP.

2:00 p.m.   *Board Meeting with Portfolio Company*

I head off to a venture fund that has co-invested with us on a portfolio company. As I walk in, I greet the CEO, the other board members and board observers that are there. The company's lawyer is on the phone and listening to the conversation. Typically, Silicon Valley lawyers will sit in on board meetings for free and will take notes as the secretary of the board meeting. In exchange for their time, they understand that they will build bonds with the board members by giving good advice to the company and will be able to bill for the work that gets generated from the meeting.

I made sure I prepared for the meeting the night before by reading the board package. It's good to be able to understand how the company has changed (both positively and negatively) since the last board meeting, which are usually one or two months apart.

For this meeting (and most meetings), we approve the prior board minutes and then go over the financial status of the company: how much cash are they burning per month? Have there been any changes to the employees? How are they doing compared to the financial plan they gave to the board? The worst thing for board members is to be surprised by drastic changes to the financial condition of the company.

We then discuss the business and some of the strategies/tactics the company will use to acquire more users. We also discuss the recent moves by our competitors and the changing needs of the market.

4:00 p.m.   *Meeting with Potential Investment Opportunity*

I'm back in our office and a prospective company is about to come in. When they come in, we exchange pleasantries and re-connect on how they came to me. Usually, a friend has referred them, which is always better than any other type of introduction. Cold calls are rarely returned. Mainly, if you trust the referrer, then the meeting goes better since your expectations are known ahead of time.

I generally start with a description of our venture fund, since it will help the company tailor their pitch to our fund's characteristics. Knowing our fund's mission also helps the company understand if there is a fit with our investment thesis.

I like to ask questions about how the founders started working together to see if they have a deep understanding of each other, which is critical during company crises (an inevitability of start-up companies). I also try to probe about competitors and compare them to other companies we might have seen. The reaction of the founders is usually very telling of how they will handle adversity in the future. To be clear—I'm not searching for reactions, but merely take note of them.

We'll also talk about the business model, although the model will also change over time as the product evolves and the market matures. I ask how much they want to raise for investment and why. Usually, this type of question elicits the person's thinking and their ability to plan. If I see a big hole in their assumptions, I'll consider their analysis when I decide whether to push for them at our next team meeting.

5:00 p.m.   *Conference Call with Potential Co-Investors*

One of our targeted companies for which we have an outstanding term sheet attracted another potential co-investor. I call the potential investor, who I happened to know and meet when I was at my law firm. We catch up since we hadn't talked in a few years. We both express surprise and delight that we may be able to work together as co-investors. It just goes to show you again just how small the world can be, especially in the VC industry.

I explain our fund's rationale for investing in the company and he goes over their rationale. It looks like we have a similar vision of what we think the company can be, which is good to know, since we want the board members to be unified in the company's direction.

We next discuss the status of the financing and the open due diligence issues. I explained some of the issues that we had found early in our process and how we resolved them. I was pleased to hear him express his gratitude for us identifying and cleaning up the open issues. All companies have complications and problems—how we deal with them helps reduce risk for future investors and increases the likelihood of a successful future financing. Frankly, my legal background helps me quickly identify these issues. Also, since I have done so many of these deals from the company-side of things, I generally will have some idea on how to resolve the issues to the satisfaction of investors—we call this "cleaning up the company."

We also talk about the management team's expectations regarding salary and then the unclear title to the intellectual property—both of course, being fairly critical issues.

We ultimately determine that neither of us has any issues that would prevent us from moving forward with the deal or make us uncomfortable.

What most companies don't understand is that we are constantly re-assessing our deals every day. On any particular day, it's possible that an investor could back out. Sometimes, one investor backing out means that we would be the sole investor in the deal—this certainly adds risk to the investment and would also trigger additional analysis on whether we wanted to continue with the transaction.

Generally, investors will sit on the board of the company and will have to work with each other over the course of the next couple of years—if not five to ten years. So it's very important that the investors and the management get along and share similar milestones for the company.

6:30 p.m.   *Company Pitch Session*

I head to my old law firm, which is hosting a company pitch session. Various organizations in Silicon Valley help incubate companies. When they are ready to debut their incubated companies, they invite venture capitalists to listen to ten to twenty companies, each of which get five minutes to deliver their value proposition.

I really enjoy these sessions. There is always a lot of energy and buzz in the room. While we eat finger food, we get to hear some of the best and brightest stand up in front of hundreds of people to try to convince us that they will change the world and make a ton of money at the same time. This is the sort of occasion where revolutions in the tech industry could happen—you never know.

Five minutes is never enough. I always hope that I hear enough to get me interested in learning more. In this case, I find one company (of twenty) that I really like. I want to hear more because I think they are doing something that could be game-changing. I see a couple of friends from the venture capital world and explain to them why I liked this one particular company. They get curious and we track down the entrepreneur to spend more time with him. We spend the next twenty minutes going over his background and the genesis of the idea that spawned the technology. It's fascinating to me to hear why they decided to risk everything and become an entrepreneur.

9:30 p.m.   *Prepare Investment Case*

I go home and start preparing the investment memo for one of the companies in which we decided to invest at today's team meeting. We try to move as quickly as we can to fund the company, since we know that the company does not have the money to pay employees or grow. The investment memo will be reviewed by the team and we try to pull together as much information as we can to include in the memo. Once we finish the memo, we will deliver it (hopefully within a week) to our investment committee, at which point the investment committee will (again, hopefully) approve the deal.

11:30 p.m.   Answer E-Mails, Go to Sleep

Before going to bed, I check my e-mails one last time and answer anyone that has a time-pressed issue. I try to flag e-mails during the day that "must" be answered by the end of the day. I try to get to them while I can throughout the course of my jam-packed day, but this is my last chance. Old habits die hard—and answering e-mails at all times of the day and night is one of my carry-over habits of when I was a lawyer. Fortunately, there are only a few that require deep-thinking—the others are more easily answered.

6:30 a.m.   Gear Up for Another 24 Hours in Silicon Valley

I repeat the same routine as the day before. Except for the routine, no day is like any other day, and that variety is a great aspect of my job. Also, hearing an entrepreneur's reasons for why he or she will change the world for the better always energizes me and makes me appreciate the work I get an opportunity to do. Getting up really isn't that hard.

Final Thoughts

The road to becoming a lawyer, the training I received in my career as a lawyer and all of the deals that I did while I was a lawyer—all of it led me to what I do today. While I can't point necessarily to one particular thing that directly connects my former legal profession to my job as a venture capital investor, the sum of the legal parts is a major contributing factor to my overall abilities to do my job well.

When I started my career as a lawyer—I originally had no idea or desire to be a venture capitalist. My core ambition was to help entrepreneurs become part of the Silicon Valley story. When I first entered my first law firm in

Silicon Valley, I had a ten-year plan (i.e., to make partner at my law firm). I gave up my plan in my third year as an associate when I received an offer to join a start-up company. Since then, rather than sticking to any specific game plan, I've tried to maximize the different opportunities presented to me, including a return to the legal profession (I returned to a law firm after my time at the start-up).

I attribute these opportunities to the fact that I try to do the best I can at all times—so that when the opportunities came—I was at least ready to think about them.

One last parting thought is that I really believe that I am lucky to have become a lawyer, which allowed me to do what I am doing now. I feel that some of my luck comes from helping others (for example, free advice—both legal and non-legal). Even when we cannot (or will not) fund a company, I will always try to help them in some way (i.e., comments on their business plan, connections to potential business partners, introductions to other venture capitalists, and so forth). Helping others, I believe, will eventually help yourself.

9

Profile 9
Melinda: Mediator/Arbitrator

Executive Summary

Name: Melinda
Profile: Mediator/Arbitrator
Location: Dallas, Texas

One might wonder how an arbitrator is different from a judge. As a mediator and arbitrator, Melinda carefully assesses the differences and uses it to do her job better and more fairly. Some of the attributes for becoming a successful arbitrator—as Melinda clearly is—include being a gifted legal writer and persuasive negotiator, as well as having previous experience in litigation while representing conflicting parties. Melinda's trained experience observing how other arbitrators operate in the field has given her plenty of accumulated know-how and invaluable insights, the most notable of which includes being constantly committed and dedicated to each and every case on behalf of the client. As a successful and devoted sole practitioner, Melinda takes care to seize opportunities to network, be punctual to all meetings, and provide thorough legal analysis—all this in exchange for the opportunity to be in control of her own schedule. Finally, Melinda is not shy about sharing her strategies in order to make sure that she gives the appropriate attention required to satisfy both parties if it can lead to a shorter, more efficient and fair arbitration process. So if you're planning a possible career in mediation or arbitration, you should find it worthwhile to spend a twenty-four-hour day with Melinda.

Profile

Career Field:	Mediator/Arbitrator
Current Position:	Sole Practitioner
Institution:	Solo Law Practice
Location:	Dallas, Texas
Previous Position(s):	In-House Counsel/Partner at Large Law Firm
Education:	JD, University of Texas, School of Law
	BA, University of Texas at Austin
Licensed (Y/N):	Yes
Jurisdictions:	Texas

Schedule

6:30 a.m.	Wake-Up
6:45 a.m.	Prepare for the Day
7:45 a.m.	Off to the Office
8:00 a.m.	Check Voicemail/Settle into the Workday
8:15 a.m.	Return Call on Possible New Case
9:00 a.m.	Review Summary Judgment Motion Papers and Cited Cases for Telephonic Hearing Tomorrow
11:45 a.m.	City Bar Association for Bar Continuing Education Luncheon
1:15 p.m.	Final Review of Filings and Notes for Discovery Hearing
2:00 p.m.	Hearing on Discovery Motions
3:45 p.m.	Back to the Office
4:45 p.m.	Exercise
7:00 p.m.	Fundraising Dinner with Friends
10:30 p.m.	Go Home
11:30 p.m.	Get Some Sleep, Finally
6:30 p.m.	Wake-Up and Begin Another Day

24-Hour Schedule

6:30 a.m.   Wake-Up

My alarm is set to ring in fifteen minutes. But as usual, I'm up before it goes off and I take a few minutes to think about my plan for the day. One nice thing about running a solo practice is that I set my schedule. And by focusing primarily on mediation and arbitration, I have a lot more control over setting my daily schedule than when I was litigating on behalf of clients. As a morning person, I'd be thrilled to start hearings and mediations at 8:30 a.m. But I always have to keep in mind what's realistic and manageable for the parties and their attorneys. I need to follow a schedule that's going to work for their schedules, and start and end hearings and conferences at times that work for everyone. So I don't normally start a hearing or a call before 9 a.m. Instead, I use the time before 9 a.m. to clean up the odds and ends of the prior day's work and deal with the never-ending barrage of e-mails.

So first things first. I check my phone to be sure that no e-mails came in overnight that I need to address right away. Work really never stops (and I still wonder if I would have preferred to work back in the 1960s when people worked only at their offices and left everything there). Some litigators send e-mails late at night to raise an issue, so I halfway expect to see at least one of those every morning in my inbox. But none today, so the day is starting well.

6:45 a.m.   *Prepare for the Day*

I start my usual morning routine: shower, do my hair, makeup, and while doing this, decide what to wear. To choose the right thing to wear, I have to think about what I'm doing today. If I'm only working on cases through telephone conferences or reviewing papers, I might just wear jeans (one of the benefits of a solo practice). But I have an in-person conference this afternoon to hear an argument and rule on several discovery disputes in an arbitration with lots of dollars at stake, multiple parties, and at least three lawyers for each party participating in every phone conference. I expect a packed room today. So today, I'll dress more "court-like," bearing in mind that it could be an intense and potentially argumentative afternoon. That means I won't wear my highest heels.

Having decided on the footwear and moving upwards, I opt for a solid color pantsuit that says, "I'm there to work," but with a multi-color knit top that doesn't bore me. Add some jewelry, nothing too flashy, but not boring also. I always try to strike the right balance. When I was actively litigating—

like every other lawyer does—I tried to read between the lines of every question a judge would ask and what the judge's demeanor or attire might say about him. So I try to walk the line between boring and flashy so no one tries to read me based on what I'm wearing. And then I think, "Well, if you were hearing a case out of town, you sure would look stuck in a rut" because then I'd be wearing the same basic look and jewelry every day. And when I travel by air, I never check-in a bag (only carry-on). So the only jewelry I bring on business trips is a watch that's easy to read at a glance. This way, when my phone is shut off, I can still know the time. I also bring a pair of "work" earrings, a short chain necklace, and a bangle bracelet. They've served me well as my business travel jewelry for years and I expect will continue to do so for years to come.

If an arbitration is long and in a city where I want to stay over the weekend, I have to be selective enough to carry all my clothes for two or three weeks in a carry-on bag. This is not impossible, but it does require careful thought. And when that happens, I'm sure I do look boring—a few solid colored skirts and pants, some coordinating knit tops, a dark jacket, and maybe only one pair of heels. But at least I don't have to do the dreaded "Did my luggage show up?" dance at the airport baggage carousel. I travel fairly often out of state for cases, so I'm glad arbitrators don't need to worry about state licensure issues in most states because of the private nature of our work. I don't have any out of town hearings scheduled until next month, so I needn't think about what I'll have to pack for that trip, at least not yet.

Now that I'm dressed and almost ready to go, the next order of business is food. I usually eat breakfast at home—orange juice, a blueberry muffin, and a cup of yogurt. I'm not a person who eats a big "fix it yourself" breakfast. Breakfast is quick and easy. And I don't drink coffee. So there's no need to waste time stopping at a coffee shop for me.

One last look in the mirror, and I'm ready to leave.

7:45 a.m.   Off to the Office

As I drive the few blocks to my office, I think about the different places I've worked and how much more convenient and easy my drive is now.

When I worked downtown, it took time to get to and from the office because the highway was always congested. And then the multiple levels of parking lots under the buildings are all so tightly constructed that just claiming a parking spot where my doors wouldn't be dinged could be a challenge in and of itself. I still can't get over having my car hit a few years ago while it was parked in a downtown parking lot because someone was talking on his phone and not paying attention—but at least the person who hit me realized he had to do the right thing and left me his insurance information on a note! With my office now in an executive suite not far from my home, my commute is now much quicker and less stressful than before, and I pull into the parking lot shortly after leaving home. They say that the average person spends seven years of his or her life waiting—including waiting when stuck in the middle of traffic—so I'd rather be waiting outside the confines of my car where I have the option to do something else more productive.

8:00 a.m.   Check Voicemail/Settle into the Workday

When I checked earlier this morning, there weren't any messages on my phone. But once I get to the office, I quickly notice there's a message light flashing on my phone. So the first thing I do is check it to see who called. It turns out the voicemail was from an attorney I know calling to check on my availability to be a party-appointed arbitrator in a new case that's going to be handled "ad hoc" by a panel of three arbitrators, with two party-appointed and the chairperson whom the party-appointed arbitrators jointly select. This is great—I like being a party-appointed wingman. Some people think that if a contract calls for each side to an agreement to appoint its own arbitrator, and then those two select the arbitration panel chair, this gives the parties the opportunity to appoint their lawyer's sibling or their neighbor and get a vote in their favor guaranteed. In reality, the arbitrator ethics rules generally require that party-appointed arbitrators be "neutral" after appointment and not favor or communicate about the substance of the case with either side. So appointing the lawyer's best buddy isn't the way to go—at least not since the latest AAA/ABA (American Arbitration Association / American Bar Association) ethics rules were issued. These rules have really benefited the arbitration process because we now don't have lawyers selecting just anyone to be an arbitrator, assuming his or her vote will be a sure thing.

This new case sounds like an interesting one, and I jot down a note to call the attorney back as soon as possible. Returning calls quickly for services is important to all lawyers, but even more so for a solo practitioner.

8:15 a.m.   *Return Call on Possible New Case*

I return the call on the new case, using my standard initial conflict check approach before talking about the case. First, I ask for the names of all the parties to the dispute, to be sure I'm not currently serving in a case in which any of them are involved (which would be a disclosure item for me if I decide to go further in taking the new case). Even though in a party-appointment, an arbitrator may not be subject to removal just because he has another case involving a same party, you still want to assess and disclose any situations that might create an appearance of non-neutrality or bias. This particular case doesn't involve any party whose name rings a bell from any case I'm currently arbitrating or scheduled to mediate. But I'll want to check my conflicts list of cases I've handled over the years to see if any party might have been involved in a closed case I handled in the past. I make a note to check my records for that information.

Once the parties have been tentatively cleared, I next ask the names of all the attorneys and their law firms to see if any of them create a disclosure situation for me. It turns out the law firm on the other side in this new case also is appearing before me in another case, one in which I was appointed through an alternative dispute provider organization's list selection process. No big deal, I can disclose this, see if anyone involved has a concern, and then deal with whether to proceed or not after the disclosure. I still need to check my conflict system to confirm any other possible disclosure issues. But so far, the conflicts for this case don't seem to be overly complicated or insurmountable.

Following this, I ask for the names of witnesses—a lot of the time the attorneys who call me directly haven't even thought about who their witnesses will or will not be, as well as whether a conflict of interest could arise for an arbitrator in serving in their case once they name their witnesses. Getting the names of possible witnesses is one area in which working on an ad hoc case can be very different from when I am selected from an alternative dispute resolution (ADR) provider organization's list.

Many of those organizations ask the lawyers to provide the names of their clients' potential witnesses when the case is first filed so that arbitrators can check conflicts of interest on the potential witnesses as well as the parties and attorneys before we agree to take the case. But when that doesn't happen at the outset, often we have to clear the witnesses for conflicts and disclosures later. But the likelihood that there's such a conflict involving a witness here seems small, and so I decide we can move on.

After I get all the appropriate information, I tell the lawyer I'll send him my conflicts disclosures in writing the next day after I've checked my records to be sure I've confirmed that there's nothing else I need to disclose based on the information I have. I assure him the disclosure obligation is continuing. If anything else comes up, I'll disclose it. Then I tell the attorney how the other party's appointed arbitrator and I will choose the panel chair (the third member of the arbitration team). After this, I ask the attorney who called me to coordinate disclosure exchanges with his opposing counsel after each has his or her arbitrator's written disclosures so this case can get moving. This is a good start to the day.

9:00 a.m.   *Review Summary Judgment Motion Papers and Cited Cases for Telephonic Hearing Tomorrow*

Tomorrow morning I have a telephonic hearing on cross-motions for summary judgment in a case that's been pending for ten months. Arbitrators like to schedule cases for hearing on as quick a basis as the parties will agree to because a speedier resolution than they may receive in court (which can take years) is a hoped-for benefit of arbitration. If none of these summary judgment motions is granted, the case goes to hearing at the end of next month for three weeks straight—unless, of course, the lawyers either settle the case or agree at the last minute to reschedule the hearing. The "settle at the courthouse steps" approach to litigation applies as much in arbitration as it does in court cases. So even if a case doesn't settle early, it still can settle right before the hearing, during it, or even afterwards. As a solo attorney who spends most of my work time dealing with arbitrations, I know the possibility of a case settling on the eve of the hearing and then leaving me with a gap in my schedule that can be a problem—but if the parties decide they want to settle, I always believe that whatever settlement is satisfactory to them is a good event and I always encourage parties to keep working toward that goal if they can. I hope that doing this lets them recognize that alternative dispute resolution is their process, and that at the end of the day, they (the clients) have control over what occurs.

But in the event parties settle at the last minute, many arbitrators protect against those gaps in their schedules by including a cancellation fee provision in their retention agreement. This is to offset some of the lost billings when a case settles right before the hearing. This can be a fine line to walk—personally, I think a cancellation policy that's overly protective of the arbitrator's interests sends the wrong message. My view right now is that having a modest cancellation fee may get the lawyers to focus on settlement potential for a case a little bit earlier than the courthouse steps. So something that's not excessive actually may help the parties work out their dispute earlier. Oh well, all that doesn't matter right now because what I'm looking at this morning are summary judgment papers, nothing about the hearing date, as of yet.

After grabbing a juice from the fridge in the break room, I sit down with the door closed to focus on the submitted papers. First, of course, I check my phones for new messages and computer for new e-mails just so I'm caught up on these first. Reviewing and thinking about the papers takes time and focused concentration—just like for a judge, the parties expect their arbitrators to read and assess every word in their motions and affidavits, and presumably also the cases they cite, which I do. As a general rule, I like lawyers to submit copies of their key cases to me rather than having to spend time accessing them myself—unlike a judge, many attorneys who arbitrate are solo practitioners who don't have a team of law clerks or associates to research the issues and write a memo on the law for them. So getting copies of the key cases straight from the lawyers without having to search for them myself just helps to speed the process along.

Each side's lawyers generally aren't shy about telling the arbitrator in a filing if they believe the other side is misstating the law. So I don't start out doing my own independent research on issues presented—sometimes unendingly, with replies and sur-replies, and whatever else they want to submit. All in all, having more rather than less information can be helpful in rendering my decision. But I know judges don't have to deal with the unending submission of supplemental information because court rules on submissions are stricter than in arbitration. Sometimes lawyers do a better job of saying everything they want a judge to know all in one filing in court. In comparison, in arbitration, the filing rules are looser. So some lawyers just keep on submitting papers after papers in a seemingly endless way while a motion is still pending.

Also, as arbitrators, we may not deal the same way as judges with an issue we think matters, but which the lawyers didn't raise. If I think there's an issue that no one's addressed, I may raise it by e-mail to the lawyers to provide me their analyses, or ask for it during an argument and set a deadline for their responses. A judge might do something similar, but because a judge may have a judicial clerk who writes those memos for the judge, he or she may be able to get the answer from the assigned clerk's research instead.

So as I read the papers, I make my notes and comments. Today I'm doing this the old-fashioned way, with pen on paper copies the lawyers sent to me by FedEx (express mail) instead of by e-mail because they were so bulky. I'll make notes about each side's position with comments raised by the other—this will help me when I ask questions tomorrow.

Suddenly, I realize it's time to leave for a lunch meeting at the city bar association. One more quick check of my e-mails, and I'm off.

11:45 a.m.   *City Bar Association for Bar Continuing Education Luncheon*

I'm now off to hear a speaker talking about e-discovery. Every law organization sponsors seminars about this subject, and all of them always point out how difficult and expensive the process can be, even if it's just reaching an agreement on search terms. It'd be great to say I don't need to bother with e-discovery issues because I rarely represent parties these days. But in reality, I need to think these issue through more carefully than do the lawyers who appear before me—either when I'm acting as part of a panel or as the sole arbitrator—in which I have to decide disputes over e-discovery all the time. Again, I wonder if lawyers were better off before computers, being stuck in conference rooms full of boxes of files tediously looking through hard copy records for relevant evidence. Then I think— wait a minute—lawyers still have to do that to produce hard copy records.

So e-discovery simply adds another layer of legal work as part of the discovery process.

There are two reasons to attend this lunch seminar. First, maybe there'll be a new tidbit I can apply in a case to help streamline the e-discovery process for the attorneys involved. Second, the Bar's a great place to network. The world of arbitrator and mediator solo practitioners has grown a lot since I started doing this. But some of the people trying to be an arbitrator or mediator don't realize that the best background to do this the right way is to have first practiced law representing parties in a great many cases. Doing that, you learn how to litigate, how to figure out the validity of claims, and how to assess evidence. Whether a case is a mediation or an arbitration, those basics matter.

Some people are deciding to become an "ADR provider" without even attending law school by just taking those quickie classes for a "certification." But with all the trained lawyers who have the basics down already, I think those non-lawyers should really re-think their career plans if they think they'll become a favored choice of lawyers to resolve their clients' disputes without having formal law school training. Understanding the law really does matter when lawyers are selecting ADR providers for their clients. In specialized cases—construction cases, accounting, or technology—people may prefer someone who also has substantive expertise in the field at issue, but substantive understanding of the law isn't gained in a forty hour quickie course.

Just last week I saw someone whose brother was planning to take a quickie mediation course and then go to the courthouse to get on the list of county-approved mediators, thinking work magically will roll in for him. Even though I don't want to be the one to burst his bubble, people's lives and rights are involved and I can't imagine who would hire someone to help resolve their rights if all he's done is take a quickie course somewhere. As an arbitrator, you have to be just as analytical and meticulous in thinking through issues, being fair to all participants, weighing the evidence, writing your award, and everything else you do as do judges and the lawyers representing parties. And the parties' appeal rights from your arbitration decisions are so much more limited than if they deal with their dispute in a public court setting. For mediation, do those quickie mediation courses even train people in the differences between evaluative and facilitative mediation? When a case is mediated, parties look to the mediator for guidance about settlement—so if you don't understand the legal issues and the parties want an evaluation, how can you competently help them? I don't understand how, with all the trained attorneys practicing ADR, someone taking a quickie course will succeed in ADR work.

Now, back from my musings—attending Bar activities is helpful, and I select my food from the not-so-great lunch buffet and sit down at a table with other lawyers to hear more about e-discovery. This will be over just in time for me to go to this afternoon's hearing.

Because of that hearing, I jump out of my chair as soon as the speaker is finished and leave, even though I'd like to stay around a few minutes to chat with some attorneys who were sitting across the room. As an arbitrator or mediator, I always prefer to be ten minutes early to the hearing/meeting locale rather than even a minute late. So I'm off.

1:15 p.m.   *Final Review of Filings and Notes for Discovery Hearing*

I tend to review filings in a fairly set process that's worked well for me thus far: I initially review a motion right after it comes in so that I know what the issues in dispute are, can set a schedule for the parties to respond to the motion, and decide if we need a hearing to argue the motion or if the issues are the type that I can decide on the papers. Whether a hearing is needed (or not) can make a difference in how quickly a response should be filed. I like to set arbitration schedules fairly tightly so that the lawyers and parties don't let the case languish. This usually helps because either the parties will decide to resolve the dispute amicably and it'll be over through a settlement, or everyone will be engaged mentally and ready for the hearing when it's set rather than asking for continuances. Last minute continuance requests create difficulty in everyone's schedule. As an arbitrator, I don't double-book two hearings on the same days in the hope that one will settle. As a result, last minute continuances and settlements on the eve of a hearing will cause gaps in my schedule.

Arbitrators are divided on how best to deal with continuances and settlements because it's a real business issue for us. Some arbitrators enforce strict cancellation fee policies so they still get paid something—or everything—as if the hearing happened even if the case settles. Others double book and hope it all works out. Others include a relatively small cancellation policy when they're retained. And some just see what happens. I've worked with arbitrators who follow all variations. I chaired one panel that had an arbitrator who was so sure that a two-week case would settle that he double-booked many days that we'd reserved for the hearing, to also be in depositions for a client. And then when the arbitration and the depositions both went forward (with another attorney covering for him), he wanted way too many breaks in the hearing so he could check in on the depositions. I've also been on panels where one arbitrator required parties to pay him his full fee if the case settled or was postponed in the last thirty days before the hearing date.

The first of these approaches isn't a good strategy because parties can sense when an arbitrator isn't fully engaged in a hearing. I can't imagine the attorneys who represented the parties in that case would ever choose that arbitrator for a later case based on that experience. And the second approach can be really irritating to the other arbitrators. This is because the others may have to try to convince the arbitrator with the more extreme cancellation policy that his or her policy is harmful to the case's progress and causes unnecessary pressure on everyone else involved in the case. I've come down on the side of being conservative—I have a modest cancellation fee if a case cancels in the last days before hearing, which is what most good solo practitioner ADR people seem to do.

Anyway, back to preparation for the hearing: I review the motions when they first come in and set the schedule for responses and the hearing soon after receiving the motions. In this case, I received four different discovery motions in a short timeframe, with each claimant filing a motion or cross-motion against each respondent and vice versa. That's pretty typical—once one party opens the floodgates on a discovery issue, all the others follow that lead. This is why I like to hold these hearings in person occasionally when I can—then the lawyers are in one room at the same time and have to look at the other parties' lawyers while they argue the issues. Being together incentivizes the lawyers to stop arguing extremes, and instead, offer compromises they're willing to accept. This also cuts through the excess puffery that may occur in the filings as well as in the arguments during a conference call.

I quickly review my notes, which I made as the motions were first sent to me and as each response was received. Because we have so many motions to deal with today, I reviewed everything I had received yesterday, and am organized for the order in which I want them addressed. The notion of "first served gets heard first" sometimes is a good system, but the ways the motions inter-relate can make a different approach more logical. And because I'm the arbitrator, whatever approach to the argument I want is the one we'll follow.

As the lawyers join me, I organize my highlighted copies of the pleadings and move to the head of the table. The time to begin the hearing is now here.

2:00 p.m. *Hearing on Discovery Motions*

The hearing begins. I start by thanking everyone for all the helpful briefing they provided. Even though it sounds trite, it's true: without all the briefing or without really well-written briefings from the lawyers representing the parties, I'd have a lot more questions and, who knows, maybe would need to ask for more information and wouldn't be able to rule immediately. If a hearing is over discovery, I always like to rule during the hearing so the parties know right away what else, if anything, they have to go searching for in their clients' files and electronic records.

One motion today was filed by the claimant over e-discovery received from one respondent. Then a cross-motion was filed. No matter how often I hear these issues and no matter how many seminars lawyers attend about how to deal with e-discovery, I've concluded that computers have really complicated the discovery process. Nevertheless, this is an important issue, and will take up more time than the remaining motions. So I plan to deal with these two together, right off the bat.

The argument's flow is going to be improved in several ways by holding this hearing in person. First, I get to see everyone as each makes his or her arguments, so I see the nuances of expression I'd miss if we were on a telephone conference call. Second, when people are in a room together, it's much more personal than by phone. So the tendency to interrupt each other's arguments is more restrained. Third, when I pose questions to the attorneys, I can say that I want to hear from all parties in response. Normally, when I say this over the phone, the response might be strategic silence on both sides, as each lawyer waits to hear what his or her opposing counsel will say first. But by looking directly at the lawyer I want to solicit an answer from first, I get the response that I want, from the party I want, when I want it. This helps to preserve the flow of the process. Fourth, like anyone else, lawyers tend to be more likely to make workable proposals about the discovery at issue if they're physically sitting across a table from each other than if they're on a more impersonal conference call that doesn't involve face-to-face contact.

Because there's a roomful of people (yes, as I anticipated, each party sent three lawyers to the hearing today), I draw the table on a piece of paper and ask everyone to write each of their names where he or she is sitting, so that I have a record of this as reference. Sometimes company representatives come to discovery hearings, and sometimes only the outside lawyers appear, but it's easier to keep the participants straight with a seating chart. Once that's handed back to me, I thank everyone for participating and tell them the titles of each motion response and reply I received and reviewed, so we're sure there's not a filing that was lost in transit. With those housekeeping issues taken care of, I tell the parties the first motions on which I want to hear argument. And we're off.

The process starts with the claimant's lawyer explaining what additional e-discovery he wants, and why. Then the lawyer for the respondent who didn't provide the discovery responds and incorporates the issues from his client's cross-motion into his response. Sometimes these discovery hearings are simply a re-hashing of what was submitted in writing already. That's not really very helpful—what I want to hear is a succinct and focused explanation of why, notwithstanding all the pages that may have been submitted by each side (keeping in mind that, whichever lawyer is speaking, is presenting the legal position that's better supported or more justified from his or her particular vantage point). Also, when the subject matter is discovery, I want the lawyers to direct me to the exact document request or issue under which the discovery was requested. I'm still amazed at how often lawyers forget to attach a copy of the written document request and response or relevant correspondence to their motion papers, in which case I have to request this documentation. Setting aside all other issues about scope and burdensomeness, whether an issue or search terms really have been vetted appropriately in the papers is critical to a fair ruling.

This case has had several prior hearings on discovery—all by telephone—so the lawyers knew to provide me the necessary background information as part of their written submissions. I don't have to ask for any additional requests or correspondence to ask my questions, hear their answers, and rule on what e-discovery each party is to provide. This was a hot button item and I knew neither side was going to offer up a solution to which everyone would agree. So I listen to both sides' positions about the search terms each proposed should be used to locate more electronic documents appropriate for the scope of manageable discovery. I quickly realize that, as often happens, the party seeking the discovery is requesting records based on search terms that are so broad that both sides will drown in computer files, and as a result, will spend far too much time and money chasing down search terms that should be more specifically tailored to the case.

Conversely, the party opposing the discovery is arguing in the opposite direction: for such narrow search terms, so specialized to the case's subject matter and unlike the way people write in e-mail, that it's possible that really substantive correspondence directly on point would be missed if I agree with its position. So even though I don't like when people say arbitrators split the baby, I rule on search terms that fall between the parties' positions. The truth is that attorneys often take extreme positions in arguing for their clients. As a result, an arbitrator often has to come down in between what each party asks for in discovery in order to be fair and give each party the reasonable opportunity to prepare its case.

On to the next motion—this time it's about the location of a third-party witness oral deposition, whether it was to occur in person or over the phone, and which side would pay for that third-party witness's travel costs if he travels for the deposition. The third-party witness lives several states away, and both sides agree they received a letter from him (the third-party witness) stating he was willing to appear for deposition in person so long as it didn't cost him any money and was done at his convenience. Though I wonder if the witness knew that he's technically outside the subpoena power of the arbitration, he offered to appear voluntarily. It's not appropriate for me (as the arbitrator) to advise the third party—or any— witness about whether he can refuse to appear. And he doesn't have an attorney participating in the hearing. So I ask if anyone knows what the witness's preference is—did he want to be deposed in his hometown, or travel to where the parties' lawyers are?

I remind the lawyers that the witness's expenses if he traveled would be paid by the parties, but the lawyers didn't seem concerned about that (of course not, their clients would be paying for them to travel to the witness's locale, so having the witness travel instead and the parties divide that expense is cheaper for their clients). So I rule that the witness is to appear at the site selected by the parties, with each party to advance equal amounts of funds to cover all the witness's expenses. But I also rule that if his preference is to be deposed in his hometown and have the lawyers travel to him, then the lawyers all have to travel to where he lives, and that each side has to notify the witness in writing of this ruling.

Then we move on to the last motion, which relates to hard copy documents that were requested many weeks ago by one party, to which the other objected on the basis that the documents were privileged. The motion has been pending for a few weeks while the lawyers tried to resolve the issue. The issue is pretty simple actually, relating to whether the documents are privileged or exempt from production as attorney-client or accountant-client communications. This is an issue with which I'm quite familiar. I'm surprised to hear the positions the lawyers are taking. But I resolve this motion on a document-by-document basis, and we're done.

I tell the parties that I'll provide an order to them within two days memorializing each ruling I made—as always, I take detailed notes as we went along in the hearing—for the record. We say our good-byes and everyone packs up to leave.

3:45 p.m.   *Back to the Office*

After leaving the hearing, I turn my phone back on and quickly check for messages before deciding nothing is so urgent that I need to respond before

I get back to the office. And I wonder again as I'm driving what practicing law was like back in the 1960s when everyone worked only at an office and was out of reach everywhere else—that must have been nice!

After getting back to the office, I return calls and messages and check what's on the calendar for the following day. Nothing out of the office, primarily the hearing on the summary judgment motion I prepped for earlier today, reviewing pre-hearing briefs and motions (for a case that's set for hearing next week), preparing the order on the hearing I held today, and reviewing a final billing statement (for a case that's been time consuming but has now settled). So I decide that I have time to get to the gym this afternoon and this work day is mostly done.

4:45 p.m.   *Exercise*

I'm now at the gym trying to burn some calories. I try to do at least an hour of cardiovascular exercise and a circuit around the machines at least three days a week. A lot of the time, I fail at this because work and other activities interfere, but I have a good workout today, and I've arrived early enough at the gym that I can jump on a treadmill right away. By 6:00 p.m., I'm done and all the workday issues are out of my head.

7:00 p.m.   *Fundraising Dinner with Friends*

That workout made me feel really good and I had time to freshen up. So I'm in the right mood to meet friends at a charity dinner at 7:00 p.m. tonight. I'm not necessarily in the mood for the speech at a fundraiser this evening, but it's important to support certain organizations, and going in with friends for a table at these events is a good way to do that. So I'll turn off my phone, see some acquaintances during the pre-dinner wine reception, go to our table, catch up with friends during dinner, and get home.

10:30 p.m.   *Go Home*

It's now 10:30 p.m. by the time I get back home. What a long but eventful twenty-four hours! Although it's on the late side for me, I still find time to check my e-mails and messages one last time before truly saying the day is done.

11:30 p.m.   *Get Some Sleep, Finally*

It's been quite a day. For me to be effective tomorrow, I really need to get some sleep. I fall asleep almost as soon as my head hits the pillow.

6:30 a.m.   *Wake-Up and Begin Another Day*

On to the next day!

Final Thoughts

In addition to having experience understanding legal issues and the ebbs and flows of the litigation process, specializing in ADR work requires one to be a self-starter with the ability to manage people who are angry with each other before they ever step in one's door. Having an ability to work efficiently and collaboratively with the parties and counsel, an understanding that the needs and timetables of the parties are paramount, and a desire to effectively resolve problems for parties are extremely valuable. This work can be rewarding and intellectually stimulating. And it can give one a tremendous sense of satisfaction at the conclusion of a successful mediation or issuance of an arbitration award that one has resolved issues the appropriate way for all concerned.

10

Profile 10
Sylvia: Litigator (General and Commercial)

Executive Summary

Name:	Sylvia
Profile:	Litigator (General and Commercial)
Location:	Dallas and Fort Worth, Texas

The life of a commercial and general litigation attorney is never thought of as easy. After all, the image of a litigator is one of endless hours of document review, drafting, and, of course, court appearances, often before a highly inquisitive judge and panel of jury members. Add to this, being a minority female in Texas makes things even more potentially challenging. But as you will see from Sylvia's profile as a litigator, she makes the seemingly difficult challenges seem quite manageable as she strategizes with partners in her law firm in preparation for an important deposition. Sylvia also gives some hints to the increasing number of female law students and would-be attorneys in terms of how to conduct oneself as a professional. Even for the male readers of this section, understanding and becoming aware of different perspectives can come in handy. For these reasons, reading Sylvia's profile should prove both interesting and useful.

Profile

Career Field:	General and Commercial Litigation
Position:	Law Firm Attorney
Institution:	Mid-size Law Firm (General and Commercial Litigation Section)
Location:	Dallas and Fort Worth, Texas
Previous Position(s):	Legal Billing Analyst
Education:	JD, St. Mary's University, School of Law
	BA, University of Texas at Austin
Licensed (Y/N):	Yes
Jurisdiction(s):	Texas

Schedule

4:30 a.m.	Wake-Up and Exercise
6:00 a.m.	Get Ready for Work
6:30 a.m.	Catch Up on the News and Chat about Work (with husband)
7:00 a.m.	Drive to Work and Listen to National Public Radio (NPR)
7:45 a.m.	Arrive at the Office/Pick Up a Cup of (Strong) Coffee
8:00 a.m.	Check Voicemail and E-Mail (and take notes on important requests)
8:15 a.m.	Check E-Mail (and respond to any urgent requests)
8:30 a.m.	Review My Time from the Previous Day (and make revisions)
8:45 a.m.	Prepare for Summary Judgment Hearing (scheduled tomorrow)
9:00 a.m.	Meet with Partner T (to discuss summary judgment case)
9:15 a.m.	Meet with Partner F (to discuss today's deposition in Marshall, Texas)
9:30 a.m.	Return Voicemail Messages
9:40 a.m.	Review Deposition Notes of Plaintiff Doe
10:00 a.m.	Drive to Marshall, Texas (for a deposition in a toxic torts case)
12:00 p.m.	Lunch – Fast Food (eat while driving)
12:15 p.m.	Arrive at Law Offices of Opposing Counsel for Deposition
12:30 p.m.	Discuss Case with Counsel Representing Co-Defendants

1:00 p.m.	Depose Plaintiff (along with multiple co-defense counsel)
2:30 p.m.	Break (check voicemail and call secretary to get updates on any urgent e-mails)
3:30 p.m.	Complete Deposition/Fine-Tune Notes
3:45 p.m.	Drive to Dallas (to law firm)
6:15 p.m.	Return to Law Firm
6:20 p.m.	Check Voicemail and E-Mail (and take notes)
6:30 p.m.	Work on Deposition Summary
7:30 p.m.	Review and Prepare for Tomorrow's Summary Judgment Hearing
8:00 p.m.	Meet Co-Workers (to celebrate a birthday)
9:15 p.m.	Depart the Building/Drive Home
10:35 p.m.	Prepare for Summary Judgment Hearing
11:30 p.m.	Go to Bed
4:30 a.m.	Wake-Up and Exercise

24-Hour Schedule

4:30 a.m.   *Wake-Up and Exercise*

I wake up and prepare for a run in my neighborhood. At this hour, it's still completely dark. But somehow, I manage to get out of bed. The reason for today's exceptionally early rise is that I am currently training for the Chicago Marathon. And my running partner K is—for better or worse—always punctual and ready to roll. We typically run our short distance runs during the week and a long run on Saturday mornings. This morning's run is a fast-paced four-miler through my hilly neighborhood. Though it always takes me a good mile to get into a groove, I love running. It relieves stress, gives me a boost of energy, and helps me mentally prepare for the workday.

6:00 a.m.   *Get Ready for Work*

After my early morning run and some time to get ready, I put on a charcoal gray suit (jacket and skirt), a pink Oxford blouse with cuff links, and black leather pumps. For jewelry, I will wear my tried-and-true pearl necklace, pearl earrings, watch, and wedding ring. Our firm dress code is business casual unless, of course, there is one of the following: a client meeting, deposition, hearing/trial, or any other setting where formal attire is more appropriate and expected. I will wear a suit today because I have a deposition in the afternoon.

A word on formal work attire: you can never be too conservative in the law profession, especially in Texas. As a female, this entails a nicely tailored suit (of the navy, charcoal, or black variety), a neatly pressed shirt or silk blouse, and, of course, pearls are always a safe bet. To be sure, the legal arena is not the venue to test out a plunging neckline, a cheerleader-length skirt, or an outrageously bright color. Save that instead for an evening out with friends if that's your cup of tea.

6:30 a.m.   *Catch up on the News and Chat about Work (with husband)*

My husband and I typically read the paper and listen to the news. We also talk over breakfast and discuss our work in general terms. My husband is a management consultant in a large global consulting firm and both our professions require a level of confidentiality. It is great to talk to someone about our work—to the extent we can—as well as, of course, non-work related matters.

7:00 a.m.   *Drive to Work and Listen to National Public Radio (NPR)*

My commute to work is approximately forty-five minutes. I normally listen to NPR for news. Sometimes I take this opportunity to make personal calls. Today, however, my mind is on two things: today's deposition and tomorrow's summary judgment hearing.

7:45 a.m.   *Arrive at the Office/Pick Up a Cup of (Strong) Coffee*

I arrive at the office and pick up a large cup of *strong* coffee, a virtual necessity. By this time, I've been up for more than three hours.

8:00 a.m.   *Check Voicemail and E-Mail (and take notes on important requests)*

One of the very first things I do once I step into my office is to turn on my computer and then check my voicemail. I grab my legal pad and take notes for each phone message. Today there are no urgent messages. But I will respond to each call either by phone call or e-mail.

Of the calls and messages, there are two issues of particular importance this morning. The first is from a client involving his *pro bono* (work performed for the public good without compensation) child support/custody case. As a new attorney, you may be asked to handle *pro bono* cases for your firm. It is you and the firm's way of giving back to the community by providing free legal aid. The nature of the message involves my client's tax returns and other relevant documents needed in the case.

The second message is from a partner asking that I fly (along with two other associates) to Houston, Texas to inspect one hundred boxes of documents in a complex commercial litigation case. For this particular document inspection, there will be twelve lawyers (including attorneys representing other companies) culling over thousands of pages.

As a young litigation attorney, you will often be asked to inspect documents belonging to your client, opposing party(ies), co-counsel, and other documents related to a lawsuit. This probably does not sound like the most exciting task, and in truth, it is often tedious and boring. But a case can win (or die) by a single piece of document; therefore, even this task is an important aspect of litigation. You learn to sift through thousands of documents and identify relevant and/or privileged documents to protect and advocate for your client.

I then check my e-mail and respond to legal queries and/or status updates on cases.

8:30 a.m.   *Review My Time from the Previous Day (and make revisions)*

When you work in a law firm, you must account for every ten minutes of your day. Your time is money—as the work you perform and the time it takes is billed to the client. For this, I review my time entries and edit the language on the firm's computer time program. My secretary typically inputs my time (via my handwritten time sheets). But I always follow up and make edits to the entries. I have to craft the language carefully and sufficiently describe the task that I performed; for example, "Work on motion for summary judgment; specifically, that plaintiff's claim fail as a matter of law because he signed a proper waiver of liability." Another example might read: "Review [large accounting firm's] accounting documents for attorney-client privilege for fiscal years ending 2001-2003."

8:45 a.m.   *Prepare for Summary Judgment Hearing (scheduled tomorrow)*

I prepare for tomorrow's summary judgment hearing, which pertains to a case involving an injured patron at my client's indoor rock climbing facility. A court will grant a summary judgment if a moving party (our client) presents evidence that establishes that there is no issue of material fact to be tried. In other words, if the judge grants the motion for summary judgment, then he rules in favor of my client (without the case going to trial).

In the case, the plaintiff is a professional rock climber and former employee of the facility. I have already prepared and filed a motion for summary judgment arguing that the plaintiff's claim fails as a matter of law because he signed a waiver of liability for any potential injuries; and therefore, the case should be dismissed. The motion also contains alternative arguments as well as case precedent to support this argument (case precedent refers to authority used in common law jurisdictions, i.e., as in American courts, whereby a legal case establishes a principle or rule that a subsequent court may use in deciding a case based on similar issues and/or facts).

A word on litigation: As a young associate at a mid-size to large law firm, you will probably not sit first chair on a case. You are likely to appear before a judge regarding motions or other discovery matters in a case. Even so, you must understand a few key things:

1.   Learn what you can about the judge and seek advice on how to approach the court. Be sure to be prepared to argue your case and make several copies of motions, etc. Nothing irritates a judge more than a disorganized attorney.

2.   Always be professional and cordial to the judge and all legal counsel including opposing counsel. In the early days of my career, I recall attending a trial with a partner and observing a super heated court battle. I immaturely

viewed the other side as "the enemy." At the end of the first day, however, I was surprised to see my partner walk over to opposing counsel and warmly shake hands with him. They talked about each other's kids and whatnot. In fact, we (i.e., our side along with opposing counsel) even grabbed a beer after court. It was a good lesson on professionalism that day—advocate fiercely for your client, but leave the gloves off at the door and don't take things personally.

3. Learn to be relatable to folks on different levels. When drafting a motion or addressing the court, always write and speak in a professional manner. When presenting before a jury, speak to be understood and don't throw complicated legal jargon (legalese) that might confuse them. Just be aware of your audience and be respectful no matter who they are. Being emotionally savvy with people will bode well for you in this profession— and in life. You would think that people would get this, but unfortunately, I've met with some pompous and arrogant attorneys. And trust me, it's an unpleasant experience.

9:00 a.m.   Meet with Partner T (to discuss summary judgment case)

As a young attorney, you may work for a few different partners in a law firm. Hopefully, you will meet at least one partner who takes mentoring seriously. A good mentor will engage you in their high-profile cases and he or she will give you opportunities to branch off on your own. My mentor is a natural teacher and provides explanations as he discusses cases with me. I wish that I could say that all partners were effective communicators such as he is, but that is not always the case.

I am quite fortunate to have such a good mentoring relationship with Partner T. After working for him several months, Partner T decided to give me total responsibility over a case (albeit a small one where the amount in controversy is $200,000, which is the summary judgment case discussed earlier). I prepared 100 percent of the case—met with the client, researched case precedent, drafted the motion, and will argue before the judge the motion on behalf of the client. Today's meeting is a final briefing before tomorrow's summary judgment hearing.

9:15 a.m.   *Meet with Partner F (to discuss today's deposition in Marshall, Texas)*

Although I am technically in the commercial litigation section of my law firm, I am also assigned depositions in the general litigation section. Our firm allows new attorneys to gain valuable deposition experience this way.

Our corporate client—a global manufacturer of safety products—is a defendant in mass tort lawsuits for allegedly defective products. These cases are mostly asbestos- and silica-related lawsuits and are designated multi-party litigation due to the sheer volume of parties involved. I will depose one of the plaintiffs this afternoon. I meet the partner and present a brief synopsis of the plaintiff providing her important information regarding the claim—work history, health records, and other notable facts.

9:30 a.m.   *Return Voicemail Messages*

I go to my secretary's desk, which is right outside my office, and check for any messages. My secretary gives me new messages and hands me a draft copy of a memorandum of law that I dictated (and she transcribed) regarding the issue of non-competition agreements. We have a five-minute chitchat, and then I return to my office.

A note on how to treat the administrative staff—treat them with respect and as team members vital to your practice! They can make your work run efficiently and effectively *or* they can stall your performance.

9:40 a.m.   *Review Deposition Notes of Plaintiff Doe*

Multi-party litigation requires an organized system of case management. Our firm developed an eighteen-page information gathering deposition questionnaire. Some of the questions about the plaintiff have been answered through other discovery tools such as interrogatories and requests for production.

It will be my job today to obtain many (if not all) of the answers at today's deposition. At this time, I am reviewing the plaintiff's work history, health records, and other relevant information to the case. I make note of any special and unusual issues involving his particular case.

10:00 a.m.   *Drive to Marshall, Texas (for a deposition in a toxic torts case)*

With regard to asbestos-related cases, many of the plaintiffs worked and resided in manufacturing cities such as Marshall, Beaumont, and Tyler (all cities in Texas). During the two and half hour drive to Marshall, I make calls regarding other cases. I call my secretary and give her instructions regarding tomorrow's summary judgment hearing. I also ask her to book a flight for me to Houston for the document inspection project.

12:00 p.m.   *Lunch – Fast Food (eat while driving)*

I normally eat healthy meals due to marathon training (or I pay for it during my runs!), but today's meal is fast food. There is no time to stop and eat, and so, I eat while driving. Talk about serious multi-tasking—driving, eating, and phone calls—the virtues of technology and a demanding career as a young litigator!

12:15 p.m.   *Arrive at Law Offices of Opposing Counsel for Deposition*

I arrive at the hotel where the deposition of the plaintiff will take place. In mass tort litigation, it is not unusual to have depositions in a hotel conference room. There will be forty other defense attorneys present today representing their respective clients (yes, forty!).

12:30 p.m.   *Discuss Case with Counsel Representing Co-Defendants*

The co-defense counsel and I have become good acquaintances. We talk about non-legal related matters and then quickly engage in discussing today's plaintiff. Naturally, we do not divulge any privileged and confidential information about our clients during our discussion.

1:00 p.m.   *Depose Plaintiff (along with multiple co-defense counsel)*

Another defense attorney takes the lead in this deposition. She filed on behalf of her client the request to depose the plaintiff, and invited other parties to attend. Once she has completed her set of questions, each counsel has an opportunity to depose the plaintiff. My main objective is to ask questions that, if possible, would extinguish my client from any liability. This particular case involves my client's safety masks and other safety related equipment. The plaintiff, however, neither identifies my client by name nor does he sufficiently describe any of my client's products. With the information that I learn, I will likely prepare a motion to dismiss with regard to this particular plaintiff in the case.

2:30 p.m.   *Break (check voicemail and call secretary to get updates on any urgent e-mails)*

After nearly ninety minutes, a fifteen-minute break is called. People use this time for various things. But with the advent of smartphones, most lawyers use this time to make calls and check their e-mail. I'm no exception. So I pick up my phone and call my secretary to get an update on any urgent matters. I also check my e-mail to see if anything extremely urgent has occurred. Fortunately, no issues need an immediate response. So I put my phone back in my purse and walk back into the conference room with the other attorneys.

3:30 p.m.   *Complete Deposition/Fine Tune Notes*

Part of the litigator's role is to complete depositions and deposition questionnaires. I fill out the deposition questionnaire as best as I can for my client. Once the plaintiff leaves the room, he enables us defense attorneys to clarify and discuss points made in the deposition. It is an informal evaluation of the plaintiff's case; for example, did he make a good witness (was he credible in other words), how extensive are his injuries, etc.?

3:45 p.m.   *Drive to Dallas (to law firm)*

After the deposition ends, I get in my car and call my secretary to check for any messages. This leads me to return a call to a partner regarding a non-competition agreement I had worked on earlier. I then dictate over the phone a letter to a corporate client regarding document inspection dates.

6:15 p.m.   *Return to Law Firm*

It takes me a little while to drive back to Dallas, where my firm is located. It's one of those few rare times where I am left alone, pretty much free of the constant barrage of e-mail and phone calls.

Naturally, clients and fellow colleagues can reach me on my mobile. But generally, this is only done if there is an urgent issue. I tune the car radio to NPR for thirty minutes to keep updated on the latest events. I also take this time to go over the arguments in my head regarding tomorrow's summary judgment hearing. After nearly two and a half hours of Texas highway driving, I arrive back to my firm.

6:20 p.m.   *Check Voicemail and E-Mail (and take notes)*

Just as I generally do when I enter my office, I check my voicemail and e-mail, all the while taking notes so I can refer to specific details later on. Some young litigators may think taking copious notes of voicemail and e-mail isn't necessary. But I find it to be a highly effective way to remember key details on behalf of my clients.

6:30 p.m.   *Work on Deposition Summary*

I prepare a deposition summary of today's deposition, which also includes an analysis of the deposition. It is critical to work on this as soon as possible while the plaintiff's deposition is fresh in my mind.

7:30 p.m.   *Review and Prepare for Tomorrow's Summary Judgment Hearing*

I review the motion and practice stating my arguments. I still recall one professor in law school telling the class, "Keep your eyes on the prize, the path to the prize is preparation." For me, the more prepared I am, the less nervous I will be (an obvious statement I know but it rings true in the practice of law). Put another way, I advocate most effectively when I let the law and facts marinate into my system. Lastly, I review my file and make sure there are copies of the cases that I cite in the motion. Oftentimes, a judge will ask to see a copy of the case. I make sure that I highlight the court's copy of the language that supports my arguments. It is also important that I bring cases that opposing counsel included in their response to my motion. This way, I can argue to the court that their case does not apply in our case.

Tomorrow's hearing will be before a state court judge in Fort Worth, Texas. I have not appeared before this judge, but my partner has on several occasions. In the partner's opinion, the judge is no-nonsense, intelligent, fair, and expects you to be fully prepared. I also take the time to meet the judge's staff and ask them about the judge's specific preferences that he expects attorneys to follow. Every judge has his or her "rules" on how he or she wants things done. While at the courts, I sit in on a couple of hearings to see how he conducts his court as well as get a layout of the courtroom.

Here's what I can expect at tomorrow's hearing: I will enter the courtroom and the judge will ask the attorneys to approach the bench. My summary judgment motion is simple and will not take up too much of the court's time. In relatively short hearings, judges will often conduct the hearing at his or her bench—where the attorneys walk up to the bench and conduct their arguments in close proximity of the judge. Because I filed the motion, I will present my arguments first. I will present other cases that are similar to my client's, which show that the court should rule in my favor. It is important to have these cases with me tomorrow in the event the judge wants to see them. I will then close my arguments and then the opposing counsel will speak. In this type of hearing, you need not make objections; it is more of a take turns procedure. The judge may or may not make a ruling on the same day, and may want to review the cases and other discovery documents. Once the hearing is over, I will thank the judge and shake hands with opposing counsel. Then I will exit the courtroom.

8:00 p.m.   *Meet Co-Workers (to celebrate a birthday)*

It's 8 p.m. and I remember that it's time to meet several other attorneys at a nearby TexMex restaurant to celebrate a colleague/friend's birthday. We catch up on life and work and make a toast to our friend. Shortly thereafter, I excuse myself early to get home and prepare for tomorrow's summary judgment hearing. Don't get me wrong, I wouldn't mind some good TexMex food with a frozen margarita. But duty comes first!

9:15 p.m.　　　　　*Depart the Building/Drive Home*

I go back to my office and check my voicemail and e-mail one last time. I know I should just turn off the computer without looking at my in-box. But it's just too tempting to see if anything urgent has come up during the time I was away. Fortunately, there are just a few e-mails that can wait for later. So I shut down the computer, grab my briefcase, and go to my car. The one positive about leaving later in the day: no traffic. I am home in thirty minutes.

10:35 p.m.　　　　*Prepare for Summary Judgment Hearing*

This time in the latter part of the evening is usually my down time where I do the following: watch a recorded television show, catch up on personal e-mail, and surf the Internet. Tonight, however, I head into my home office and open up my laptop to work—I am seemingly never done! I am able to work from home because I can connect to my firm's mainframe.

11:30 p.m.　　　　*Go to Bed*

After finishing up some work, I close my laptop for the day. It's past 11 p.m. and it's about this time that my husband returns home. I'm obviously not the only one in this household who has high work demands. But I think we both enjoy what we do, which tends to make the whole thing worthwhile. After he walks in, we check in with some of what transpired throughout each of our day. We both would love to talk more. But we know that we both need our rest to have a productive day tomorrow. So we get ready for bed. And before we know it, it's lights out and we're both sound asleep.

4:30 a.m.　　　　*Wake-Up and Exercise*

The alarm bell rings. I look up at the glowing digital clock, which reads "4:30 a.m." I can't believe I have to get up when it seems I just went to bed. But this doesn't deter me from putting on my running shoes for my usual early morning run.

Final Thoughts

If you are interested in attending law school, study hard your first year. I was lucky to have a third-year student tell me this my first semester of law school. If you end up in the top tier, you will then have an opportunity to work for a judge or assist a professor. You may also be asked to become a member of a law journal, which is a prestigious and a competitive advantage post-law school. Once you have one of the above experiences, you will then have offers to become a summer associate for a law firm. All of these opportunities in general begin with your first year grades. I recall some colleagues who realized this late, and although their grades were strong the end of second year, it was a bit too late for them because the opportunities at the larger firms had passed.

Squeeze the life out of law school like a sponge. Visit your professors if you're unclear about the law. However, always be prepared to speak intelligently about the matter. Join law clubs and programs: law journal, clinics, trial advocacy, etc. Learn all you can about "how to be a lawyer" before you graduate. My biggest regret was not taking a trial advocacy class (e.g., mock trial experience). The more time you spend learning the courtroom ropes, the more confident you'll be when faced with a real case.

I would also suggest that you always study with folks who are smarter than you, but work just as hard as they do. Nothing annoyed me more than when a member of one of my study groups didn't pull his or her own weight. Time is so limited, and it is not fair when you have to teach folks because they simply didn't prepare.

Moreover, I would recommend perhaps working two years before law school. Those of us who did this were used to sitting in the library a full day. We treated studying like a job. Those who came directly from graduating from college could not sit still for long periods of time. They often took multiple breaks. We may have sat for hours, but our brains were always working!

Lastly, make time for exercise. You don't have to train for a marathon, but find something that relieves stress and keeps you healthy (both physically and mentally). This is important because both law school and the legal profession provide an environment that can be conducive to stress.

11

Profile 11
Stephen: Military Judge

Executive Summary

Name: Stephen
Profile: Military Judge
Location: Camp Pendleton, California

As a member of the US military, no one—not even Stephen who holds a title as a the Marine judge advocate (military judge)—can be exempt from the regimented and disciplinarian ways often found in the military. Some moments in Stephen's typical day might look more like a day in the life of an FBI agent rather than a judge. He goes through annual pistol checks and undergoes intense physical training with all the other members of his US Marines. As Stephen mentions in his twenty-four-hour career profile, being a military judge is not for everyone. It requires thicker skin than a normal civilian judge, since he is dealing with military officers and cases that often revolve around issues such as assault and fraud. There are also trial procedures that are specifically unique to a military tribunal such as special and general court-marital. However, despite the somewhat intimidating vocabulary involved, Stephen leads a dynamic lifestyle as a government/military employee and emphasizes that being able to travel around the world is one of the many benefits of being a military judge in the US Marine Corps.

Profile

Career Field:	Military/Criminal Law
Current Position:	Military Judge
Institution:	US Marine Corps
Location:	Camp Pendleton, California
Previous Position(s):	International/Operational Law US Forces Korea, Prosecutor Camp Lejeune, North Carolina
Education:	JD, William and Mary School of Law LLM, The Judge Advocate General's Legal Center and School BA, University of Arizona
Licensed (Y/N):	Yes
Jurisdictions:	Virginia, Navy-Marine Corps, Court of Appeals for the Armed Forces, US Supreme Court

Schedule

5:30 a.m.	Wake-Up/Shower/Put on Uniform
6:10 a.m.	Eat Breakfast
6:50 a.m.	Arrive at Pistol Range (re: annual pistol qualification)
8:00 a.m.	Complete Pistol Qualification/Head to Office
8:10 a.m.	Change into Service C Uniform/Prepare for Court
8:30 a.m.	Conduct 15 Minute Rule for Court-Martial 802 (re: pretrial conference with prosecutor and defense counsel for guilty plea later in the week)
8:50 a.m.	Move to Courtroom
9:00 a.m.	Conduct Two Arraignments: One Special Court-Martial/One General Court-Martial
9:45 a.m.	Conduct Guilty Plea (re: special court-martial assault case)
11:30 a.m.	PT (physical training workout)
12:45 p.m.	Eat Lunch at Desk/Preparation (re: afternoon *voir dire* for courts-martial)
1:00 p.m.	Move to Courtroom
1:05 p.m.	Conduct *Voir Dire* (re: contested general court-martial)
3:45 p.m.	*Voir Dire* Complete/Recess Court (until 0830 (8:30 am) tomorrow for opening statements)

4:00 p.m.	Return to Office/Review Motion Briefs (re: unrelated case)
6:00 p.m.	Head Home
6:30 p.m.	Have Dinner with Family
7:15 p.m.	Help Daughter with Homework
8:00 p.m.	Review/Authenticate Record of Trial
9:30 p.m.	Send E-Mail to Colleague Stationed in Afghanistan
10:00 p.m.	Go to Sleep
5:30 a.m.	Wake-Up (for another 24 hours!)

24-Hour Schedule

5:30 a.m.   *Wake-Up/Shower/Put on Uniform*

Since I will be doing my annual pistol qualification in the morning, I need to wake-up a little earlier than usual.

6:10 a.m.   *Eat Breakfast*

Time is short. And I'll be doing my pistol qualifications in an hour or so. So I decide to go for a very light breakfast.

6:50 a.m.   *Arrive at Pistol Range (re: annual pistol qualification)*

I drive to the armory, draw my Beretta 9mm pistol, and head to the pistol range to qualify. The weather is a little cold. But it's not raining, so it should be a good day to shoot. All US Marines—regardless of their military occupational specialty—must demonstrate their proficiency with the use of weapons, particularly with the rifle and pistol. Additionally, the Marines have a robust martial arts program that all Marines train and are tested on. The martial arts program is based on a variety of different martial art disciplines, such as boxing, jujitsu, and wrestling. Training with weapons and martial arts builds discipline, self-confidence, and esprit de corps while preparing all Marines for the rigors of the job, particularly in a deployed environment. It's important that Marine attorneys go through the same training and hardships that all other Marines experience. This is because it provides a frame of reference for the attorney to view client issues. It also goes a long way toward developing rapport and confidence with other Marines (who are my potential clients). Keeping up with these and other requirements—while still satisfying the requirements of your primary job—can be challenging. But it is a challenge that all Marines share. This is partly what binds us together: facing challenges and overcoming adversity in the spirit of defending our country.

8:00 a.m.   *Complete Pistol Qualification/ Head to Office*

By this time, I'm done with the pistol qualification. At the pistol range, we wear our camouflage utility uniform (which is in the digital camouflage design—sometimes called "MARPAT"—which is a camouflage pattern devised by utilizing small micropatterns, as opposed to larger macropatterns, for effective camouflage).

8:10 a.m.   *Change into Service C Uniform/ Prepare for Court*

For court, we typically wear the service "C" uniform (also called, "Charlies"). This uniform is more formal and it allows the attorneys, the judge, the jury members, and especially the accused to wear any decorations (awards) that they have earned during their service. Judges in the other services (Army and Air Force) wear ropes to court in the same tradition as civilian court proceedings. The chief judge of the Navy-Marine Corps has made the decision that Navy and Marine judges should wear their service uniform for courts-martial. Most Marine Corps judges prefer this approach.

8:30 a.m.   *Conduct 15 Minute Rule for Court-Martial 802 (re: pretrial conference with prosecutor and defense counsel for guilty plea later in the week)*

Because of mission requirements, frequent assignment transfers and the forward deployed nature of the Marine Corps and Navy, it is not uncommon for counsel and witnesses in a case to be spread out all over the world. These types of pretrial conferences are essential for handling administrative and logistical matters associated with preparing for a court-martial and for the parties alerting the court to potential problems.

RCM is an abbreviation for "Rule for Court-Martial." These rules govern the procedures and punishments in all courts-martial as well as preliminary, supplementary, and appellate procedures and activities. The rules are intended to provide for the just determination of every proceeding related to trial by court-martial. The intent behind the drafting is to "secure simplicity in procedure, fairness in administration, and the elimination of unjustifiable expense and delay."

8:50 a.m.   *Move to Courtroom*

I don't have much time. So I move quickly to the courtroom. This is the place upon which most of my schedule is based upon. Court days typically begin with arraignments because they usually do not take that much time (typically ranging from fifteen to thirty minutes).

9:00 a.m.   *Conduct Two Arraignments: One Special Court-Martial/One General Court-Martial*

This morning, I will conduct an arraignment for a special court-martial (similar to a civilian misdemeanor) assault case and a general court-martial (similar to a civilian felony) sexual assault case. Although crime rates in the military and aboard military installations are much lower than that in the civilian sector, the sheer populations aboard installations make it realistic to expect that some level of crime would occur. As an example, Camp Pendleton (located just north of San Diego County) on an average work day would be the second largest city population-wise in San Diego County with well over 100,000 people living and working aboard the base. Military jurisdiction extends to military personnel all over the world whether on or off an installation or vessel.

Whether a court-martial has jurisdiction over a case frequently turns on issues such as the status of the accused at the time of the offense or the status of the accused at the time of trial. If the offense is chargeable under the Uniform Code of Military Justice (UCMJ) and the accused is a service member at the time the offense is committed, subject matter jurisdiction is satisfied. Personal jurisdiction focuses on the time of trial: can the government court-martial the accused? The answer is "yes" so long as the accused has proper status (i.e. that the accused is a service member at the time of trial). Often military jurisdiction runs concurrent with state federal or foreign jurisdictions. Our judicial circuit covers court-martial cases for all Marines and sailors in the Western United States.

9:45 a.m.   *Conduct Guilty Plea (re: special court-martial assault case)*

Guilty pleas in the military typically take considerably longer than guilty pleas in the US federal or state systems. This is in large part due to a lengthy providency inquiry that the military judge is required to conduct to ensure that an accused is pleading guilty voluntarily, and that he understands exactly the meaning and effect of his guilty plea. In this case, the accused is pleading guilty to using marijuana and 3,4-methylenedioxymethamphetamine (ecstasy). Illegal drug use is strictly forbidden in the Marine Corps and can often lead to the premature end of a Marine's career as well as other punishments, such as confinement or a punitive discharge. This case ended in a guilty plea after the prosecution's motion to pre-admit Prosecution Exhibit 1 for Identification (PE-1 FID) was granted at an earlier session of court.

The main issue in the case was based on concern about how the recent US Supreme Court ruling in the case of *Melendez-Diaz v. Massachusetts* will be interpreted by the court to affect PE-1 FID's admissibility in this case. The defense moved to compel production of all lab personnel at the Naval Drug Screening Lab, based on the Sixth Amendment and the US Supreme Court case of *US v. Melendez-Diaz*. The court-martial ruled that the prosecution had produced the analyst required by the Sixth Amendment of the US Constitution (which sets forth rights related to criminal prosecutions).

The Marine in this case had a rather long track record of misconduct that led to a sentence of a bad conduct discharge and sixty days of confinement. His pretrial agreement capped the confinement at thirty days and suspended the remaining thirty days of his sentence. Two witnesses from his unit testified during sentencing and both the prosecutor and defense counsel made sentencing arguments.

11:30 a.m.   *PT (physical training workout)*

All Marines, regardless of rank or position, are required to maintain a high level of physical fitness and stay within designated weight standards. Every

Marine must be physically fit, regardless of age, grade, or duty assignment. Fitness is essential to the day-to-day effectiveness and combat readiness of the US Marine Corps. Furthermore, physical fitness is an indispensable aspect of leadership. The habits of self-discipline required to gain and maintain a high level of physical fitness are inherent to the Marine Corps way of life and must be a part of the character of every Marine. Fitness levels are periodically evaluated by the physical fitness test consisting of a maximum set of pull-ups, maximum set of crunches in two minutes, and a three-mile run. A perfect score requires twenty pull-ups, one hundred crunches in two minutes, and no more than eighteen minutes on the three mile run. The combat fitness test tests sprinting ability, ammo can lifting, fireman's carry of another Marine, and other physical combat-related skills. Daily PT (physical training) in one form or another is very encouraged.

For me, I have always enjoyed physical training and pushing myself in this regard since my youth. When I was an undergraduate, I played football. And even these days, I try to surf when I get the time—one of the virtues of being stationed in Southern California.

12:45 p.m.   *Eat Lunch at Desk/Preparation (re: afternoon voir dire for court-martial)*

Today I eat lunch at my desk. It would be nice, of course, to be able to enjoy a leisurely lunch with colleagues or friends. But due to my heavy commitment load, I can get more things done when I eat a fairly quick lunch. With what little remaining time I have, I prepare once again for my afternoon *voir dire*.

1:00 p.m.   *Move to Courtroom*

It's 1:00 pm already. It's time for me to get quickly over to the courtroom for the afternoon court-martial.

1:05 p.m.   *Conduct Voir Dire (re: contested general court-martial)*

Voir dire (i.e., the process where jury members are questioned to see if a basis for challenge exists) and jury selection in the military is conducted in similar fashion to many civilian jurisdictions. First, an initial panel of potential jury members arrives at court and is questioned by the military judge and counsel for the prosecution and defense. Prior to arriving for court, the members will have submitted their answers to an eight to ten page questionnaire. Today, the issue is a fraud case where a Marine involved in government contracting is alleged to have conspired to defraud the government for her own personal gain. Several of the panel members are challenged for cause, one because she knew a witness, one because he knew the prosecutor, and one because he was married to a Naval Criminal Investigation Service (NCIS) agent who was assigned to the base field office. The defense also exercised a peremptory challenge against the senior member, a colonel. The *voir dire* process takes the entire afternoon. Afterwards, I recess the court until opening statements in the morning.

NCIS is the primary law enforcement and counterintelligence arm of the United States Department of the Navy (which includes the Marine Corps). NCIS works closely with other local, state, federal, and foreign agencies to counter and investigate the most serious crimes: terrorism, espionage, computer intrusion, homicide, rape, child abuse, arson, procurement fraud, and more. The stated mission of NCIS is the following: to prevent and solve crimes that threaten the warfighting capability of the US Navy and Marine Corps. It also pursues three strategic priorities: prevent terrorism, protect secrets, and reduce crime. NCIS' entire mission is supported by the Multiple Threat Alert Center and Infrastructure Protection/Computer Investigations.

3:45 p.m.   *Voir Dire Complete/Recess Court (until 0830 (8:30 am) tomorrow for opening statements)*

Voir dire is complete. So I order that the court will be in recess until 0830 tomorrow for opening statements.

4:00 p.m.   *Return to Office / Review Motion Briefs (re: unrelated case)*

Although contested courts-martial can take a considerable amount of time to prepare for and conduct, they cannot be addressed to the exclusion of the remainder of the docket. When I arrive back to my office, I review a defense motion to suppress the government response, the statement of an accused to NCIS, and all derivative evidence derived from a search based on the statement. The case involves a Marine accused of sexual assault in a "date rape" scenario. The defense is alleging that the statement that the accused Marine gave to NCIS was involuntary in violation of his Uniform Code of Military Justice (UCMJ) Article 31(b) rights. In the military, a suspect is required to be advised of his rights even if an interview is done in a non-custodial setting.

The military justice system provides an accused rights and due process that in many ways offer additional protections to those provided a defendant in civilian criminal courts. Pursuant to Article 31, Uniform Code of Military Justice (Section 831 of Title 10, United States Code), service members have a right against self-incrimination and an entitlement to be informed of the suspected offense(s) before questioning begins. In addition to protections against self-incrimination, service members have a right to free military counsel when questioned as a suspect of committing an offense, upon preferral of court-martial charges, or initiation of arrest or apprehension.

In the military justice system, these rights are afforded much earlier in the criminal justice system than in civilian practice. These rights and protections apply whenever the service member is questioned as a suspect of an offense. In civilian practice, Miranda rights or warnings are not required, unless there is custodial interrogation by law enforcement personnel. In fact, the US Supreme Court referenced the military's "warning rights" practice under Article 31, UCMJ, when deciding to establish the Miranda Warning requirement.

A showing of indigence is required before a defendant is provided counsel without cost in the civilian system. An independent military defense counsel is provided free of charge regardless of the accused's ability to pay. The accused may also employ civilian counsel at his or her own expense, or request a particular military counsel, who will assist the accused if reasonably available. The accused has the right to be represented by counsel at the magistrate hearing when a determination is made regarding continued pretrial confinement, at the Article 32 investigation, and during all court-martial sessions. After trial, the accused has a right to free military counsel to assist with his appeal through the military appellate courts, and potentially to the US Supreme Court.

6:00 p.m.   *Head Home*

It's 6:00 p.m. Fortunately, today there are no immediate crises that need to be resolved, although I could be contacted at any time in the event a crisis does occur. So I take this opportunity to make my way home, which is in the Carlsbad area (located in San Diego County, not too far from Camp Pendleton). I look forward to now spending some quality time with my family.

6:30 p.m.   *Have Dinner with Family*

My wife has made one of my favorites: Thai green curry chicken. One of the benefits of being in the Marine Corps is that my family and I have had the unique opportunity to live all over the country and the world. My wife has developed a knack for preparing cuisine from many of the places we have lived or traveled to. And to me, her Thai recipes are her best.

7:15 p.m.   *Help Daughter with Homework*

Part of my quality family time is now spent with my daughter. She has some homework that needs to be done. And I try to help her navigate through what her teacher assigned her.

8:00 p.m.   *Review/Authenticate Record of Trial*

One of the important yet tedious duties of a military judge is to review the records of trial for cases we preside over to ensure completeness and accuracy. I try to fit in time to complete these whenever possible because our appellate courts enforce strict timelines for post trial case processing and appellate review.

The Uniform Code of Military Justice provides for several tiers of appeal. All cases are reviewed by the commander convening the court (the convening authority) who, as a matter of command prerogative, may approve, disapprove or modify the findings and/or sentence. The commander may not approve a finding of guilty for an offense of which the accused was acquitted nor increase the sentence adjudged. A convicted service member may submit a request for leniency to the convening authority prior to the convening authority's approval of the court-martial sentence.

Each military service and the Coast Guard have a Court of Criminal Appeals, which is composed of panels of three appellate military judges. These courts review all cases in which the approved sentence includes death, a punitive discharge, or confinement for at least a year, and all cases referred to it by the service judge advocate general. The court of criminal appeals "may affirm only such findings of guilty and the sentence or such part of the sentence, as it finds correct in law and fact and determines, on the basis of the entire record, should be approved. In considering the record, it may weigh the evidence, judge the credibility of witnesses, and determine controverted questions of fact, recognizing that the trial court saw and heard the witnesses." Article 66(c), UCMJ.

The Court of Appeals for the Armed Forces (CAAF) consists of five civilian judges appointed by the President of the United States, with the advice and consent of the US Senate, to fifteen-year terms. The CAAF must review cases from all of the military services in which the court of criminal appeals has affirmed a death sentence, cases the Judge Advocates General order sent to the court, and cases appealed from the court of criminal appeals by the accused (in which the CAAF finds good cause to grant the petition for review). Unlike the service courts of criminal appeals, the CAAF "shall take action only with respect to matters of law." Article 67(c), UCMJ. Decisions of the CAAF are "subject to review by the Supreme Court by writ of certiorari" per Article 67a, UCMJ (which merely confirms Article III, Section 2 of the US Constitution, granting the Supreme Court appellate jurisdiction in all US cases where it does not have original jurisdiction).

9:30 p.m.   *Send E-Mail to Colleague Stationed in Afghanistan*

Marines are constantly deployed around the globe. This applies to Marine judge advocates (attorneys) as well. One of my good friends from an LLM program we attended together was recently deployed to Afghanistan with the 1st Marine Division. So I dropped him a line to see how he was doing and if he or his family needed anything.

10:00 p.m.   *Go to Sleep*

It's been another eventful day. This is usually the time I go to sleep, along with my family. It may seem a bit early for some. But given my early rise (at 5:30 a.m.), it's better for me to get a full night of rest so I can concentrate on the tasks at hand tomorrow morning.

5:30 a.m.   *Wake-Up (for another 24 hours!)*

I hear the sound of my alarm clock. The sunrise has barely begun, which means it's the beginning of another twenty-four hour day for me.

Final Thoughts

The life of a Marine judge advocate can be exciting and rewarding. It is not for everyone, however. The position can require long hours, long periods away from family, and assignments to desolate and even dangerous places with spartan living conditions. Having said this, I've never met a Marine judge advocate who regretted his or her decision to join the Corps.

12

Profile 12
Yong: Marine Judge Advocate

Executive Summary

Name: Yong
Profile: Marine Judge Advocate (US Military Defense Counsel)
Location: Quantico, Virginia

Yong is a proud Marine and puts this in the heart of his job, as a defense counsel of the US Marine Corps (Marine judge advocate). He describes this title as one of hard work and discipline and believes that his multiple-layered position as a legal professional becomes more meaningful to him and differentiates him, by being a Marine first. Among the numerous military jargon that you have to get used to, Yong emphasizes that you truly undergo spiritual transformation by joining the Marines. On a day-to-day basis, he oversees operations of the legal defense section, performs legal counseling, and trains other defense counsel on trial techniques. His schedule doesn't permit a wasted moment with all the other physical requirements he has to meet. If you are a person who has passion for the law and believes in serving your country, Yong shows how it is done. Properly and with pride.

Profile

Career Field:	Federal Government/Military
Current Position:	Senior Defense Counsel
Institution:	US Marine Corps
Location:	Worldwide (currently stationed in Quantico, Virginia)
Previous Position(s):	Chief Trial Counsel, US Marine Corps
	Administrative Law Attorney and Ethics Counselor, US Army
	Chief of Client Services, US Army
Education:	JD, Brooklyn Law School
	BA, New York University
Licensed (Y/N):	Yes
Jurisdictions:	New York/New Jersey

Schedule

5:30 a.m.	Wake-Up
5:55 a.m.	Battalion Run
6:30 a.m.	Still Running
7:00 a.m.	Getting Ready for the Day
7:30 a.m.	Start of Work Day
8:00 a.m.	Arraignment
8:25 a.m.	Old Acquaintance from the Past
8:45 a.m.	Brig and IRO (Internal Reviewing Officer) Hearing Notification
9:00 a.m.	Promotion and Reenlistment Ceremony
9:25 a.m.	Work Load and Case Review
10:00 a.m.	Unscheduled Walk-In Counseling
10:30 a.m.	Drafting Motions and Responses to Motions
11:15 a.m.	Witness Interview
12:00 p.m.	Quick Chow (Lunch) and a Little Reprieve
12:45 p.m.	Walk to the Medical Clinic (re: annual physical health assessment)
1:30 p.m.	Meeting with the Trial Counsel
2:00 p.m.	Office of the Staff Judge Advocate Section Head Meeting
3:00 p.m.	New Cases

3:15 p.m.	Article 32 Hearing Preparation
4:00 p.m.	Quick Physical Fitness Training
5:00 p.m.	"802" Conference Call with the Military Judge
5:20 p.m.	Back at the Office for More Work
6:20 p.m.	Drive to the BX (Base Exchange)/Commissary and Back to the Office
7:00 p.m.	PME (Professional Military Education)
7:30 p.m.	Call from My Brother
8:00 p.m.	Review and Submit Page 57 Matters
9:00 p.m.	Drive to the Lodge
9:30 p.m.	Call Wife and Daughter
10:00 p.m.	Watch TV and Read
11:00 p.m.	Time to Sleep
5:30 a.m.	Wake-Up for Another Day

24-Hour Schedule

5:30 a.m.   *Wake-Up*

I got up earlier this morning than I usually get up for work because my battalion has a unit run today. I have been up for almost an hour now and I have been standing outside wearing my OD (olive drab) green colored skivvy shirt and shorts for the last fifteen minutes or so waiting for the battalion of Marines to form up and start on our four or five mile jog across the base.

5:55 a.m.   *Battalion Run*

It's a brisk spring morning, but the smell of the air is refreshing. As I look across the stadium field where we were supposed to report to this morning, I see several hundred Marines in their OD green skivvy shirts and shorts waiting for our commanding officer to lead us on our run.

From one end of the field to the next, there are Marines from all different cross-sections of the United States. The Marines may be different in size and color, with different backgrounds whether they be an officer or an enlisted person. But each Marine has been forged from the depth of the

Marine Corps "training" to become a warrior of our country's premier expeditionary force that is capable of fighting our country's battles in every climate and location. I think to myself that it's been a while since I ran with my battalion. I look at my watch and see that we are five minutes away from beginning our run. Suddenly, I hear the battalion sergeant major shout, "A-Ten-Hut!" Every Marine falls into his rightful place in the formation. We are about to start our run together. There's a Marine standing in front of me, behind me, and left and right of me. For the love of our corps, our country, and our family, we stand together and run together—and I know that, come hell or high water, a Marine would stand with me till the end.

6:30 a.m.   Still Running

We're more than halfway through our run. I am sweating, but my lungs feel good from the fresh morning air. I can hear the loud motivating cadence from a gunnery sergeant—a staff non-commissioned officer—from the left. I can also hear the shouting of the Marines next to me, and my own voice, repeating the gunnery sergeant's cadence call. Each step I take is virtually automatic, one step after the next. As I continue to run, I'm reminded of the importance of physical fitness and the application of warrior ethos in my daily life. After all, every Marine is a rifleman, and all Marine officers are rifle platoon commanders first.

7:00 a.m.   Getting Ready for the Day

After the battalion run, I take a quick shower at work and ensure that my face is still clean shaven—if it's not still clean shaven from my early morning shave before the run, I would shave again. Once I'm done with taking care of my hygiene, I get dressed in my service Charlie uniform, which consists of short sleeve khaki shirt with ribbons, white T-shirt, dark green slacks, and black shoes. Normally, I would wear my desert MARPAT (Marine pattern) digital camouflage uniform, but I have an arraignment at 0800 (8:00 a.m.) and the rules of court requires me to be in my service Charlie uniform. I check to ensure that my ribbons are correctly aligned and my khaki shirt fits properly. I look in the mirror and see that I still have a clean high and tight haircut from yesterday. Overall, I'm satisfied with my look and I turn on my government computer. I also take out a yogurt from the small fridge in my office for a quick morning chow.

7:30 a.m.   *Start of Work Day*

I open up my Outlook folder and see that I have about ten new e-mails since late last night. But before opening any e-mails, I call my wife to see if she is awake. I call my wife every morning because she and I have been living separately due to my military service and her career obligations being incompatible in terms of location, at least for now. My family and I have been living apart for the last several years, and I only get to see my wife and two-year-old daughter mostly on weekends when I'm able to visit them in New York City. One difficulty with serving in the military is the continued possibility of being separated from family and friends. I sometimes complain about only being able to see my family on the weekends, but I quickly realize how lucky I am to see them at all.

I speak with my wife briefly and it seems that both she and my daughter are doing well. I then turn my attention to the e-mails I received since last night. I quickly skim through them to see if anything important needs to be addressed right away. There was nothing urgent to address. So I quickly review the case file for the arraignment this morning—which I already reviewed the night before—and wait for the Marine who I'm representing in the arraignment to show up.

A few minutes later, the Marine shows up. I go through with him the arraignment procedure, his constitutional and other procedural rights, and answer any questions that the Marine may have at this time. The Marine tells me that he understands what I have told him. Shortly thereafter, we walk to the courtroom, which is just next door for his arraignment.

8:00 a.m.   *Arraignment*

Today, we have a Navy judge presiding over the arraignment. Navy judges often preside over Marine Corps cases, since both military services fall under the Department of the Navy, and because our judicial circuit is subject to the jurisdiction of the Navy and Marine Corps trial judiciary.

The arraignment takes about fifteen minutes. During arraignment, the judge makes certain that the Marine understands his constitutional and other procedural rights. The government trial counsel—also known as a prosecutor—reads the jurisdictional data into the record. I, on the other hand, ensure that the Marine's pleas, forum selection, and motions are properly reserved in accordance with the trial schedule previously ordered by the judge.

It was a routine arraignment this morning and there were no real issues. The Marine waived the formal reading of the charges against him, which consisted of several violations of the UCMJ (Uniform Code of Military Justice) for being absent without leave, disobeying orders, and disrespecting an officer. After arraignment, the Marine and I return to my office. I further explain to him what will happen next and answer any questions that he may have. Shortly thereafter, the Marine leaves.

8:25 a.m.   Old Acquaintance from the Past

I quickly change into my MARPAT uniform since I do not have to wear my service Charlie uniform for any other reason today. I check to see that my MARPAT blouse sleeves are rolled up neatly to my biceps and look down to see if my MARPAT trousers are fitted properly. I also check to see whether my rank insignias are aligned correctly in the collars of the blouse. The MARPAT uniform is much more comfortable than the service Charlie uniform. And I do not have to worry about it being dirty or wrinkled.

When I open the door to my office after changing over uniforms, I notice someone wearing a dark business suit walking by. The individual goes to the end of the hall and speaks with one of the defense counselors from my office. He talks about his role as a DNA expert in a court-martial that is starting today. His voice sounds familiar, but I ignore him thinking that he is just one of the witnesses in a court-martial. So I go over to my office inbox and retrieve some documents, which were served on my office this morning by the Military Justice Office—the Military Prosecutor's Office— as a part of an ongoing discovery process in a case that I am detailed to. As I say my morning greetings to my Marine legal specialist—equivalent to a civilian paralegal/law clerk/legal secretary combined into one—I hear a voice from the end of the hall say, "Is that you, Captain?" I turn around and notice that the man in the business suit is trying to get my attention.

After a brief conversation with the man, I realize that he was one of the civilian DNA experts from United States Army Criminal Investigation Laboratory (USACIL) who I worked with in a previous rape case, when I was a trial counsel a number of years ago with the United States Army stationed in Seoul, Korea (I was a captain back then). I think to myself what a small world this is while meeting this person after almost four years. Then again, I think to myself, that it wasn't too uncommon to meet people who work for the government in my line of work—this was not the first time and I'm sure that it will happen again in the future. The biggest differences between four years ago and now is that I have been promoted to the rank of major, and now, I am serving as a defense counsel instead of a trial counsel.

8:45 a.m.   *Brig and IRO (Internal Reviewing Officer) Hearing Notification*

I see several new e-mails in the last hour. I review them and notice that one of the Marines who I am representing was placed in pretrial confinement in the brig. Apparently, the Marine's commanding officer thought that the Marine was a flight risk and was likely to commit further serious offenses if the Marine was not placed in such pretrial confinement. Pretrial confinement in the military is equivalent to the civilian criminal courts placing a person in jail without bail to ensure that person's presence at trial.

In the military, there are several procedural requirements that must be met before an accused service member can be placed in pretrial confinement, and subsequently, continue to be kept in pretrial confinement. There are several safeguards against illegal pretrial confinement under the Rules for Courts-Martial, to include an initial reviewing officer (IRO). This is where a neutral, impartial, and detached officer reviews the detained Marine's case to see if continued pretrial confinement is warranted. I notice that the IRO hearing is tomorrow and quickly write it down in my Outlook calendar. I also pull out the Marine's case file and review the new accusations against him. Upon my review, if the new accusations against the Marine were based on probable cause, then there will be a slim to zero chance for the Marine to be released from pretrial confinement. Having been a part-time military magistrate in the past, I was pretty certain that the Marine would stay in pretrial confinement until his trial.

9:00 a.m.   *Promotion and Re-Enlistment Ceremony*

Every month or two, there is a Marine or two who gets promoted to the next higher grade/rank or re-enlists to serve our country a little longer. Today there is a Marine being promoted from the rank of lance corporal to corporal, and a Marine staff sergeant who is re-enlisting to serve our country for four more years. Whenever a Marine gets promoted or re-enlists, it is a special moment not only for that Marine, but for those Marines around him or her. Today was no different. There were a number of Marines and federal civilian employees who showed up to pay their respects for the Marine who was being promoted and the Marine who was re-enlisting. We held a formation in the quarterdeck and the promotion/re-enlistment ceremony were carried out. The promotion warrant was read and a Marine was promoted to the rank of corporal—a non-commissioned officer. The re-enlistment oath was executed and a Marine pledged four more years in service of our country. The Marines were properly congratulated before returning to their normal duties. I too congratulated them and then returned to work.

Walking back to my office, I'm reminded of my own promotion to the rank of major, the oath I swore, and the responsibility that came with the office, which I undertook. As a leader of Marines, I repeated to myself that I must have a strong sense of the great responsibility that comes with my position since the resources I will expend in war are human lives—lives of Marines.

9:25 a.m.   *Work Load and Case Review*

I review the latest Military Justice Report, which lists all active UCMJ cases in our office. Each Marine defense counsel in our office carries about fifteen cases. Fifteen cases seem relatively low compared to the thirty or forty cases I had as a trial counsel about a year ago. However, while the number of cases was relatively low compared to last year, the charges in the cases that we currently have are more complicated and more serious. Our office not only represents Marines at court-martial, but we also represent Marines in Administrative Separation Boards. Each Marine defense counsel also provides legal counseling to an average of about five to ten Marines a week. As the senior defense counsel in the office, I am also responsible for overseeing the day-to-day operations of the defense section in all aspects as well as training defense counsels on new legal development and trial techniques.

After reviewing the Military Justice Report, I pulled out one of my most serious cases, which involves a Marine officer who is being accused of committing child sexual abuse by his estranged wife. There were about 2,000 pages of investigative and discovery materials that I need to review again in preparation for the formal investigation under Article 32, UCMJ. I went over the list of work priorities for the case, which I prepared a few days ago, and made additional notes for the investigation (about two weeks away).

10:00 a.m. *Unscheduled Walk-In Counseling*

I'm reading a sworn statement of a potential witness in one of my cases when my Marine legal specialist knocks on my door. She tells me that a Marine who is currently under an investigation for several suspected UCMJ violations, and is being sought out to be questioned by NCIS (Naval Criminal Investigative Service), wants a few minutes of my time. Although today is not a walk-in counseling day and the Marine does not have an appointment, I decide to meet with the Marine in order to offer him advice as to his possible courses of action.

After listening to the Marine's story, I was convinced that it was in his interest not to waive his Article 31b rights—similar to *Miranda* warnings seen in civilian court cases. Having served as the chief trial counsel, and having worked with several law enforcement agencies in the past, it was apparent to me that this Marine's story was fraught with falsities and misleading statements, which could serve as the basis for additional charges against him for providing false official statements. What was supposed to be a short counseling session was extended and turned into a meeting lasting half an hour. I was not surprised by this since, in my line of work when someone asks you for a few a minutes, they're really asking you, "Can I have your undivided attention until I finish my entire story?" Although I knew that it would be like this, I met with the Marine anyway. In fact, if anything, I was surprised that it only lasted half an hour.

10:30 a.m. *Drafting Motions and Responses to Motions*

Once the Marine who came in for the unscheduled walk-in counseling session left, I turned my attention back to the cases that I was reviewing earlier. I notice that there was a motion due in a case that needed to be filed with the court by no later than close of business tomorrow. Thankfully, I'd started on the motion several days ago and the first draft was already completed. It is a motion to dismiss several charges against a Marine under the principle of multiplicity and unreasonable multiplication of charges. Multiplicity is a concept found under the Fifth Amendment of the United States Constitution, which forbids a person from being tried twice for the same type of crime under the same set of facts—better known as the "Double Jeopardy" clause. The principle of unreasonable multiplication of charges is different from the principle of multiplicity in that it is not a constitutional doctrine. But it is a presidential policy that prohibits prosecutorial overreaching by imposing a standard of reasonableness against prosecutors who may charge several offenses against a service member under one set of facts.

After making my final revision on the motion to dismiss, I read over the government's motion *in limine*, which seeks to prevent me from asking questions under Military Rules of Evidence 412—equivalent to *rape shield* rules in civilian court cases. I read over the government's motion thoroughly, make several notes along the margins, and start to think about ways to respond to the government's motion.

11:15 a.m.   Witness Interview

As I was thinking about how I should write my response to the government's motion *in limine*, my telephone begins to ring. The person on the other line is returning my call from several days ago. This person is a very important witness in one of my case and it has been extremely difficult getting in touch with her since she lives and works overseas. I knew that I would have a hard time getting in touch with her again if I didn't take this call. So I drop what I'm doing and start to go over the case with her. I wanted to get as much information from her as possible and develop a good rapport with her in anticipation of the trial. After speaking on the phone for about forty minutes, I'm satisfied with the information I received. Before hanging up, I review the notes I took and ask her a few more questions for clarification and confirmation.

12:00 p.m.   *Quick Chow (Lunch) and a Little Reprieve*

I'm very hungry since I haven't eaten anything more than a plain yogurt earlier this morning. However, I'm lucky because I have a mini fridge in my office and I have a box full of microwaveable cooked rice that my brother got for me last weekend. For lunch today, I decided to eat rice, dried salted seaweed, and kimchi (Korean spicy cabbage) that my wife packed for me when I last visited New York City. I do not eat like this every day. Sometimes I pick up a Subway sandwich or go out with my colleagues to eat at the Officer's Club. However, today, I just wanted to sit behind my desk, eat a quick chow, browse the Internet, and just relax a little bit. After eating my lunch and having read some Internet news, I close my eyes and put my feet up on top of my desk thinking about nothing for the next twenty minutes or so.

12:45 p.m.   *Walk to the Medical Clinic (re: annual physical health assessment)*

I wake up from my short siesta (rest) and it's time for me to go to the Base Medical Clinic for my annual physical health assessment (PHA). The purpose of the PHA is to review each service member's current health and to ensure that any possible health issues are spotted and properly cared for. This is one of several annual requirements that I must complete.

The clinic is only about five minutes away by foot. I grab my things (which include my Marine Corps cover and ID card) and start to walk toward the clinic. It's a nice spring day. As I walk toward the clinic, I think to myself how fortunate I am to be where I am instead of being under the desert heat of Iraq or Afghanistan. As I near the clinic, a sudden emotion swirls me—a feeling that makes me think that I too need to be with my brothers and sisters in arms in countries like Iraq or Afghanistan fighting our country's battles. My day to serve there will come one day, I think to myself. And as much as my family and friends may not want this for me, I know that when the time comes, I would heed the calling of my country and the US Marine Corps. Every Marine to the fight!

1:30 p.m.   *Meeting with the Trial Counsel*

I returned to my office after my PHA appointment and I walk toward one of the trial counsel's office to discuss a possible pretrial agreement in a case that I have been detailed to. The Marine I was detailed to represent confessed to committing barracks larceny, which amounted to several thousand dollars and his involvement in an illegal prescription drug distribution ring. The evidence looks solid from the government's point of view. And the Marine is facing a potential sentence of more than thirty years in the brig, if he is convicted of all charges and specifications. After negotiating with the trial counsel, I am able to convince him to endorse a deal for the battalion commanding officer in charge of the Marine to send the case to a special court-martial—equivalent to a misdemeanor in a civilian court—in exchange, the Marine would make full restitution, serve as a NCIS informant, and give other concessions requested by the government. Of course, the deal would not finalize until both parties agreed and signed a written agreement to that effect. Unlike the civilian prosecutors, military trial counsels do not have prosecutorial discretion and must ensure that the appropriate court-martial convening authority approves a pretrial agreement. On the other hand, I must make sure that the Marine understands the terms of the deal and agrees to it, knowingly and voluntarily.

2:00 p.m.   *Office of the Staff Judge Advocate Section Head Meeting*

Once a week, there is a meeting between the director of the law center (also known as Office of the Staff judge advocate) and the section leaders. The director is a full bird colonel and he is a judge advocate with more than twenty years of experience. The director is responsible for several sections. But my office is unique in that we are only administratively controlled by the director and he does not have full supervisory authority over my office because of potential conflicts of interest. The director hears reports from each section. I also provide non-confidential information relating to the operation of the defense section to the director. As with the rest of the Marine Corps, the director uses the concept of decentralized command when issuing orders or directives. Using the decentralized command concept, the director gives us his orders or directives, but he does not tell us how to carry out those orders or directives. Instead, it is left to the individual Marine to fulfill the mission using his own initiative and knowledge.

There was a lot of news passed by the director this afternoon. Apparently, many Marines—both officers and enlisted members alike—are going to be moving to another duty station this summer. This means that many new faces would be replacing these Marines as well (this is what happens to Marines and other service members every few years—we move from one duty station to the next). During the meeting, the dates for the pistol and rifle qualification ranges are announced, as well as the dates for the physical fitness test. The director finally concludes the meeting after passing several other pieces of news and information. Once I return to my office, I send an e-mail to all Marines in my charge, along with my direct supervisor—the regional defense counsel for the East Coast—informing them of what I learned from the meeting today.

3:00 p.m.   New Cases

Every couple of days, I receive several new cases that require detailing of a defense counsel. Today, there were three new cases (two courts-martial and one administrative separation board). An administrative separation board is different from a court martial in that it is a hearing convened to decide on whether a Marine should be discharged from the Naval service. As the name suggests, it is an administrative and not judicial process. While an administrative separation board does not result in a conviction, it can still have a tremendous affect on a Marine's career such as affecting the type of benefits the Marine may receive at discharge.

Typically, I would review each case thoroughly trying to discern the surfaces and gaps of each case before detailing it to a defense counsel. The terms "surfaces" and "gaps" are used in MCDP (Marine Corps Doctrinal Publication) 1, Warfighting. *Surfaces* are the hard spots—enemy strengths. *Gaps* are the soft spots—enemy weaknesses. I examine the surfaces and gaps to better understand the "critical vulnerability" and the "center of gravity" of the government's case. By doing so, I can properly analyze the strengths and weaknesses of each case and detail it to the right defense counsel.

I decide to hold off reading the cases and leave it in my inbox for review later on. I did this in order to work on other priorities of work.

3:15 p.m.   *Article 32 Hearing Preparation*

An Article 32 hearing is a formal investigation under the UCMJ—similar to a preliminary hearing or a grand jury proceeding in civilian criminal courts. An Article 32 hearing is required before an accused's charges can be referred to a general court martial. During the hearing, a fair and impartial investigating officer is supposed to thoroughly examine the evidence and give a report of detailed findings, as well as recommendations, to the commanding officer who convened the Article 32 hearing. Based on the Article 32 report, and the advice from his legal counsel, the commanding officer may take several actions with respect to an accused (i.e., dismissing the charges or referring the charges to a general court martial).

The charge in tomorrow's Article 32 hearing include one specification in violation of Article 120, UCMJ, for aggravated sexual assault. A Marine is being accused of sexually assaulting a soldier who was supposedly either too intoxicated to consent to sexual intercourse or who was incapable of consenting to sexual intercourse. Having worked on the Article 32 case since last week, I felt confident in cross-examining the alleged victim and other witnesses in the case. However, regardless of how well I do tomorrow, unless the alleged victim recants, I know that this case will likely be referred to a general court martial. This is because sexual assault cases have been highly publicized in recent times and because the Marine Corps takes these allegations very seriously.

4:00 p.m.   *Quick Physical Fitness Training*

Having been stuck in the office since 0730 (7:30 a.m.) I feel like getting out of the office a bit to get some fresh air. Instead of going for a walk, I decide to change into my "rainbow" PT gear (i.e., civilian physical fitness gear—a Uniqlo T-shirt and black running shorts) and decide to go for a run along the trails. I warm up and stretch out my muscles for about five minutes. I do about two sets of fifteen pull ups and two sets of fifty crunches before going on the run. Once I'm done with my sets, I start jogging toward the trails slowly. Once at the trails, I go at a steady pace because I know that it'll get tougher along the way. After about two or three miles, my left ankle starts to feel weird. It's nothing new. My left ankle often feels this way when I go run on the trails—it has been like this ever since my left ankle broke my fall during an obstacle course I was doing several years back.

5:00 p.m.   *"802" Conference Call with the Military Judge*

I return from my late afternoon workout and barely make it in time for the 1700 (5:00 p.m.) "802" conference call with the military judge regarding a guilty plea next week. The trial counsel was already waiting for me, and because I did not have a chance to take a shower, I show up at the trial counsel's office in my "rainbow" gear drenched in sweat. The trial counsel looks at me, smirks, and gives me a little nod. The smirk and nod is not meant as any sign of disrespect, but it is a way for the trial counsel—a Marine—to acknowledge and approve of what I was doing. A Marine knows that PT is an important part of being a Marine. And in this case, I think the trial counsel was jealous that he didn't do PT along with me before the conference call.

An "802" conference is a discussion between the military judge and counselors outside the formal recorded session of the court. Often, defense counsel, trial counsel and a military judge would conduct an informal "802" conference before a court session to address any outstanding matters before the actual formal court session. This time was no different. We discussed some scheduling issues as well as a minor issue involving a sentencing motion. Once we were all satisfied that there were no other issues needed to be discussed, we ended our "802" conference call.

5:20 p.m.   *Back at the Office for More Work*

After the conference call, I take a quick shower and change into my civilian clothes—jeans and a polo short-sleeve shirt. I changed into civilian clothes because it was after duty hours. I look at my Outlook inbox and see that there are about a dozen new e-mails. The topics of the e-mails range from a reminder about Fitness Reports that I have to write by the end of the month for the officers under my charge (a Fitness Report is a Marine's evaluation report for a specified time period); information on my DLPT (Defense Language Proficiency Test) in Korean that I have to take annually; my potential future assignment next year; various questions from Marines asking about their individual cases; and a training opportunity at the Naval

Justice School. As I read and respond to the e-mails, I also listen to several voice messages left on my office phone. After I'm done going through my e-mails and listening to the voice messages, I think about what I need to do before I can call it a day. Although most of my work for the day was done, I realize that I still need to finish some matters before going home.

6:20 p.m.   *Drive to the BX (Base Exchange)/Commissary and Back to the Office*

I get out of the office to drive to the BX (base exchange) and the commissary before they close for the day. I grab some food and drinks from the commissary and buy some uniform items from the BX. I listen to some music to and from the BX/commissary and also try to call my wife using my BlackBerry device's hands free option. My wife didn't answer and I assume that she's probably either busy or has her phone on vibrate mode. In any case, lucky for me, my Blackberry isn't connected to the government server. For that reason, I don't have to worry about getting work e-mails all throughout the day and night.

7:00 p.m.   *PME (Professional Military Education)*

I return to the office and I make myself a sandwich. While I eat, I log on to www.Marinenet.usmc.mil to complete the MCPP (Marine Corps Planning Process) course, which I started a few months ago as a part of my PME. Because my primary duty for the last several years dealt almost exclusively with military justice matters, it felt good re-engaging in military subject matters that Marine officers are expected to be proficient in. After several attempts to complete the course during the last few months, I finally finish it today.

7:30 p.m.   *Call from My Brother*

My BlackBerry rings and I see it is my brother calling me. I answer the phone and he asks me where I am. I tell him that I'm still at work. He asks me if I need anything. Fortunately for me, my brother works and lives about an hour and half away. He's a good brother and I see him about once a week. He asks me about how my wife and daughter are doing and gives me some updates on our parents. As I speak with my brother, I realize how very fortunate I am to have a brother like him. I also reflect on how grateful I am to our country. My brother and I were not born in the United States. We immigrated when he was fourteen and when I was nine. Today, my brother is a doctor and I am an officer in the Marines. My brother and I talk about the past and become a little nostalgic. By the time we're ready to hang up the phone, we agree that our family is very fortunate to be where we are today. Without saying anything else, we both understand how important our family and country are to each of us.

8:00 p.m.   *Review and Submit Page 57 Matters*

The last thing I need to do before going home is complete the Page 57 matters for a court-martial next week. Page 57 matters include several documents: the final witness list; *voir dire* questions for potential jury members (to confirm the jury's impartiality); any requested judicial notice and instructions; and any notices of defense. It takes me about an hour to finish the Page 57 matters, scan it and then send it via e-mail to the clerk of the court. After sending the Page 57 matters, I grab my things, and get ready to leave for the night.

9:00 p.m.   *Drive to the Lodge*

I leave the office and realize that it's dark and really quiet outside. I get into my car and start the engine. Once in the car, my BlackBerry rings. It's my wife. I answer the phone and tell her that I will call her back shortly once I get to the base lodging. I've been using the base lodging because my family and I are living separately, and it's more convenient for me in many ways. I drive toward the base lodging and wonder what my wife and daughter are doing tonight. I drive very carefully toward my destination. It's a cool and calm night tonight. The moon was already up and shining brightly. I think to myself that it's hard to see a moon like this in New York City where I grew up.

9:30 p.m.   *Call Wife and Daughter*

I drop my stuff on the floor of my room and call my wife right away. I ask her about her day and how our daughter is doing. My wife and I talk for about the next thirty minutes. She tells me about all the things my daughter did today and it brings a smile to my face. I can't wait to see my family again this weekend.

10:00 p.m.   *Watch TV and Read*

I turn the TV on and log on to the Internet. I take care of some personal matters, which include paying some bills online and going through my finances, and then catch up on some reading.

11:00 p.m.   *Time to Sleep*

I feel very tired after the day. And without realizing it, I fall asleep on top of my bed.

5:30 a.m.   *Wake-Up for Another Day*

Still dressed in my clothes from the night before, I wake up to the sound of the alarm clock going off. I decide to hit the snooze button on the alarm clock to sleep in another hour or so. An hour passes by. I get up and get ready for another day.

Final Thoughts

If you think you want to be a "Marine lawyer," think again and think hard about why you want the position. In the Marine Corps, Marines who are qualified and certified to practice law are given a military occupational specialty title of judge advocate. While the words "judge advocate" tell us what a Marine does, the title of Marine is what truly defines an individual. It isn't easy earning this title. And it's not easy subsequently qualifying and being certified to be a judge advocate.

There are reasons why the Marines are called "the few and the proud." It's not just a slogan, but rather a classification of who we are. It's also our state of mind—our state of being. It's a tough and hard road for those who accept the challenge to become a Marine and to live as one. However, once a person earns the title of "Marine," that individual will not only know the true meaning behind the words "the few and the proud," but that individual will always be a Marine—for once it is earned, you can never lose it.

For most of us, it will be the hardest challenge we will ever face in our lives. In fact, a number of us will lose the challenge and never become a Marine. Some of us will never even try or give up before taking a step toward facing the challenge. I, for one, once also failed in this challenge. Moreover, even if you overcome the challenge, you will likely find out a lot about yourself— a part of you that you probably never knew and a part that you probably did not want to know. While my words may sound cryptic, I am not purposely trying to be. It is just an experience that words cannot properly explain. However, I know that a Marine, wherever he or she may be, would know what I mean.

It was once said that, "America today wants a Marine Corps because she knows not only what we do, but also something about who we are, and what we believe—the standards of our ethos and our values. The nation wants its Corps of Marines because we are a force she can trust. Consequently, it has been the duty of every Marine to reserve that trust." (Ethos and Values, *Marine Corps Gazette*, November 1995.) Consequently, it has been the duty of every Marine to reserve that trust. It is a very important and serious duty that exacts a Marine to be held to the highest standards of both professional and personal conduct. It is what the nation expects of us.

The Marine Corps will not entice you to join its ranks by offering you money as an incentive. While money may be offered as an additional benefit of a person signing up to become a Marine, the Marine Corps does not want anyone who places material gain above a person's desire to serve his country and fellow citizens. The Marine Corps will also not give you a cushy job or a duty station. To the contrary, you will likely be offered the most challenging jobs in most difficult of places. This is not to say that the Marine Corps will not take care of you and your family—this is because Marine Corps does take care of its Marines and the Marines' families as best as it can. What I am trying to convey here is that, if you truly want to be a Marine (whether you are qualified and certified to be a judge advocate or not), you better be able to face yourself and overcome the most lowly and selfish feelings that you may have—because you will be tested in mind, body, heart, and soul when training to be a Marine and when living as a Marine.

In general, I believe Marines who are qualified and certified as a judge advocate, whether on active duty or not, have the confidence and bravado like no other professionals. These Marines will be successful in any matter that he or she sets their mind to. These Marines will never stop running until his goal has been achieved.

The foregoing thoughts, comments, and information, has been provided to you in my personal capacity and is neither endorsed by nor represents the view of the United States Marine Corps, Department of the Navy, Department of Defense or any other component of the United States government. I further omitted the general military compensation and other federal government benefit information, because I believe anyone can research this information, and because I wanted to focus on the intangible aspects of my profession.

13

Profile 13
Spiritas: Lobbyist

Executive Summary

Name: Spiritas
Profile: Lobbyist
Location: London

We think we know what a Lobbyist does. But the truth is we don't really know what it takes to be a lobbyist or how they work in specific detail. Simply put, in general, a lobbyist tries to persuade the government to better meet the needs of the public or certain corporate actors, which Spiritas does for her particular organization. Based in the UK, Spiritas's day is full of meetings and events, informing counterparts, and drafting documents to help benefit her company's operations in various countries. Lobbyists can also influence new laws being proposed by the government, which is where her law background gives her a competitive edge. Above all, one of Spiritas's significant roles is to meet and know a wide range of political figures including ambassadors, government ministers, and policymakers. She also must maintain good relations with them, which make communication skills and the ability to persuade and influence a vital skill set. In her career profile, Spiritas also advises how important it is to be observant, well-informed, and of course, capable of moving the minds of other people. If you like what you hear so far, then spend twenty-four hours with Spiritas in her typical day as a lobbyist.

Profile

Career Field:	Government Affairs/Legal
Current Position:	Government Affairs Manager
Institution:	UK-Based Global Financial Corporation
Location:	London, UK
Previous Position(s):	Same firm (In-House Counsel)
Education:	Postgraduate Diploma, King's College, University of London
	LLM, University of Melbourne
Licensed (Y/N):	Yes
Jurisdiction(s):	New York/England and Wales/New South Wales and Victoria, Australia

Schedule

6:30 a.m.	Get Up and Get Ready
6:45 a.m.	Cycle to Work
7:30 a.m.	Arrive at Work/Shower and Change
8:00 a.m.	Arrive at My Desk/Turn on Computer
9:30 a.m.	Team Meeting
10:30 a.m.	Teleconference with Asia
11:30 a.m.	Back at My Desk/Check E-mails
12:30 p.m.	Attend Lunch at Asia House
1:30 p.m.	Ambassador's Speech
2:00 p.m.	Head to Westminster
2:30 p.m.	Meeting at Department of Trade
3:45 p.m.	Head Back to the Office
4:15 p.m.	Draft Memorandum
5:30 p.m.	Review White Paper
6:30 p.m.	Review Research and E-Mail
7:00 p.m.	Leave for Industry Association Meeting
7:30 p.m.	Arrive at Mansion House
8:00 p.m.	Dinner and Speeches
9:45 p.m.	Leave Mansion House
10:15 p.m.	Arrive Home
10:30 p.m.	Pack Suitcase/Watch *Newsnight* on TV
10:50 p.m.	Research/Collate Papers/Review

12:00 a.m.	Set Alarm/Go to Sleep
5:00 a.m.	Wake Up/Get Ready
6:30 a.m.	Board Eurostar to Take to Europe

24-Hour Schedule

6:30 a.m.   *Get Up and Get Ready*

I am usually up at 6:30 each morning, unless I am traveling, in which case it is likely to be earlier (I don't usually need an alarm clock to get up). As soon as I am up, I get ready, get into my cycling gear, pick up my bag (that I packed the night before), and go to the basement of my flat to get my bike out of the lock-up area (where most people lock-up their bicycles).

6:45 a.m.   *Cycle to Work*

Unless the weather is terrible or if I have some other obligation (such as attending a breakfast meeting, hosting an event, or something similar), I try to cycle to work every day. This is one way to combine commuting and exercise. When I first moved to London, I was a bit hesitant to ride my bike because there are not many bike paths and the traffic can be dangerous. But London has made efforts to improve conditions for cyclists and although it's not great (and certainly doesn't compare to a city like, say, Melbourne or Munich), it's a lot better than it used to be. The route to work is quite picturesque. I ride mostly along the Thames River and pass the Tate Modern, St. Paul's Cathedral, the Millennium Bridge, and Shakespeare's Globe. I then cross over the Tower Bridge and ride along the canals. As long as the weather's nice, it's a good ride.

7:30 a.m.   *Arrive at Work/Shower and Change*

I lock up my bike in the basement of the building where my office is located and head for the showers. Usually, it doesn't get very crowded before 8 a.m. So I have a quick shower, get changed, and head for my office. On the way, I grab some breakfast at the canteen, which is usually a piece of toast and a piece of fruit.

8:00 a.m.   *Arrive at My Desk/Turn on Computer*

The first thing I do once I arrive at my desk is to turn my computer on and to start reading the day's newspapers. I subscribe to the *Financial Times, The Wall Street Journal* (both European and Asian editions), and the *Times*. There are also a couple of specialist journals such as the *European Voice* that focuses on the European Union (EU) and industry-specific journals, as well as the weekly *Economist*. I also like to check the BBC website and news wire sites such as Reuters for any breaking news. For my job, being a news junkie is a prerequisite.

I scan the headlines first, tick the articles that are the most relevant or significant (such as new regulatory developments or changes to existing regulations), and then go back and read the articles in detail. My team produces a weekly report summarizing the major regulatory developments around the world that are relevant to my industry. So I summarize the main items for the newsletter and e-mail them to Ben who works on the newsletter. I also note if there are any leads that need follow-up, such as new legislative initiatives by the EU or the UK government, or other countries that may affect my company.

9:30 a.m.   *Team Meeting*

On Mondays, we start off with a team meeting, reviewing existing projects, giving updates on where we are at, prioritizing tasks that need to be followed up, and the like. Ours is a very small team of four people and we manage all government affairs related matters from around the world, except for the United States. Often there are so many urgent issues that the "important-but-not-urgent" projects keep getting put on the back burner. So it is vital to have a regular review of all projects to make sure that things are being progressed on the non-urgent, but important projects, too. On other days, in the morning when my brain feels relatively fresh, I usually try to do tasks that require more thinking, such as writing position papers.

10:30 a.m.   *Teleconference with Asia*

There is a telephone conference with one of the Asian country managers. Our company's global headquarters is in London and it has its Asian headquarters in Singapore (located in Southeast Asia) with representative offices all around the region. I hold telephone conferences regularly with the various country managers to find out whether there are any regulatory barriers that they experience in those countries. Because of the time difference, I try to schedule the call in the morning for Asia.

As a note, being located in London is good in that it has a reasonable number of hours of overlap with both Asia and the Americas. I've heard many international executives say that it is easier to be global if one is based in London simply because it is easier to contact the rest of the world. If you're based in Asia and you are trying to work with New York, more effort is required because of the greater time differential.

When participating in the telephone conference, it turns out that they (the firm's Asian country manager and office) are indeed experiencing some difficulties with accessing the market with a particular new product that they have developed. It seems that a license from the government is required to market the product. And although we satisfy all the requirements for the license, the government is unwilling to grant us the license. The reason seems to be that there is a domestic producer of a similar product being championed by the government and they do not want foreign competition. I explain that there may be a few avenues that we can explore to address this problem. Most Asian countries have introduced laws to attract foreign direct investment (FDI), especially after the Asian financial crisis of 1997. Under the legislation, discriminating against a foreign company would be illegal. Separately, there may be a bilateral investment treaty between the UK and that country, which would also make it illegal for UK companies operating in that country to be discriminated in this manner. If the country is a member of the World Trade Organization (WTO), that can also help us if they have agreed to open up that particular market.

I ask the country manager if he can find a copy of the local FDI related legislation and send us a copy of it, preferably in English, so I can then follow-up on the bilateral investment treaty and the WTO. After I get off the phone, I summarize in bullet points what we discussed so that I can e-mail it to the country manager as reference. The task is made easier by the fact that I was able to take notes on my laptop while we were on the call. I found that it's always important to make a memorandum of any meeting, especially if there are any tasks that need to be followed-up. Otherwise, people often forget. I ask my researcher to see if there is a bilateral treaty between the UK and the Asian country in question. I also ask her to find out if that country is a member of the WTO and to find its schedule of commitments listed by sectors.

11:30 a.m.   Back at My Desk/Check E-Mails

After I arrive back at my desk, I open my e-mail. I used to check my e-mail constantly and reply immediately to any e-mail that landed in my inbox. But later, I found that doing it this way was quite disruptive and a really inefficient use of my time since I couldn't focus on other activities for any length of time. So now, I try to limit the time I spend checking e-mails when I'm at my desk, especially if I have tasks that requires real thinking. I've even turned off the pinging noise that alerts me when a new e-mail hits my inbox. Initially, I was concerned that I might miss something really urgent or important. But people call rather than e-mail if there is something really urgent. So it turns out that this way works quite well. I quickly scan the subject headings to prioritize answering them according to urgency. If there is a thread (a series of related e-mails), I just go to the most recent one. I make sure I file away any important e-mails electronically.

12:30 p.m.   Attend Lunch at Asia House

Lunch is usually a sandwich at my desk while I continue working through my e-mails. But more often than not, there is an event I need to attend. Today there is a lunch being hosted at Asia House to welcome the new Chinese ambassador to the UK. China is an important market for everyone now. So it's crucial to keep abreast on any new developments there and to develop good relations with the relevant representatives. Asia House is a useful association that fosters business and investment links with Asian countries. I take the Tube (London's public subway system) to Bond Street and walk to Asia House, which is housed in one of the fine eighteenth century townhouses lining the streets of Marleybone. These gatherings are a great way to network, get to know people, and to develop better relationships. There is a pre-lunch drinks reception followed by a seated three-course lunch. I refrain from drinking any wine though.

1:30 p.m.   *Ambassador's Speech*

The Chinese ambassador makes a short speech between the main course and dessert. It is a very articulate, clear, and well thought-through speech, peppered with humor. It's clear that everyone in the room is impressed by the new ambassador. After the lunch, I go up to the new ambassador, introduce my company and myself and exchange name cards. I also meet the new diplomatic attaché.

2:00 p.m.   *Head to Westminster*

After the ambassador's speech at Asia House, I need to leave straight away for a meeting at the trade ministry in Westminster. It's only a short Tube ride away from Bond Street. In the city center, I tend to avoid taking a cab because of the traffic. At least with the public transport during the day, it is more likely that you will get to a meeting on time. My bag is always full of reading material that I need to get through. So I use the time while on the Tube to read.

2:30 p.m.   *Meeting at Department of Trade*

I arrive at Westminster and get out of the station. The area is always full of tourists visiting the British Parliament and taking pictures in front of Big Ben. Sometimes it gets very crowded on the street, which is the case today. After making my way through the crowds, I walk to the trade ministry building near Westminster.

There is an upcoming meeting between the trade minister and my company's CEO. Today, I am seeing the minister's team to prepare for the meeting. I bring with me a draft memorandum that I have prepared, which outlines the issues my CEO will raise in the meeting with the minister. It is a laundry list of barriers to doing business that we experience in the UK that cover a whole range of issues from the lack of foreign language skills of UK graduates to power supply issues. Normally, for a discussion like this, I would use either e-mail or hold a teleconference. But there is also an upcoming industry roundtable that my company has agreed to host. So we also need to discuss the organization of the event, speaker and guest lists and so on. So we ultimately decided to meet face-to-face, which will facilitate the discussion.

3:45 p.m.   *Head Back to the Office*

There were a number of items to get through in the meeting with the trade ministry. As a result, the meeting overran a little bit in time. We finish after more than an hour and I hurry back to the office.

4:15 p.m.   *Draft Memorandum*

I resume working on a memorandum I will be providing to the new British ambassador who will be taking up his appointment next month in a South Asian country where my company has a large presence. He has agreed to meet with us before his departure to get a clear understanding of where we experience difficulties in operating in that country. Our meeting is scheduled for tomorrow morning. So the memorandum needs to be finished tonight. With written documents like these, sometimes it is useful to send it ahead of the meeting, but sometimes, it is better to follow-up by sending it after the meeting. It depends on the situation and the person receiving it. This time, given the new ambassador's unfamiliarity with our business, I decided it would be better to send it after our meeting. This way, I will first have a chance to explain to him various related details in person.

5:30 p.m.   *Review White Paper*

I finish the memorandum, then start reviewing the new white paper produced by the EU on cross-border transactions. A white paper is the official document proposing new legislation. As a result, it is important to provide input at this stage. There are a few provisions that are of concern and I make note of these. I know most of my company's business well enough so that I can judge if something may have an impact on the business or not. But if I am not certain whether a new proposed law may have an impact or not on a particular area of business, I will contact the business manager of that area to discuss it with him or her.

The white paper calls for a response in four weeks' time. So I put these in my diary with prompts. I have to consider whether the issues raised by the white paper are generic enough that I can rely on the relevant industry association to make a representation on our behalf, which will reduce the work we need to do, or whether the paper raises specific issues concerning my company that I need to prepare an individual response. I decide that the issues in this instance raise concerns shared by the industry. I call the chair of the industry association and speak to him briefly about the content of the white paper. He also shares my view and says he will be preparing a draft position paper by next week, which he will circulate for the review by the members. I thank him and tell him I look forward to receiving the document.

6:30 p.m.   *Review Research and E-Mail*

I start working through my e-mails again. My researcher has sent through the result of her work from this morning. It turns out there is no bilateral treaty between the UK and the Asian country in question. But the country is a member of the WTO and it has made commitments in the relevant sectors. This is a good start. I e-mail the country manager I spoke with earlier this morning about the result and suggest a couple of ways to follow-up. I remind him to send me the legislation. There is also a draft of the minutes of the meeting from the trade ministry. I fill in a couple of points and send it back.

7:00 p.m.   *Leave for Industry Association Meeting*

Tonight, there is an industry association dinner in the City of London, which I decided to attend a while back. So I leave the office to attend the dinner event. As it is a formal function, I change my jacket for the occasion (I keep a change of clothing in the office for occasions such as this). I get a lift with a colleague who is also attending the dinner.

7:30 p.m.   *Arrive at Mansion House*

People are often unaware of the fact that there are two mayors for London. There is the mayor for the greater London city, with a population of approximately 8 million people. Then there is the other Mayor of the City of London. The City of London—or simply "the City" or the Square Mile—is a smaller area within Greater London that is the financial center of

London. A separate Lord Mayor of the City of London governs the area and Mansion House is the official residence of this Lord Mayor. It's an imposing looking building in Palladian style situated near the Bank of England. Once we arrive, we are ushered in by attendants into the Mansion House banquet room.

8:00 p.m.   *Dinner and Speeches*

Seated at my table is my counterpart from a member of one of the industry associations to which my company belongs. I ask him about his views on the recent proposals made by the EU to change laws in a particular area, which concerns both our companies. He doesn't think it's a major issue, but one that needs to be clarified. While we chat, dinner is served—I skip the starter and pass on the wine. Too many formal dinners and lunches can have a detrimental effect on one's waistline. My view is to take everything in moderation always. The highlight of tonight is the keynote speech by the governor of the Bank of England. The governor was in good form as usual tonight. But in the speech, there were no revelations or additional insights.

9:45 p.m.   *Leave Mansion House*

During the event, I recall that I have an early start tomorrow morning. So I leave the dinner as soon as the speeches are over and then hail a cab to go home.

10:15 p.m.   *Arrive Home*

There was very little traffic on the cab route home. I arrive home in less than half an hour. I wash, change into my pajamas, and turn on the TV to catch up on the last bit of the evening news.

10:30 p.m.   *Pack Suitcase/Watch Newsnight on TV*

I am not looking forward to the trip tomorrow, but it has to be done. It's going to be a slightly longer trip than my usual one-day or overnight to Brussels trip. This is because I have to go on from Brussels to Strasbourg to appear as an expert advisor at a roundtable at the European Parliament the next day. I have the toiletry kit always packed and ready to go. So it's just a matter of selecting a suit, tops, and underwear. It takes me no time to do this. Over the years, I've become extremely good at packing and I travel very light. But I must admit I seem to have acquired a bit of luggage fetish! I watch *Newsnight*, a news and political commentary program, while I finish packing. I like the program for its presenter, who is an irascible, caustic type of journalist who gives no quarter to any politician he interviews, but he was not really in high form tonight.

10:50 p.m.   *Research/Collate Papers/Review*

I go over all the papers that I need for tomorrow to make sure I've got everything. My assistant is usually incredibly organized and makes sure I have everything I need. But there were a couple of things that I spotted in today's newspapers that I wanted to follow-up on. So I go online and do a bit of research to locate the new initiatives papers that the article referred to. This could be quite useful for the meetings tomorrow in Brussels and Strasbourg the day after. I review the papers, and then review once more the people I am meeting and their backgrounds (to think about how best to approach the problems given their interests and background).

12:00 a.m.   *Set Alarm/Go to Sleep*

I set the alarm for 5 the next morning (a mere five hours from now) since a car will be coming to pick me up thirty minutes thereafter at 5:30 a.m. to take me to St. Pancras to board the Eurostar (a high-speed passenger train between the UK and continental Europe). As I mentioned earlier, I usually don't need an alarm clock to wake me up. But no matter how remote the chance may be, the last thing I want to do is miss a business trip. I turn the lights off and try to go to sleep.

5:00 a.m.   *Wake Up/Get Ready*

I hear the alarm clock, get out of bed, and start to get ready. In thirty minutes, I am all prepared for my trip and leave my flat to the awaiting car that will take me to St. Pancras to board the Eurostar.

6:30 a.m.   Board Eurostar to Take to Europe

It's been twenty-four hours since my day began yesterday. But with such a packed and busy schedule, it seems to go by very quickly. I board the Eurostar to my designated seat. I use this time to scan the newspapers and review the materials for my upcoming meetings in Europe.

Final Thoughts

Some days involve many more internal and external meetings, with senior managers, government officials, industry associations, my counterparts from other companies, and so on. I also spend quite a bit of time preparing for meetings and receptions with ambassadors, ministers, and other visiting dignitaries (once I even had to host a meeting for the president of Mongolia!). I travel about twice a month, although this also depends on what needs to be done. Because so much of my work does involve the EU, I have to visit Brussels regularly and other cities in Europe as well where EU institutions are based such as Strasbourg where the European Parliament is based or Paris, where some of the regulatory authorities are located.

I've also had to go to Bonn, Dublin, Vienna, Frankfurt, Zurich, Prague, and other cities around Europe on various occasions for different projects. Less often, I have also had to fly to various parts of Asia. This is one aspect that is very different from lobbying in the US where most things are based in Washington D.C. Traveling to Brussels or Paris is easy thanks to the Eurostar. Whenever I can, I try to take the train instead of the plane to try to reduce my carbon footprint, but it's not always easy. Also, taking the train is much less of a hassle than getting aboard a plane, particularly due to the increasingly intrusive and restrictive baggage checks and security inspections in the current environment. From London, however, it is really only Paris and Brussels that are easily reachable by train. The rest of the time, one has to fly.

I cannot say I enjoy the traveling much. The novelty and glamor wears off very quickly and you discover that work doubles when you are traveling since you have to do all the routine work as well as prepare for the trip and attend to any new work generated by the trip. In terms of work, sometimes there is really high-octane stuff where you are working with senior government officials and executives on high profile matters. But most of the time, my work involves a lot of reading, analyzing, and drafting of documents.

To be a good lobbyist, you need to know about policy, process, and politics. But most importantly, you have to be able to communicate well. At the heart of lobbying, is making the other person understand what your issue is and making them want to help you. I do not make campaign contributions or do anything else of that nature. So it is really through information exchange that you hope to influence policymakers. This is because it is their (the policymakers') job to ensure that the policies they formulate and implement have a positive impact on the industry while avoiding any undue negative ones.

Although there is no one typical day as a lobbyist for a multinational company, one of the aspects that I really enjoy about my work is the variety of issues, type of work, and the people I get to meet.

14

Profile 14
Akiko: Intergovernmental
Organization (IGO) Chief

Executive Summary

Name: Akiko
Profile: Intergovernmental Organization (IGO) Chief
Location: New York, New York

If you consider yourself a patron to world peace and security, environmental protection, or human rights and are interested in working in the public law sector, surely you may have thought about working for the UN (United Nations) at one point or another. But before you get your cape and start to fly off to an exotic destination, you should realize that the cooperative nature of IGO's (intergovernmental organizations) often require much more administrative work and conferences than you might expect. It could also be a slow-paced, often time-consuming environment, leaving little time to focus on actual legal drafting and other pertinent issues in the spirit of helping provide "peace and security" for the international community. In most instances, this career field often demands a schedule no less hectic than other private law firms, which may be counter to what some people may think. After all, promoting meaningful legal changes—especially when dealing with issues transcending many borders—often demand considerable time and communication. The multicultural working atmosphere between other international offices also motivates people in the UN to brush up on their language and negotiation skills. Above all, the fact that you can use your legal skills to pursue a higher and nobler cause—such as protecting the rights of women and the disabled—as you will see in Akiko's twenty-four-hour career profile, could very well be the ultimate merit of working for the United Nations or other IGO, which Akiko does with great integrity and pride, as you will see in her twenty-four-hour profile.

Profile

Career Field:	Intergovernmental Organization (IGO)
Current Position:	Chief, Secretariat for the Convention on the Rights of Persons with Disabilities, Department of Economic and Social Affairs
Institution:	United Nations
Location:	New York, New York
Previous Position(s):	Legal Advisory
Education:	LLM, University of California at Berkeley
	MA, University of Chicago
	LLB, Sophia University (Tokyo, Japan)
Licenses (Y/N):	No

Schedule

6:15 a.m.	Wake-Up/Take Care of the Family Dog
6:45 a.m.	Leave for the Metro North Station
7:06 a.m.	Take the Metro North Train to Grand Central Station (NYC)/Skim through *The New York Times*/Check and Reply to E-Mails
8:05 a.m.	Arrive at the UN Plaza DC2 Building (where my office is located)
8:15 a.m.	Check E-Mails (in detail)/Review Follow-ups
8:30 a.m.	Start Taking Action on the Priorities for the Day (send e-mails to confirm the day's schedule, request each member to take action on urgent issues in their respective fields of work)
9:15 a.m.	First Conference Call (with UN office in Geneva)
10:15 a.m.	Second Conference Call (re: MERCOSUR meetings - Latin America)
11:30 a.m.	Chiefs Meeting with the Assistant Secretary-General
12:30 p.m.	The Unit's Meeting
1:15 p.m.	Luncheon Meeting with Experts (who will work on DESA's projects)
2:30 p.m.	Meeting of the UN Focal Points for Women
3:30 p.m.	Reviewing Policy Documents/Legislative Analysis (submitted by the Unit Members)

4:30 p.m.	Meeting with Individual Members of the Unit (re: to discuss their respective responsibilities)
5:30 p.m.	Review Urgent Priorities (for the rest of the evening)
7:00 p.m.	Leave for home (in Westchester County, New York)
8:00 p.m.	Cook Dinner (for the family and the dog)
8:30 p.m.	Dinner
9:30 p.m.	Resume work (checking and replying to e-mails)
11:00 p.m.	Prepare for the Following Day
12:15 a.m.	Go to Sleep
6:15 a.m.	Wake-Up (for another 24 hours!)

24-Hour Schedule

6:15 a.m.   *Wake-Up / Take Care of the Family Dog*

When the alarm clock goes off, I'm always in disbelief how morning returns so quickly. My dog, Mupsha, is still in bed (she is not a morning dog), and I need to wake her up by greeting her very gently—even at home with the dog, I always try to exercise gentle diplomacy.

After my dog is up, I get ready for work. It's extremely difficult to choose what to wear, as New York weather is so unpredictable. I usually choose suits of either black or gray, or of relatively bright color, depending on the season.

As I walk out the door near the reception area of my condominium, I leave instructions for the building staff to walk my dog during the day. At least that makes one of us getting some fresh air and exercise during working hours!

6:45 a.m.   *Leave for the Metro North Station*

Even before I step outside, I brace myself for the ensuing weather conditions that abound once I leave the warm confines of my residence. And sure enough, contrary to what the news forecasted, it seems like rain, snow, or a combination of the two. It's a brisk ten-minute walk to the Metro North Station where I need to go to commute by rail to my workplace. And given the weather conditions, snow/rain boots are very good friends for one's feet, especially in January and February.

7:06 a.m.   *Take the Metro North Train to Grand Central Station (NYC)/Skim through The New York Times/Check and Reply to E-Mails*

One part of being a professional is trying to balance work and family. This holds especially true for me. So despite the weather, and the cold and early morning hour of the day, I make time to call my father (who lives in Tokyo) right before I get on the train. I call during this time because he is almost always at home in the evening. And the timing works, since Tokyo is usually about 13 thirteen hours ahead of New York. While riding the metro, which is the quickest and easiest way to get to Manhattan from upstate New York where I leave, I use the time to skim through *The New York Times*, while also checking and replying to e-mails in the train as much as I can within the hustle and bustle of commuters all around me. I also finish some routine paper work, as I usually try to do during this time, such as editing public information materials for my unit at the United Nations (UN).

8:05 a.m.   *Arrive at the UN Plaza DC2 Building (where my office is located)*

Before I know it, the train has already made its stop at New York's Grand Central Station—one of the city's busiest stations, located not too far from the UN headquarters. Because it's about an hour before 9 a.m., it's not as busy as it could be. But it's definitely busy enough with people in rush mode to get where they need to be. It's about a ten-minute walk from Grand Central Station to the office. There's actually a few ways to get to the UN once I get off the train. But first things first, I need to pick up my morning coffee and a pastry or two at one of my favorite bakeries/cafes. My purchase of several bottles of mineral water is also a standard purchase I make during my morning routine to work.

8:15 a.m.   *Check E-Mails (in detail)/Review Follow-Ups*

I get to the UN DC2 building and take the elevator to the thirteenth floor—where my office is located—near the corner with a fairly decent view of bustling downtown Manhattan. Right next to my building is the main UN headquarters—the historic tall structure designed by the famous architect Frank Lloyd Wright located next to the Hudson River found on many a postcard—surrounded by the various flags of the UN member states. It's still quite a spectacle to behold for me.

Upon my arrival to the office, I always remind myself that I should organize my workspace, but honestly, it's impossible to find time. I check my latest stream of e-mails, but due to the stream of accumulated e-mails from the previous night and even from the time I got off the train, there are usually around twenty or so that I need to attend to on an urgent basis.

Because limited time means prioritization is critically important, I attend to the most urgent issues first, involving requests from the office of the secretary-general or the office of the under secretary-general of our department, since our unit is directly and substantively responsible for the work and activities related to disability, human rights, and development within the UN secretariat in New York.

8:30 a.m.   *Start Taking Action on the Priorities for the Day (send e-mails to confirm the day's schedule, request each member to take action on urgent issues in their respective fields of work)*

I now focus on other matters. And on this particular day, I start off by requesting each member of the unit to take action in their respective fields of work. In my unit, there are a total of six professionals (including myself) and two general staff members. Each professional has his or her own specialized areas of designated responsibilities. The unit meets at least once a week for over one and a half hours. There are also frequent small meetings as part of this process since we (the unit and its members) all need to support each other's work as most of the members of my unit are new to the United Nations or to the field of disability. Recruitment for each post takes anywhere between three and six months.

9:15 a.m.   *First Conference Call (with UN office in Geneva)*

There are a number of collaborations related to activities concerning the UN Convention on the Rights of Persons with Disabilities. This is an historic piece of UN legislation that I've been dedicating myself to for quite some time—in short, it essentially is a new international public law that provides certain rights and responsibilities for disabled persons.

Due to the time difference, I try to schedule my first conference call with my European colleagues. Due to this time difference (Europe is a few hours behind New York time), it makes it a bit of a challenge sometimes to coordinate such calls between our offices, but it is much easier to coordinate than for conference calls with my colleagues from the Asia-Pacific region (which, as mentioned with my call to my father earlier in the morning, can be something like thirteen hours ahead of New York time).

10:15 a.m.   *Second Conference Call (re: MERCOSUR meetings - Latin America)*

On issues concerning the rights of persons with disabilities and development, which I am spearheading, there are always official requests from various governments and civil society organizations to organize conferences and arrange for various regional meetings. Working with Latin American partners, one realizes that competency in the Spanish language is essential. And I always feel that I should improve my Spanish so that I can conduct the meetings and organize conferences in Spanish. As you could probably guess, being multilingual, especially in one or more of the UN's six official languages—Arabic, English, French, Mandarin, Russian, and Spanish—helps not only to get hired at the UN, but to also succeed after you get in. After all, working to pass legislation among so many different cultures, languages, borders, and even legal systems can be daunting, and requires consensus building. And consensus building is often much easier when making an effort to speak in your partner's language. In my case, I speak English in addition to my native tongue of Japanese, while making continuous efforts to polish my Spanish and French language skills.

11:30 a.m.   *Chiefs Meeting with the Assistant Secretary-General*

Our division is overseen by the assistant secretary-general (of economic development) of our department, which is not typically the case, except for the fact that the director post has been vacant for quite some time. Since he (the assistant secretary-general) is the chief economist of our department, I am beginning to learn to speak like an economist. But as a lawyer, it is sometimes an impossibility! Since I am one of the two human rights lawyers in my department, one task I have is to translate my work into the policy language we use in social development. But this is easier said than done. Given all the nuances, among other things, I find it very difficult to translate the substantive work of my unit into the type of policy language that is required. Hence, it's one of the various challenges embedded in the type of work I do.

12:30 a.m.   *The Unit's Meeting*

I always enjoy working with both my professional and general staff members that comprise my unit. When distributing assignments, I always try to combine the work and priorities of our unit with the skill and professional development of my younger colleagues. It's important for me to make sure that each staff member is improving his or her skills in all areas of our work, while accumulating experience in their specialized areas. I try to make the unit's meeting interesting as well as hopefully motivating. But it tends to get intense because we have so many requirements and a whole host of expectations from our various partners, despite the relatively limited number of staff on hand in the unit. Nonetheless, we somehow seem to manage the tasks that need to get done.

1:15 p.m.   *Luncheon Meeting with Experts (who will work on DESA's projects)*

For me, it's important to make use of lunch time for consultations on upcoming projects. I'm very fortunate that I have many professional colleagues who are established authorities in many different fields in human rights, social development, and even in peace and security. So when we embark on a new project that requires a high level of expertise and recognized authorities, I turn to my friends and colleagues in the particular area needed for their intellectual insight and assistance. For example, my former colleagues are working together with my Unit as consultants to provide a road map for crucial technical issues concerning the human rights of persons with disabilities in development. It's also a great pleasure to be able to work with my friends and colleagues to create "something new" to "add value" (yes, a term used even in IGOs like the UN, not just in the private sector) to the work of the organization.

2:30 p.m.   *Meeting of the UN Focal Points for Women*

My personal and professional commitment to gender equality and empowerment of women has made me decide to keep my position as the Departmental Focal Point for Women, which assists the UN Focal Point to ensure that UN policies achieve an equal 50/50 balance in all professional categories and to promote empowerment of women staff members. In this spirit, we meet regularly to discuss implementation of the organization's policies to promote gender equality. The meeting also takes the form of luncheons and other activities. I believe it's vitally important to develop and strengthen networks of women professionals to reach the stated goal of the United Nations. So I'm glad that my contribution in this important effort can make a difference to the organization, and hopefully beyond.

3:30 p.m.   *Reviewing Policy Documents/Legislative Analysis (submitted by the unit members)*

Because of my duty as the chief in my unit, I need to review all the work done by the staff members of my unit. In other words, I review the final product of the assignments that I assign to my unit. Our work ranges from reviewing policy documents, legislative and policy analysis, as well as public information to organizing major conferences and event planning. All our tasks require review and feedback at every stage. So this times careful review, which is where my legal training to pay attention to detail on the important issues at hand, comes in handy. But even despite having such a legal skill to review lots of intricate documentation and language at any given time, this task is still one of the most time-consuming aspects of the unit and thus my day.

4:30 p.m.   *Meeting with Individual Members of the Unit (re: to discuss their respective responsibilities)*

In terms of being a good manager, for me, it's important to set aside sufficient time so that I can discuss with each staff member in my unit his or her areas of work and their progress in that area. Reviewing their work and conducting their performance review is another important dimension of management of the unit. As you would expect with this, it can be very sensitive, but it's critical for all parties involved to get this type of feedback.

5:30 p.m.   *Review Urgent Priorities (for the rest of the evening)*

It's past five already. Fortunately, today I'm nearly done with all my urgent tasks for the day. But despite this, my attention is drawn towards deciding what needs to be done before the end of the day. Often people say that they need things done by COB (closing of business). In the old days, this meant 5 p.m., but in my case, it means midnight. So for those wishing to work in the UN or other similar IGO, you should bear in mind that the working hours are not always a nice and tidy nine to five day. I think maybe those days are over for many, if not all, sectors, due to e-mail and other forms of global connectivity that lessens the costs of communication.

7:00 p.m.   *Leave for home (in Westchester County, New York)*

Although there's always something more to do, one more e-mail to send, I dash out of the office to catch the train (reassuring myself that tomorrow will be the day I tidy up my office). I take the Metro North train to Westchester to return home. I try to make an arrangement for dinner before I get on the train, for example, deciding on what to cook. Some people cook to eat, but for me, I have always enjoyed the virtues of cooking and finding new recipes. I always like to be inspired by new recipes I read in one of my cookbooks, or by the dishes I enjoy during one of my mission trips to different countries. I only have approximately forty minutes on the train to think, ponder, and then execute my culinary game plan!

8:00 p.m.   *Cook Dinner (for the family and the dog)*

After giving instructions to my husband on how to start preparing the dinner ingredients, I take a shower in about ten minutes. Afterwards, I follow exactly the culinary idea I had planned while riding the train. Sometimes it takes much longer than I anticipate to cook what I have in mind, which can sometimes be frustrating since I'm often quite tired by this time. But at the same time, it helps me leave my work behind while I prepare a freshly cooked dinner that gives me nutrition and enjoyment. Maybe it has something to do with working and creating something with my hands, along with the ability to use some culinary creativity from time to time. It's really hard to say, but regardless, I quite enjoy the moment.

I also cook a special dinner for my dog, Mupsha. She eats lightly cooked meat and broccoli with kibble and supplements fit for her stage of life. A meal fit for a king, or shall I say, queen.

8:30 p.m.   *Dinner*

During the dinner, I talk with my husband about what transpired throughout each of our days. In many ways, our worlds are quite complementary, since he is an actuary who is very numbers focused and quantitative based, compared to the qualitative nature of my legal work. So this makes things interesting to share viewpoints.

Afterwards, I try to relax after dinner while my husband cleans up. As you can see, we've formed a comfortable division of labor that would make Adam Smith proud—my husband does the dishes (labor intensive) and I cook (capital intensive)—which suits me just fine. I also take this time to catch up on the news, such as the BBC or NHK. Every once in a while, I see some figures I know appear to do an interview on one of these channels. One evening, I was surprised to see one of my former interns on TV, who has since become department chair at a very large and prominent university in South Korea!

9:30 p.m.   *Resume work (checking and replying to e-mails)*

After dinner and watching the news, I again check my e-mails, replying to as much as I can. This way, I can try to streamline my inbox before it gets too huge by the next morning. Like other legal professionals, it's a constant struggle against the constant barrage of incoming mail. Fortunately, the task of walking the dog is given to my spouse (another handy division of labor), which gives me the needed time for me to continue to focus on finishing my day's work.

11:00 p.m.   *Prepare for the Following Day*

Although it's late, I take a bath and then do yoga, which is essential for my health. For those of you who are yoga skeptics, I highly recommend giving it a try.

One of my habits is my need to decide what I should wear the following day (more or less). But as it usually turns out, I often change my mind in the morning, depending on the weather and my mood.

12:15 a.m.   *Go to Sleep*

It's way too late for my own good. But I feel relaxed and ready to snuggle into bed, along with my husband, and Mupsha, the other love of my life!

6:15 a.m.   *Wake-Up (for another 24 hours!)*

6:15 a.m. already (it is a cliché, but yes, indeed, how time flies!). Okay, here comes another day—in the global effort to help raise awareness in the areas of persons with disabilities, human rights, and gender issues—it's not easy work, but I'm very glad to be able to do it.

Final Thoughts

My priority setting for my twenty-four hours is done in accordance with the UN General Assembly (the legislative arm of the United Nations) mandates and expected political dividends.

Almost 30 to 40 percent of my time is taken by managerial/administrative work. So there is very little time for me to engage in meaningful legal or policy analysis for our work to support the Convention on the Rights of Persons with Disabilities. Work-life balance is not ideal due to endless tsunami-like workloads. For example, when we are supporting the intergovernmental processes—namely negotiations for resolutions during the General Assembly (or the Commission for Social Development under the Economic and Social Council), preparing for major conferences and events, continuing with various collaborations (with stakeholders, governments, civil society and academic institutions) while also sometimes trying to meet a plethora of internal deadlines (for policy briefs and other related matters)—my work becomes more than my life.

I have at least "three shifts" (depending on the time difference between New York, and wherever I am on mission). For example, when I am in Geneva, Switzerland, I get up and check e-mails, attend local meetings, go back to checking e-mails, and engaging in discussions (through e-mail or phone) with my colleagues in New York and Asia, among others. Lunch time and dinners are preceded and followed by phone discussions or by reviewing documents for submission to both the office of the under secretary-general and sometimes the secretary-general.

To my regret, I'm not able to fully engage with outside partners since the demands in my office are disproportionately heavy, consuming so much time for internal activities within my department, which doesn't leave much time for building new partnerships. But hopefully after reading my twenty-four-hour career profile, our partners, both current and future (along with the many other readers of this book), can have a sense of what it is I do on a day-to-day basis in furtherance of the United Nations mission.

15

Profile 15
Jasper: Law Professor

Executive Summary

Name: Jasper
Profile: Law Professor
Location: Seoul, South Korea

When many students see their law professors, it's usually just for a few hours per week for an undergraduate or graduate lecture. But do you ever wonder what happens beyond those class hours? Jasper's profile provides a rare "behind-the-scenes" look at what a young law professor can and should do as part of his or her life in academia, or as some would say, the "Ivory Tower." But, as you'll see in this profile, life as a law professor can at times often be as hectic as legal careers in the public and private sectors. The next twenty-four-hour career profile begins in the early morning hours for a live TV interview for an international news broadcaster, followed quickly by a graduate course lecture, lunch meetings with colleagues, a job talk for a faculty position interview, followed by some final touch-ups on an op-ed piece for a major US-based financial newspaper. So if you're considering a career in academics—before you make any move toward the campus courtyard—you might want to read this twenty-four-hour profile first!

Profile

Career Field:	Academia
Current Position:	Department Chair, Associate Professor
Institution:	Ewha University
Location:	Seoul, South Korea
Previous Position(s):	Structured Trading Desk, UK-based Global Investment Bank (Hong Kong)
	In-House Counsel, US-Based Global Investment Bank (Japan)
Education:	JD, Rutgers University, School of Law
	MSc, The London School of Economics and Political Science
	BA, University of California, San Diego
Licensed (Y/N):	Yes
Jurisdictions:	Washington, DC/New Jersey

Schedule

5:25 a.m.	Alarm Clock Rings (from iPhone)
5:30 a.m.	Wake-Up/Turn on TV/Light Workout (while watching news)
6:15 a.m.	Pick Clothes for the Day/Take Shower
6:35 a.m.	Eat Quick Breakfast/Gulp Ice Coffee
6:45 a.m.	Take Subway to Central Seoul (for live TV interview)
7:15 a.m.	Arrive at TV Broadcasting Network Building/Prepare Interview Setup
7:25 a.m.	Live TV Interview (with global news network)
7:45 a.m.	Finish TV Interview/Go to University
8:15 a.m.	Arrive at University/Check E-Mail
8:45 a.m.	Prepare (again) for Graduate Law Course
9:30 a.m.	Begin Graduate Law Course Lecture
10:45 a.m.	Graduate Law Course Break/Speak with Students/Check E-Mail
12:15 p.m.	Graduate Law Course Ends
12:30 p.m.	Meet Faculty Members for Lunch
1:45 p.m.	Come Back to Office/Check (Regular) Mail in Faculty Mailbox

2:00 p.m.	Office Hours for Students
4:00 p.m.	Conduct Monthly Faculty Meeting
4:45 p.m.	Job Talk (for possible faculty hire)
5:45 p.m.	Finish Edits for Op-Ed Piece
7:05 p.m.	Meet Friends for Dinner
10:35 p.m.	Arrive Home/Greet Wife and Mini Dog
11:15 p.m.	Check E-Mail (again)
11:45 p.m.	Try to Catch the Late Night News/Fall Asleep
5:25 a.m.	Alarm Clock Rings (press the snooze button)

24-Hour Schedule

5:25 a.m.   *Alarm Clock Rings (from iPhone)*

The alarm clock on my iPhone goes off. I look outside and it's still pitch black. And for a split second (but not more), I wonder how I could have agreed to get up so early this morning—to give a live TV interview for a global news network for later this morning—in almost exactly two hours. Fortunately, I'm a morning person. And so it actually works out that the interview time is set for 7:25 a.m., a time that would be a deal breaker for most other academics to speak on issues concerning their area of expertise.

I did most of my research for the interview last night. And of all the mass information I gathered from various sources, I narrowed the main points to a couple of "talking points." So I go over this in my head as I make my move toward a cluster of free weights for a quick (and I mean quick!) workout before the interview.

5:30 a.m.   *Wake-Up/Turn on TV/Light Workout (while watching news)*

I try to work out at least three times a week. I find that it helps clear my head and provides me focus. Also, I'm a firm believer of maintaining a balance between body and mind. To me, the two are highly correlated.

I turn on the TV and flip through the main news channels—BBC, CNBC, CNN, and Bloomberg. Having the news on gives me a jolt of energy, as my mind tries to ingest all the information from the various breaking headlines and news flashes. I choose one of the channels, and then I start my workout regiment with a few repetitions of sit-ups to get my body warmed up for about ten minutes. And then I move to the weight regiment for about thirty minutes. By this time, I'm fully charged and ready to go.

6:15 a.m.   Pick Clothes for the Day/Take Shower

The type of clothes I choose depends on the type of meetings and events I have scheduled for the day. Because of the interview—with potentially millions of people watching—I'll choose a fairly conservative suit, sometimes with a necktie, sometimes not, depending on how I feel that day. I usually have a couple of outfits I have in mind the night before. I make the final "executive decision" in a spur-of-the-moment decision when I'm actually getting dressed. Last night, the two outfits consisted of: (1) a dark blue suit, white shirt, and blue tie combo (I call it the IBM "Big Blue" conservative look), and (2) a dark gray suit, light pink shirt, and dark tie.

I take a shower, which is a time of rest and relaxation for me. Some people claim to do their best while thinking in the shower or while taking baths (e.g., John F. Kennedy, Alan Greenspan). But I'm not in this crowd when it comes to places to think. For me in terms of places to think and write, it's usually a coffee shop or café with good music in the background (and crisp air conditioning, if it's the summer!) and a whir of subtle background noise. It's "creative conditions" like this where I've written my best work.

After several minutes, I get out of the shower, dry myself off, and then ultimately decide on the dark gray suit, pink shirt, and dark tie combination as "the" outfit for the day.

6:35 a.m.   Eat Quick Breakfast/Gulp Ice Coffee

Time is of the essence since the countdown until the interview is ticking quickly down to the wire—only about one hour left! Yikes—that definitely helps to put a fire under my feet. By this time, my wife and the dog are awake. My wife asks me what I'd like for breakfast. But the easiest and quickest option for me is to just eat a quick bowl of cereal (granola oats, to be exact) and a couple bites of a lightly toasted bagel. Last, but not least, I take some pre-refrigerated coffee and pour it over a cup of ice. For some reason, hot coffee doesn't give me the jolt that ice coffee does. I don't have much time. So I basically drink the whole glass in a few massive gulps. I feel the rush of caffeine, sugar, and ice all at the same time. "Okay, let's do this," I tell myself. And I'm out the door, grabbing my talking points and iPhone on the way out.

6:45 a.m.   *Take Subway to Central Seoul (for live TV interview)*

I have about forty-five minutes to get to the TV broadcasting center. Luckily, I don't live that far away—just a few stops away on the subway (Seoul has a fairly good subway system). I take the stairs and escalators down to the subway platform. While I wait for the subway, I use every second that I can get to review my interview talking points. It's fairly hot in the platform (it's early summer). But when I step into the train, I'm instantly relieved as I feel the chill of the air conditioner on at full throttle. For some reason, when it's chilly or air conditioned, that's when I feel most mentally sharp.

I look around and see other commuters. Seoul is classified as a "megacity" since it has a population of approximately 10 million people, which makes it larger than some other more well-known cities (like Manhattan with approximately 8.4 million people). I take a subtle look around and see all sorts of people—businesspeople, students, elderly folks, and the very occasional foreigner. Most of the younger commuters are looking at some sort of digital device, which is a very "Seoul" thing to do. For most, it's looking at their cell phones for test messaging and TV (through a system called DMB, digital media broadcasting), for some it's gaming devices, and for some it's connecting to the Internet to check e-mail with their smartphones.

Before I know it, the train is at my stop (City Hall station, located in downtown Seoul). I get off the subway along with about half of the other commuters in my subway car, it seems. It's a lot of people, and I then join the herd of other people as they make their way to the subway station exit. I look at my watch—better step it up—I have just ten minutes to get to the studio! I start a slow trot to the building. And since it's early summer, I can feel the sweat beads starting to form around my forehead (oh no, not just before going on TV!).

7:15 a.m.   *Arrive at TV Broadcasting Network Building/Prepare Interview Setup*

I promised to be at the studio by 7:15 a.m., to give the station a ten-minute cushion before the actual live interview. But I'm slightly late. I arrive at 7:20 a.m. and immediately press the up button the elevator after I arrive at the building. I go to the thirteenth floor of the building—the floor dedicated to other foreign (non-Korean) broadcasters (for some reason, they are grouped together on one main floor in the Press Center building).

I rush into the press room for this particular broadcaster (based in the UK). It is smaller than you would think—probably not much larger than a typical living room and dining area in a typical house. When I walk in, I see papers scattered here and there. The floor layout of the place is long and fairly narrow. The first section has several TV screens, computers, and recording equipment. The middle section has a secluded area for radio interviews. The third and farthest section away is where my TV interview will be recorded in just a few short minutes. It's a fairly tight fit—just barely large enough for myself and the camera. Behind me is a fairly large window with a view of downtown Seoul.

After a few seconds from the time I walk in, the TV technician does a quick sound and video check with the Singapore office. But for some reason, the video link is *not* working!! I've done several interviews with this station before, but never with this type of technical hiccup right before we go live on air.

I look at the clock—just four minutes until the live interview. I have an earpiece in my left ear, which allows me to hear the live news broadcast. I hear my name mentioned by the main news announcer in London (where the news is being transmitted from). I ask the technician, "What happens if this video link doesn't work on time?" He quickly replies, "As a default, since your audio is working fine, we can just broadcast your voice and mention your name, like a radio interview, but on TV." It's not the ideal situation, I think to myself, but at least it's something.

What most people don't realize when doing these types of live TV interviews is that most of the time, you do *not* know what questions will be asked to you by the announcer/anchor. Most people assume that I get handed (or e-mailed) a list of questions the day before, and that I have plenty of time to prepare scripted answers. This couldn't be farther from the truth (and how I wish this was true!).

For whatever reason—maybe it's the spontaneous nature of the industry or announcer's desire to exercise his or her freedom to ask whatever questions he or she thinks necessary at the time—this is not the case. Instead, when the live interview begins, it's truly live, and literally anything could happen—I have very little idea of what questions will be asked, apart from the general subject matter of the interview. And in terms of getting a call to request that I do an interview, this varies from a couple days before, to a couple *hours* before the actual interview time. But for today's interview, the call came late last night, which gave me adequate time to form some opinions on the topic (I fortunately didn't need much time to prep since I was following the general subject matter of the interview anyway for my own academic interest).

7:25 a.m.   Live TV Interview (with global news network)

Today's topic is a decision by the central bank (Bank of Korea) to increase its key rate, and its possible affect in the Korean financial markets.

Recall that because of the video link breakdown, I had thought that the interview would be voice only (without video, which is a bit easier to do, since I just need to concentrate on what I'm saying—in a TV interview, I would have to do this plus worry about how it appears to the station's viewers worldwide on a TV screen). But just at the last second—just ninety seconds before air time—the video link for some reason decides to cooperate—and it works! Okay, I say, just a second before I thought that it would just be my voice broadcast over the world. But now, it's going to be my every facial feature and movement that will be broadcast as well. "Okay, it's show time!" I say to myself.

I take a quick look in a small mirror next to me. Well, I figure, "It's not going to get any better than this." And from my perspective, what I see is just a very bright light and a dark camera lens to look into for the interview. There's not even a cameraman, since the camera is on automatic mode. The only way I know that I am actually on TV is through the earpiece when I hear the announcer ask a series of quick questions to me (by the way, the sound quality from the earpiece is mediocre at best at most of these places, which is why you see some people being interviewed having to ask that the announcer repeat the question asked again—oh how I sympathize with them now!).

Doing these live TV interviews requires a particular skill set that no school trains you for (I'm still learning every time). This is because there are so many things to focus on simultaneously. First, I need to hear the question that's being asked to me, clearly and accurately. This is not as easy as you would think (remember what I had to say about the earpiece sound quality). Second, I need to give a well-informed *yet very succinct* answer to the question being asked (usually around ten seconds or less). Most academics have a hard time with these types of time constraints since, in a lecture setting, there's usually plenty of time to say what you need to say. But for me, talking in short prose comes fairly natural now. This may be due to my "previous life" (i.e., former position) as a banker and lawyer sitting in the trading floor—I learned quickly that brevity and simplicity is king. Third, since TV has become increasingly visual (since, based on what I was told by the studio, many people are watching the show while multitasking with other things, like preparing to go to work, eating breakfast, getting children ready for school, etc.), I need to "look the part" (i.e., a young but well-informed professor). Part of this requires a combination of maintaining constant direct and steady eye contact with a dark camera lens (there isn't always a monitor nearby to see how you are looking—believe it or not), along with maintaining an even and steady posture (i.e., you're not swaying or moving around during the interview).

On top of all this is the obvious—that there is no time for a rehearsal or retake—it's absolutely live. And so, once I say something, that's it, there's no Modify or Delete button to press. It's permanently memorialized and seen around the world instantly. But for some reason, this is what I enjoy about it most. I actually look forward to "the moment" when the cameras are on and it's time to go live.

7:45 a.m.   Finish TV Interview/Go to University

Although the interview seems like five hours, in actuality, it just takes five minutes. After I hear the announcer switch to the next topic, I take it as a cue that the interview is over and that I can take out my earpiece and not worry about the camera anymore.

I ask the technician, who was watching the live interview from the front section, how it went. And he seems pretty pleased. "Getting better every time," he says. I also ask for a DVD copy of the interview. I figure it's good for posterity!

After a bit of talk, I say good-bye and head down to the lobby. I feel a few buzzes from my iPhone—it's from people who have just seen me on TV— "Hope you liked it!" I type into my iPhone, and then press the Send button. I also call my wife to see how she liked it (she is my most trusted sounding board, after all). She replies (in her usual understated manner), "You did just fine." Well, that's good enough for me!

I leave the building and walk toward the subway station. I'm going against the flow of commuter traffic at this point, since most people are walking toward the building where I'm coming from (it's now peak commuting time—in Korea, people often arrive at their desks early, often to beat traffic and appease their boss). Although the day hasn't started for most people, I almost feel like I've had a full day already, in a good way.

8:15 a.m.   Arrive at University/Check E-Mail

I take the subway to my university, which is just about fifteen minutes away from City Hall station (the subway stop for the interview). The area in front of my university is known not only for the location of the world's largest all-women's university (some 24,000 graduate and undergraduate students), but also as a marketing hotbed for entry of foreign brands such as the country's first Starbucks (which is constantly packed), Burger King, and Cold Stone. Even though I've been at Ewha University for over half a decade, I'm always very proud to be able to be a faculty member at this storied institution. Not only is it a very prestigious university, but it also represents a beacon of hope for the education of women. Korea's first female lawyer, medical doctor, engineer, and prime minister have all come from Ewha, to cite a few examples.

When I tell people that I teach at Ewha—a women's university—I often get asked the same types of questions. I'll share some of them with you now. The first question is typically, "What is it like to teach at an all-women's university?" My answer is usually, "It's like teaching at any other reputable university, but you just happen to have mostly women as your students." In truth, one of the only few times that I'm really reminded of the fact that I teach at an all women's institution is when I'm entering the main gate of the university when classes have just let out – at which point, hundreds, if not thousands of female students are walking toward (and past) me to leave the university, while I walk the other into the university's main gate. The second question is typically, "Can men take classes at Ewha?" The answer is, "Yes, male students can take classes at Ewha (usually as exchange students), but the university cannot confer a formal, academic degree to male students." In actuality, several male students every year enroll at Ewha as exchange students, mostly (but not always) from Europe and some from nearby universities (like Yonsei or Sogang universities).

Another question I get is, "Why did you leave your high-paying banking and legal career to teach?" I think part of this relates to a story I can share with you now. When I was a university student (which seems like yesterday), I remember my economics professor telling me that, "Every time I pick up my check, I can't help but chuckle a little." What he meant, he went on to explain, is that he really didn't think of his job as a "job" in the traditional sense. In other words, he just loved what he did, almost like a hobby. And that he couldn't believe that he got paid to pursue his passion. Little did I suspect back then that I would be in very similar shoes as him a few years later down the road, and second, that I would feel exactly the same way about my so-called "job." To me, it's a true passion. And I love doing it. The money is gravy.

One misnomer about teaching at a graduate school as a university professor is that it's a job that just requires the professor to show up for a few hours a week for the class lecture, and then the rest of the time is basically "free" time. This may be true at certain smaller liberal arts colleges where teaching is the primary focus and mandate of the faculty. But at a "research university" like Ewha, teaching probably only represents about one-third of my typical twenty-four hour day. The other two-thirds is usually focused on publishing academic papers in "peer-review" journals (i.e., journals where submitted articles are sent out to other academics in the same or similar academic field for review and comment, to decide whether to accept or reject the submitted article) and "administrative" work (i.e., admissions, recruitment, etc.). And when a faculty member gets elevated to a predominantly administrative position—such as dean, associate dean, or department chair (as in my case)—teaching makes up probably even less of my total time, probably around 20 percent or so. This is not because I spend less time teaching, or focusing on teaching—rather, it's that my administrative duties catapult up exponentially.

Back to me walking to the campus. From the university's front gate to my office only takes about five minutes. The university has recently taken on a "green, eco-friendly" theme with a new underground building. The hallmark architectural feature is a religious chapel that is on top of the hill near the front gate (all students are required to take a "chapel" course).

My building is fairly new, and luckily the lobby has a café where I stop by to get (yet another) ice coffee. After I get my drink, I then take the elevator up to my office. I walk in and turn on the lights and my computer (along with the air conditioning and fan). My office is probably where I feel most comfortable, apart from my home. I don't know why. Maybe it's because it represents freedom to me—freedom to teach, freedom to write, and freedom in terms of how to spend most of my time in the way that I think would be most effective. This is in stark contrast to my former banking years when my "office" was a small part of a row in a long line of other people on the trading floor where privacy and freedom was probably the scarcest resource around.

My office has high ceilings. I take full advantage of this by having light colored wood bookshelves stacked all the way to the ceiling on the left side. The right side of my office is divided into two parts, first, my computer area (I have two computers and three monitors—two monitors are for my PC and the third monitor is for my Apple iMac). This setup really helps me get work done much more quickly than if I just had one computer connected to one monitor (studies have shown that dual screens increases productivity by 30 percent or so). The second part of my office on the right side is where I have a medium-sized desk with four chairs around it for meetings (usually with students). On the right side wall are a couple large prints, my favorite being a Mark Rothko framed portrait (an American abstract minimalist painter in the mid-twentieth century).

Although it varies, I try to keep my office as "paperless" as possible. I know this may clash with the image of scattered student papers in professors' offices. But I like to think I'm different. I feel like a clean and organized office reflects a clear and organized mind (I'm not saying this is actually the case, but at least it's something to aim for!).

It takes my computer a few minutes to rev up. After it does, the first thing I do is to log into my e-mail account and check my inbox. After I became department chair, the number of e-mails increased many-fold. This is partly because almost every major decision for the department needs my consideration and final signoff (among a few others). The title is nice, don't get me wrong. But it definitely comes at a price: greater visibility, which translates into greater responsibility.

This morning, I log in to see there are about eighteen e-mails in my inbox. I do my best to answer as many as possible, or else they'll pile up. I try to answer every e-mail within twenty-four hours (a vestige from my banking years). So my e-mail replies may be brief sometimes, but at least I'm returning them!

8:45 a.m.   Prepare (again) for Graduate Law Course

E-mail has a way of making time fly at supersonic speeds sometimes. After what seems like just a few minutes of going through my e-mail, I look at my computer monitor and notice it's 8:45 a.m. already—in other words, just forty-five minutes until I begin a three-hour graduate law course lecture!

I've gone over my lecture notes yesterday afternoon, including the cases that I'll cover in the class. But I also always review my notes again right before the class and read over the cases one final time (to make sure it's all fresh in my mind). I also write down on a mini yellow legal pad the main points I want to cover in class. I also look over the class roster to refresh myself on who the students are in the class.

Just five minutes left. So I put on my jacket, grab the textbooks and lectures, and I'm off to the lecture room (which fortunately is just one floor below). As soon as I step outside my office, I remember a very key thing that I cannot do without—my ice coffee! I always have an ice cold drink with me when I lecture, no matter the season. The caffeine and sugar keeps me energized and the ice-cold temperature makes sure that I'm always highly alert.

I make a quick dash back into the office, grab my ice coffee, close the door, and then take the flight of stairs down one level to the lecture room.

9:30 a.m.   *Begin Graduate Law Course Lecture*

I walk into the lecture room just a bit before 9:30 a.m. I greet the students, who number about fifteen since this is a graduate class (an undergraduate class would be much larger). Of the fifteen students, ten are female students from my university, two are female students from nearby universities (with which we have a credit exchange agreement), and the remaining three students are exchange students (two male and one female from Europe). The room itself is fairly small in size, not like the large auditorium-like lecture halls some may envision. And the desks are arranged in a square so that the students can feel more comfortable talking with each other. So it's more or less a seminar type setting. One wall is made up entirely of windows, which makes for a panoramic view of downtown Seoul with its high-rise office buildings and neon colored store signs.

I place my books, notes, and ice coffee down near the lecture podium. And I begin to write up a few "big picture" concepts on the whiteboard.

These days, more and more professors are using PowerPoint presentations for their lectures (especially in MBA programs). At first, using PowerPoint was tempting for me since it would mean that I would have to write less (my writing is barely legible even on its best days!). But what I came to discover was that students basically have a "movie theater" reaction to PowerPoint slides. In other words, they become spectators than participants, which is the exact opposite of the type of learning environment I want to create. Because of this, I basically have taken a "back to basics approach" and now write down the concepts by hand on the whiteboard. And the students, as a result, get more involved. I also use a "Socratic lite" version of teaching (i.e., I teach by asking questions to specific students). In the US, especially in law schools, this type of teaching is the accepted norm. But outside the US (and especially in Asia, which is based more on a Confucian-based, lecture-style teaching method), it's a very new type of teaching method. Some students like it, some do not.

For today, since the semester is near its tail end, I cover some concepts in international business law related to international contract law, specifically, governing law provisions.

Some professors rely heavily on their notes, almost treating it like a script. Conversely, some don't use (or have) lecture notes, and teach by ad-lib (I call it, the "structured spontaneity" teaching method). I'm probably somewhere in the middle. For me, I always admired presentations by Steve Jobs (Apple's founder). And I try to follow that presentation style somewhat, but obviously with a more academic approach. I do this by keeping my whiteboard notes and any other written materials as simply and clearly as possible. I usually focus on "big picture" concepts first (i.e., the forest) and then zoom in and out on various sub-concepts (i.e., the trees). I do this so that the students always are cognizant of how a specific concept applies in the grand scheme of things. I think that's important, especially as it applies to the real world.

10:45 a.m.   Graduate Law Course Break/Speak with Students/Check E-Mail

For many, teaching three hours in front of others can be daunting. But I love it. And once I get started, time really flies by very quickly (at least from my perspective!). So it's comes as a sudden surprise (again) when I look at the clock to notice that it's 10:45 a.m. —near the halfway point for the three hour class. So I let everyone know that we're taking a fifteen minute break until 11 a.m.

During the break, a couple students come up to me to ask about their final paper. They give me a couple of ideas that they're considering, and then I weigh in on my thoughts. I always tell them that not only must the paper topic be good, but also that the execution of the paper (i.e., the research methodology and writing—both the "art" and the "science" of it) must be done well. Some students ask me, "How do you know what's a good paper and what isn't a good paper?" There's no magic formula when it comes to this. But I think weighing the "art" and "science" elements of a paper is important. And many may be surprised how quickly a professor can tell the level of the paper's quality from even the first couple of paragraphs. It's kind of like a movie or book, you can get a rough (but not fully complete) idea of how good it is fairly quickly into it.

It's still before 11 a.m., so I still have a few minutes until I need to start the second half of my lecture. I decide to take the stairs one level up back to my office to check my e-mail again. I look and see that there are already six more e-mails just in the span of the last hour and a half or so. Some are directed specifically for me (in the "to:" section) while with the others, I am cc'd. I flag the e-mails that I can't answer right away for later. But mostly, I try to answer my e-mails as quickly as possible, or else they just accumulate, with the chance of forgetting or not returning those e-mails gaining higher with each passing day. So instead, just like with regular mail and paper, I also like to keep the number of e-mails in my inbox to a minimum (but sometimes I have little choice but to store very important e-mails in electronic files).

At 11:00 a.m., I resume the class. The previous week, I assigned some international business law cases for certain students to present to the class this week. So now, the assigned students go up in front of the class to summarize and analyze the cases assigned to them. Often they use PowerPoint. And sometimes they do role-plays. It varies, which I think is a good thing—to each, their own (to a reasonable degree)!

12:15 p.m.   Graduate Law Course Ends

I look at the clock and it's almost 12:15 p.m., the time when the class is scheduled to end. I make a few final points to the class for next week's lecture. And I let the class know that I'm available during my office hours as well as via e-mail. Then I end the class with a "Good job everyone, and see you next week!"

Some people may wonder whether teaching becomes repetitive or monotonous. I admit this was one perception that I had before entering academia. But I actually find it not to be the case at all. The course objective, topics and textbooks can all be changed at any time (and often they are). And at least in my department, I am fairly free to teach what courses I want (along with my time and even lecture room preferences). And in terms of research and publications, I'm also free to choose what topics I think I should write about.

The only caveat is that academia is largely a solo/individual effort, although of course there can be collaboration with other academics. So if you are a fairly social person who really enjoys the idea of constant interaction with other people on a consistent basis, then academia may or may not be for you. This is in contrast to, say, a business setting, where teamwork and coordination with other divisions is often needed and seen as critically important. But having said all this, at least for my case, everything so far has worked out great—probably the best career move I have ever made was becoming a professor. For a person like me, who was under constant supervision and micromanagement in the banking sector before entering academia, having this type of freedom (in academia) is priceless and even necessary (to help foster creativity and allow me the flexibility to choose the best way to maximize the use of my time). I think the guys at places like Google probably figured this out a while ago too.

12:30 p.m.   *Meet Faculty Members for Lunch*

Today, after my class, I'm having lunch with several other international faculty members. During the semester, we try to do this on Wednesdays at 12:30 p.m. The meeting place is at the front gate of the university. I arrive just a couple minutes before. And there are about three faculty members there already. After a few more minutes, a few others show up. Today, the group is composed of mostly Europeans and Americans (as well as a faculty member from China).

Our first order of business is deciding where to eat lunch. There are plenty of choices, maybe too many choices—I say this because such choices cause our group to ponder the situation almost like an academic "research question." Finally, after a few minutes of deliberation, a decision is made:

we end up choosing a nearly restaurant that's known for their spicy chicken and noodle dishes.

In terms of interpersonal dynamics, everyone's fairly easy to get along with in this group. Some of the conversation is "talking shop" about what's happening in the university, our fields, or even social lives. But because of the FIFA World Cup season fast approaching, the dominant topic is which teams have the best chance of winning it all this year. The German contingent feels good about their chances. I put in a vote for Brazil and Team USA as a dark horse for the quarterfinals (hey, why not, anything can happen, right?).

What I find refreshing about the academic setting is that things aren't so rushed. There's time to think, debate, and ponder. While working in the private sector, I always felt like we were rushing to the finish line (i.e., for the trade to close), with never a chance to take in the surroundings. For many, maybe most, the "prize money" at the end of the finish line was what counted (i.e., the deal was a means to the end—money). But I always felt like there was, or should, be more to life than just money. For those who think otherwise, then academia may not be your cup of tea.

Speaking of hot drinks, after lunch, we have another "mini conference" about where to go for a cup of coffee. It seems that almost every other store is a coffee shop these days (no complaints from me though). Ultimately, we choose a place that has an outdoor patio with shade (a must!). After ordering and talking a bit more (mostly still continuing the World Cup discussion theme), we make our way back to the university— some have office hours, some have to finish papers, and some have to teach.

1:45 p.m.   Come Back to Office/Check (Regular) Mail in Faculty Mailbox

I enter my building and press the eleventh floor button—this is where the main administrative offices for my department are located. I leave the elevator and then first check with the administrative staff whether there are any forms I need to sign off on. To which they inform me, "Why yes, there's a few waiting for you." I look at them—request to change concentration majors, request to transfer credit from another university, and a request to amend a budget issue—they all seem okay, so I sign and date the forms.

I then check my faculty mailbox. I'm the tallest faculty member in the department, yet my mailbox is near the very bottom. No problem—it will help with my dexterity! The mail is a combination of notices and invitations to various functions (such as conferences, special lectures, etc.). I sift through them quickly and throw out what I don't need (per my "paperless office" mantra!).

2:00 p.m.   *Office Hours for Students*

I hold weekly office hours for the students in my courses. When I'm teaching an undergraduate class, office hours are fairly busy (for all sorts of things, including internship and career advice, applying to graduate school, etc). I enjoy this time very much since I know I'm making a direct impact on their academic future.

As I walk toward my office, I notice that one student scheduled for 2 p.m. is already waiting for me outside my office door. In Asia, the hierarchy between professors and students tend to be greater than in the United States. So as part of this, students tend not to be late (they usually arrive slightly early) when meeting a professor. This particular student is interested in applying to US law schools after graduation. And she would like to know what the field of law (and practicing law) is "really like." I tell her, "It's a terrific question, and it just so happens that I have this book coming out soon, called *24 Hours with 24 Lawyers: Profiles of Traditional and Non-Traditional Careers* that covers exactly this issue!" We chat a bit specifically relating to why she's interested in law school, and I try to paint a picture of what certain types of lawyers do. I also let her know that the JD degree is fairly broad, which, if leveraged strategically, can add a lot of career options for her, just as the JD degree did for my career.

By this time, I hear a knock on the door—it's an "urgent" administrative form that I need to sign right away (I've come to realize that many such related things are deemed "urgent," but this one I'm told is "especially urgent"). So I look over the document and sign it. Also, I see yet another student hovering near my doorway. It turns out she has a question also.

4:00 p.m.   *Conduct Monthly Faculty Meeting*

Part of the virtues of being department chair is that I lead the monthly faculty meetings. Sometimes these meetings cover routine things like announcements. Other times, the meetings cover more contentious issues (such as faculty recruitment). Because faculty hires can and often stick around for a long time (especially after tenure), the faculty are particularly sensitive about what type of person they want to bring into the department. This can be based on all sorts of factors (as you will soon read).

Today's meeting is fairly short because it just so happens that we are having a "job talk" for a person who is applying to our department in less than an hour. So I make a few announcements, and ask the faculty what expectations they have in terms of the faculty member they want to hire. The responses are varied and slightly cautious. But as I will come to find out, there will be much more feedback about this after the job talk ends.

4:45 p.m.   *Job Talk (for possible faculty hire)*

A job talk is a nerve-racking experience for many people. Imagine having to present a paper (usually a peer reviewed, published article by the person giving the job talk) to a fairly well-informed and well-educated group of possible future long-time colleagues.

Today's job talk will be in two parts—the presentation followed by a Q&A session.

The presenter is a newly minted PhD holder from one of the premiere Ivy League schools. Before I joined academia, I had thought that what university you attend was one of the most important, if not the, most important issue considered. But now that I've been in academia for several years, I've come to discover that the main issue (in most cases) is what papers you have published, and where your papers have been published, as long as you meet a certain minimum threshold criteria (in terms of your alma mater).

The paper topic presented relates to Korea's colonial period. The presenter uses a PowerPoint presentation, which includes some interesting photos of the subject matter that he researched. The presentation is not the most exciting that I've seen, but it's clear and logical. After about thirty minutes, the presentation is finished. And then a series of questions are asked to the candidate from, "Why did you apply to Ewha University?" and "What courses offered at our department do you think you are qualified to teach?" to questions related to the research methodology of the presented paper.

After the Q&A session is over and no one has further questions, I walk the candidate out the room to the elevator and thank him for coming over to make the presentation. I then return to where the job talk was held to have our internal evaluation of the candidate.

To me, it seems that the candidate has a lot of promise and potential. And most of the others seem to agree. But one or two faculty members raise their objections, "I don't think his research interest and focus area will be interesting enough for our students," "He's too focused on Korea's historical colonial period, but most of our students are focused on contemporary issues," to quote a couple perspectives.

In our department, one objection from a faculty member is usually all that's needed to reject a candidate. And this is exactly what happens here today. Well, I think to myself, sooner or later we've got to hire somebody. But I guess that day isn't going to be today.

5:45 p.m.   *Finish Edits for Op-Ed Piece*

One thing I really enjoy about my job is the opportunity of writing opinion-editorial pieces (op-eds) for various newspapers. For me, there's just not enough time to write about all the things I'd like to. For others, it's the reverse problem (i.e., having difficulty finding a topic to write about). I must have written more than fifty op-eds in the past few years. It's not because it's required by my university or that I receive some type of research credit for it. In fact, neither is the case. It's just something I like to do. When I buy the newspaper, open it up and see my name (and sometimes picture) in print next to the article I wrote, it gives me a terrific sense of accomplishment and satisfaction—more than when I used to help close trades in banking, and more than writing a more "technical" and "academic" research article for a peer review journal. Part of this is that the op-ed readership covers all sorts of people—college students, other academics, business people, diplomats, and everything in between. For me, I've always gained a lot of pleasure knowing that I could be influencing such a potentially large group of people, apart from a select group of "experts" dedicated to a particular journal.

Since I have a half hour before my next appointment, I use it to finish the edit requests of an op-ed piece I wrote and submitted recently to a prominent US-based financial newspaper. The topic relates to real estate "bubbles" in Korea. It's a touchy subject. And at the time of the op-ed piece, most people thought that the local market was *not* in a so-called bubble. But I relish being the contrarian in some cases, especially when the commonly held view seems questionable. I look at some central bank data, along with a few other primary sources, to update and modify the piece, and then submit it back to the editor. I'm impressed just how good the suggestions from the editor are. And I get the feeling that the person who reviewed my piece had a very firm understanding of the topic at hand (which is not easy to do when you're covering so many topics as an editor does).

7:05 p.m.   *Meet Friends for Dinner*

Tonight I'm having a small reunion with some friends of mine I knew when I lived and worked in Tokyo. Most of them are from the States, but some are from Korea. We chose to meet at a TexMex restaurant near the university.

I walk in and the place is extremely crowded and pretty loud. There are people with Coronas and margaritas in hand. And most important for me, this is the one place in Korea where I can eat my absolute favorite Mexican dish—the carna asada burrito!

I am the second person to arrive. We chat about our old days in Tokyo (when we were all in banking). We were all single then. But now most of us are married with kids. After a while, the others show up and we order food as well as drinks.

It's really good to see everyone. And it made me realize just how quickly time flies by. We originally met nearly ten years ago—has it been that long? Well, I figure, as I pick up my margarita, here's to ten more!

10:35 p.m.   *Arrive Home/Greet Wife and Mini Dog*

After I say good-bye at the restaurant, I take the subway back to my home. After getting off the subway, I take a local bus that goes directly next to my apartment complex (in Korea, most younger families live in large high-rise apartment complexes since land is relatively scarce compared to places such as the United States).

When I get to open the door to my apartment—even before I begin to unlock the front door—I hear my dog, Jonny, barking his hellos (Jonny's a "mini-pin" the size of a small handbag but with the bark of a Labrador!). He was actually my wife's dog before we got married. At first, I didn't know what to make of the little (short-haired) guy. But one thing I noticed right away, he's a sharp fellow. He knows just when and how to ask for food and treats.

I walk in and my wife is there to greet me also. She's on the computer reading the latest entries from one of her favorite cooking websites. I'm glad someone in the house likes to cook, while the other likes to eat (hint: I'm the one who likes to eat!). My wife and I chitchat about the day. And then I turn on the air conditioner (it's a hot summer day, is my excuse).

11:15 p.m.   *Check E-Mail (again)*

I'm a bit of an e-mail junkie. So although it's been just a few hours since I last checked my e-mail, I can't help resist checking what's in my in-box again. Checking my e-mail with my iPhone is almost too easy and quick to do. If not for it, I'd have to grab my notebook, press the on button and then wait for several long minutes for the machine to boot up (and shut down afterwards). Now, I just press a couple of buttons and then I have instant access to my e-mail and the Internet. It's definitely part of the iPhone's charm.

So I press the e-mail button on my iPhone and in streams my latest e-mail. There's about seven, mostly from the university headquarters, none pertaining directly to me. I then can't help but check the latest sports news. In particular, I'm a huge basketball fan (NBA and NCAA). I try to stay on top of things when it comes to the latest news about players and teams. One thing that has really given me a lot of joy recently is a paid Internet service to watch regular and playoff games in real time or delayed. I know for those in the States, this can be taken for granted. But for me in Korea, it's quite a treat!

11:45 p.m.   *Try to Catch the Late Night News/Fall Asleep*

Before sleeping, I try to wind down with some TV shows on cable. South Korea has a surprising number of TV sitcoms from the United States aired, and fortunately, they are usually not dubbed (there are Korean subtitles near the bottom of the screen instead).

I'm starting to get drowsy. Maybe it's because it's late or maybe it's because I woke up fairly early this morning. At any rate, I take it as a sign that it's time for bed. My wife and dog are fast asleep by now—as I will be in just a few short minutes.

5:25 a.m.   *Alarm Clock Rings (press the snooze button)*

I must have forgotten to turn off the alarm for 5:25 a.m. yesterday morning. No early morning TV interview today means no early wakeup call needed— so I push the snooze button with glee!

Final Thoughts

I absolutely enjoy what I do. It's almost like a hobby for me, and so the pay is just a bonus. When I was in banking, I constantly thought, "They don't pay me enough to do this." But now, as a law professor, I think, "I can't believe I'm getting paid to do something I love to do."

Having said this, academia isn't for everyone. It's a much slower pace than the private sector. And if you don't like being around the university environment and with students, then that's another sign that there may be better options for you elsewhere.

For me, I always enjoyed reading, writing, and being around energetic and enthusiastic young people. I see so much potential in them—with their hopes and their dreams. I figure I can potentially be an instrumental part of their lives through the medium of higher education. In other words, I can make a difference in their lives (as opposed to making wealthier people and companies even more wealthy).

Everyone has to find his or her calling. I was fortunate enough to find it where I am today. So if you like to think and ponder things at a slightly deeper level than most, are not excessively materialistic, and like the freedom to do research and write about what interests you, then academia just may be the calling for you as it was for me.

16

Profile 16
Karen: Energy Law Attorney

Executive Summary

Name: Karen
Profile: Energy Law Attorney
Location: Los Angeles, California

After working at a large law firm and earning the big bucks, Karen left this behind to become in-house legal counsel for the primary electricity supply company in the Southern California region. Her position as an energy lawyer provides a more predictable schedule and the ability to balance work with family. As one of the senior attorneys at her firm, Karen still manages a sizeable workload relating to the complex plethora of energy laws when dealing with renewable power. Her twenty-four-hour day is filled with responsibilities such as leading ad-hoc conferences with other energy industries and meeting in-house clients to best meet the ratepayers' needs. She also gladly dedicates some of her precious time to take part in pro bono work as a way of giving back to the community. Given the importance of the energy industry, Karen considers herself lucky to work in an environment surrounded with intelligent people where her work is appreciated, as you will see when you read her twenty-four-hour career profile.

Profile

Career Field:	Energy Law
Current Position:	In-House Legal Counsel
Institution:	Regulated Investor-Owned Utility
Location:	Los Angeles, California
Previous Position(s):	Large Law Firms in Los Angeles and New York City, In-House at Fortune 100 Companies
Education:	JD, Columbia University, School of Law
	BS, University of Illinois, Urbana-Champaign
Licensed (Y/N):	Yes
Jurisdictions:	New York/California

Schedule

6:55 a.m.	Wake-Up/Check BlackBerry/Cuddle with Five-Year Old Son
7:05 a.m.	Prepare for the Day
7:45 a.m.	Drive to the Office
8:30 a.m.	Arrive at the Office
8:45 a.m.	Check E-Mail/Voicemail
9:00 a.m.	Meeting with GC (General Counsel) (re: strategy to avoid exposure to potential antitrust claims)
9:35 a.m.	Call Partner at Outside Legal Counsel
9:50 a.m.	Follow Up Call to Attorney Representing Renewable Energy Seller
10:00 a.m.	Conference Call with Industry Participants (re: document update)
10:55 a.m.	Teleconference with Renewable Energy Seller's Attorney (re: PPA)
11:12 a.m.	Impromptu Discussion with In-House Clients (re: miscellaneous issues)
11:15 a.m.	Meeting with In-House Clients (re: upcoming RFO)
12:00 p.m.	Lunch with Colleagues
1:15 p.m.	Discuss Travel Arrangements for Upcoming Conference with Assistant
1:30 p.m.	Pro Bono Committee Meeting
2:30 p.m.	Call from Son (re: after-school schedule)

2:35 p.m.	Review Novation Agreement
4:00 p.m.	Presentation to Executive Committee (re: peaker issue)
5:05 p.m.	Chat with Colleague (re: indemnity provisions)
5:40 p.m.	LA Lakers NBA game in Company's Luxury Suite at Staples Center
7:30 p.m.	Leave before Half-Time to Get Home before Son's Bedtime
8:00 p.m.	Arrive Home
8:05 p.m.	Bedtime Routine with Son
9:00 p.m.	E-Mail Friends/Spend Time with Husband/Google "damper recipe"
10:30 p.m.	Check BlackBerry (again)
10:40 p.m.	Go to Sleep
6:55 a.m.	Wake-Up (for another 24 hours!)

24-Hour Schedule

6:55 a.m.   *Wake-Up/Check BlackBerry/Cuddle with Five-Year Old Son*

Wake-up time. I check the clock (unless I have an unusually early meeting or flight, I don't set an alarm). I then grab my BlackBerry to check my morning meeting schedule and any urgent e-mails. My five-year old son has been waiting for this moment—as soon as he sees signs of waking he crawls into bed next to me and unleashes a deluge of questions, "Can I have pancakes for breakfast?" "Do I have tennis today?" "When will you be home from work?" "Can I watch TV?" After the requisite answers are provided, he skips downstairs to have breakfast.

7:05 a.m.   *Prepare for the Day*

As I shower, I mentally review my "to-do" list for the day. Unfortunately, one of my brightest in-house clients recently announced that she is moving on to another company. I ponder who her replacement will be and how much time it will take before the replacement and I are on the same page. In-house practice differs greatly from a law firm in this respect. At the firm, I handled different clients as different projects heated up. In my capacity as in-house counsel, I repeatedly work with the same clients, which makes our working rapport vitally important.

I wander into my closet with the day's schedule in mind to gauge the level of formality required for the day. I recall that I have a meeting with our general counsel (GC) and select a pale gray skirt suit and a tailored shirt. I allow myself a bit of personality by adding a colorful silk scarf that I purchased on my last trip overseas. Another interesting aspect of in-house practice is that our dress code leans to the conservative side of professional. At the firm, the number of billable hours packed into the week was often directly related to the sloppiness of an associate's attire—a disheveled appearance was the battle scar of billing eighty-plus billable hours per week. Younger law firm associates also tended to be more fashion forward. In-house at my particular organization, I sense that our GC wants his lawyers to present a conservative and professional image on behalf of the company.

My son rushes into my arms for a good-bye hug. I marvel at how fast he's grown and linger for a moment before I gather my briefcase and keys. I notice a smudge of pancake syrup on my blouse. I give him an extra kiss, then rush back upstairs to change my outfit because of this unexpected event.

7:45 a.m.   *Drive to the Office*

Los Angeles traffic is notoriously bad. My normal thirty-five minute commute to the office can take an hour (or more!) depending on traffic. I use the time in the car to listen to satellite radio and catch up on news and world events or to make personal or work-related calls. I inevitably receive a call from my husband or son regarding some detail of the day's events or a morning mishap. Luckily, panicked calls from clients are rare—unlike my days at a law firm.

8:30 a.m.   *Arrive at the Office*

Although lawyers at my company generally arrive somewhere between 8:30 and 9:00 a.m., our in-house energy and gas traders are in by 6 a.m. and most of the business personnel arrive well-before 8:00 a.m. This makes mornings a busy time for me. As a senior attorney, one of the perks I receive is reserved parking in the management lot. This doesn't sound like much until you realize that I'm competing for parking with the 3,000 or so other employees who work onsite!

8:45 a.m. *Check E-Mail/Voicemail*

As I wade through the e-mail and voicemail that has accrued and prep for my upcoming meeting with our GC, I realize there is no way I will have time to grab breakfast from the company cafeteria. I settle for a candy bar and a soda from the vending machine and make a mental note to eat better tomorrow.

9:00 a.m. *Meeting with GC (General Counsel) (re: strategy to avoid exposure to potential antitrust claims)*

As a utility company that provides power and gas service to more than 4 million customers (known as "ratepayers"), we are heavily regulated by the state's Public Utilities Commission or PUC. In addition, we must comply with the same federal and state laws that other companies face. These sometimes competing interests require us to be vigilant in ensuring that we are in full compliance with all laws and regulations while still meeting our ratepayers' needs.

The purpose of today's meeting is to touch base with our GC regarding advice we've received from outside legal counsel on avoiding exposure to potential antitrust claims. I am respectful of his time and try to keep the meeting brief—I lay out key background information, highlight the areas of concern, and present our options along with my pitch for the best approach. I field questions and jot down areas to clarify with our outside legal counsel.

9:35 a.m. *Call Partner at Outside Legal Counsel*

I call the partner at the firm handling our antitrust concerns (we work with several large outside law firms depending on their area of expertise needed) to flesh out the issues raised by our GC. The partner is smart and very experienced, but she has a tendency to present both sides of an issue and hover around the middle ground. From my perspective, we (as the client) are paying for her expertise (as our outside legal counsel) and I push her to recommend the best course of action. She promises to get me a draft of a document we discussed by the end of the day.

9:50 a.m.   *Follow Up Call to Attorney Representing Renewable Energy Seller*

In the 1990s, several changes in laws made it illegal for US utilities to own both power generation and power distribution operations. Although restrictions have since softened and my company owns a number of generation facilities, in order to provide the remainder of the power its customers need, my company must go out into the power market to purchase energy. This is especially true on the renewable front since most renewable generation is not utility owned. In order to purchase renewable power, we generally enter into a power purchase agreement (referred to as a PPA) with the seller.

One of our sellers is unable to meet a required condition by the deadline required in its PPA, giving us the right to terminate the PPA due to the seller's default. The deadline is fast approaching and we are amenable to amending the PPA to address the deficiency. However, my in-house clients have been unable to reach the seller's contact on the business side. I've placed a call to their attorney in an attempt to expedite the process, but haven't been able to reach her so far.

I leave another message.

10:00 a.m.   *Conference Call with Industry Participants (re: document update)*

In addition to PPAs, our power, gas, and financial transactions may be governed by a number of industry-standard documents, including agreements published by the International Swaps and Derivatives Association Inc. (ISDA), North American Energy Standards Boards (NAESB), and Edison Electric Institute (EEI), among others. The documents are base documents (also known as a "pro forma") that have been developed as an agreed-on starting point through the consensus of multiple parties from all aspects of the industry (marketers, sellers, buyers, public utilities, investor-owned utilities, etc.). Due to a potential change in

PUC regulations, we have formed an *ad hoc* drafting committee to modify one of the standard documents accordingly.

I'm now leading the group of more than twenty participants from a wide range of backgrounds. It's a challenging task to get a group this diverse on track and to adopt a single viewpoint, that I can then memorialize into writing. After months of conference calls, our progress is slow, but steady. After the call concludes, my in-house clients nod approvingly as they leave my office. But I feel like I've spent the hour herding cats.

10:55 a.m.   *Teleconference with Renewable Energy Seller's Attorney (re: PPA)*

As I'm about to leave my office for my next meeting, my assistant pops in to tell me that the attorney representing the renewable power seller that I've been trying to reach is now on the line. The call will make me late for my next meeting, but I really need to speak with her.

It turns out that the business contact on her side is traveling and unavailable for the day. I lay out the issue and give our range of possible solutions. But in the end, I have to tell her that this is a business issue—not a legal one— and someone from her side with the authority to make a business call will need to contact us by the end of the day in order to resolve the issue in time. Like many in-house counsel, we guide our clients regarding business matters from a legal purview. But the ultimate resolutions and decisions that affect the business lie with them.

11:12 a.m.   *Impromptu Discussion with In-House Clients (re: miscellaneous issues)*

On my way to my next meeting, I run into two clients who only need "a moment" of my time to discuss a few small issues that have arisen. This is another unique aspect of in-house practice—working in the same building as my clients makes us both more accessible to one another. We chat as I walk to my next meeting, but it's clear that their issues are larger than a moment's discussion. I ask them to work with my assistant to calendar time for a meeting since I'm already late for my 11 a.m. meeting.

11:15 a.m.   Meeting with In-House Clients (re: upcoming RFO)

In order to purchase additional gas or energy to meet our ratepayers' needs, several times each year we conduct Requests for Offers (RFOs) in which we solicit potential sellers to make formal offers with respect to certain products depending on our needs. Based on the offers, we select those sellers that look best able to meet our needs and begin PPA negotiations. Today's meeting is to discuss the parameters and details of an upcoming RFO. Although many of the issues that arise aren't legal issues per se, I am still looked to for advice and guidance. This is one of the aspects of my job that I appreciate.

At my company, lawyers are generally well respected. I say this because sometimes this unfortunately is not always the case. As an in-house lawyer, I don't represent my clients as individuals, but rather the company as a whole. As a consequence, the advice I give is sometimes in opposition to what a particular individual wants to do, but is on the whole the best approach for the company. This can cause friction, but at the end of the day, I know my input is valued.

12:00 p.m.   Lunch with Colleagues

I've been checking e-mail from my BlackBerry all day. I send off a few quick replies and then depart for lunch with some of my colleagues. There are more than ninety lawyers in our law department. We have a number of younger attorneys, a few of whom are friends of mine from law school, which makes the office environment congenial and easy-going.

We usually grab something quick in the company cafeteria, but today is a colleague's birthday, so we head out to a local restaurant for a longer lunch. At the end of lunch, we embarrass her by having the waitress bring out a candle-laden dessert to commemorate the occasion. After the festivities, we head back to the office.

1:15 p.m.   Discuss Travel Arrangements for Upcoming Conference with Assistant

In a few weeks, I will be attending an industry conference. The conference will be a great opportunity to learn more about certain aspects of my field and to get to know key players in the industry—the conference also happens to be in a well-known ski area, so I look forward to some time on the slopes. I work with my assistant to figure out the best travel arrangements and sort out my schedule.

1:30 p.m.   *Pro Bono Committee Meeting*

Pro bono work (done in exchange for little or no compensation to help society) has always been important to me so I jumped at the opportunity to head the law department's Pro Bono Committee. The Committee spearheads a variety of projects including those that help veterans and underpaid low-income workers as well as helping with the adoptions of children in Los Angeles' foster care system. I'm grateful that my company values public service. Today's meeting is to discuss which projects would be a good experience for the law department's summer interns.

2:30 p.m.   *Call from Son (re: after-school schedule)*

My son and his nanny are having a disagreement over his after-school schedule. I mediate the dispute, remind my son to do his homework, and tell him he cannot have another cookie, but he is welcome to a healthy snack. This type of scenario is becoming increasingly common, and reflects the balancing act required between family and work that a legal professional like me must face. Fortunately, unlike private practice at a large law firm, my current in-house position affords me the environment in which to keep up on family concerns.

2:35 p.m.   *Review Novation Agreement*

One of our counterparties recently underwent a merger. A variety of circumstances, including a significant change in corporate structure such as this, can trigger the need to review (and possibly amend, novate, or terminate) all of the agreements we have in place. Depending on the products that we transact with the counterparty, we may have ISDA, EEI, NAESB, and other agreements in place. The merger may mean a change in the counterparty's credit rating as well, which requires discussions with our credit and risk people. In this instance, only a straightforward novation of an existing agreement will be required, including certain changes to the counterparty's credit requirements. The counterparty's attorney sent over a draft Novation Agreement, but it doesn't address our concerns. More importantly, a novation can be an opportunity to renegotiate provisions that are no longer market standard—something we may consider here.

4:00 p.m.   *Presentation to Executive Committee (re: peaker issue)*

As a member of the transaction group in our Law Department, I sometimes deal with unusual issues. In this case, an issue has arisen in connection with construction of a PUC-approved "peaker" plant (a peaker plant provides emergency power in peak demand situations where existing generation can't keep up with demand or where there is an unforeseen transmission or generation outage).

Today's presentation to our executive committee (generally comprised of our president, CEO, and various vice presidents) gives them an overview of the situation and seeks approval of the solution the business unit and I have developed. Although my manager, as well as our assistant general counsel (AGC) and GC are all present, they let me handle the presentation. I field a number of tangentially related and unexpected questions (including "How much water does a commercial toilet use per year?"—more surprising than the question was that someone else in the session actually knew! Whew!).

5:05 p.m.   *Chat with Colleague (re: indemnity provisions)*

I run into a colleague in the hall and stop him with a question regarding the indemnity provisions in our pro forma PPA. The potential seller has some issues with the way the section is drafted. Due to the large number of transactions that we handle, our goal is to have a fair and consistent approach that adequately protects the interests of the company and the ratepayers. Since my colleague has worked on these PPAs for several years, I chat with him about possible solutions. He has some great input and I am once again reminded of what a pleasure it is to work with such smart and congenial coworkers.

5:40 p.m.   *LA Lakers NBA game in Company's Luxury Suite at Staples Center*

My company subscribes to a luxury suite at the Staples Center. My committee was offered tonight's tickets to a Lakers game as a "thank you" for our hard work on several recent projects. Tonight's event is important because I want to show my committee members how much I appreciate their hard work. In addition to outings such as these, I also receive a number of invitations to charity events for non-profit organizations sponsored by my company. I try to limit my evening work commitments to one or two events each month so that I can spend more time with my son. A key reason that I left my previous job in a big law firm was so that I could have a more predictable schedule and more time to spend with my son.

There's a full spread of hor d'oeuvres, sushi, and snacks as well as wine and cocktails. I enjoy the food and company as the pre-game show wraps up. The Staples Center is packed and I see Jack Nicholson in his usual courtside seat.

7:30 p.m.   *Leave before Half-time to Get Home before Son's Bedtime*

The game is fast-paced and exciting, but I need to leave a bit early in order to make it home before my son's bedtime. Again, another reminder of how one must constantly try to seek a happy medium between work and family demands. The suite steward comes by with the dessert cart brimming with amazing choices. I can't decide, so my friend and I opt to share two desserts—smores cake and their signature caramel apple. Once again, I make a mental note to eat better tomorrow. And to get some exercise. I'm a little sad to leave all the fun behind, and can't imagine how envious the other fans sitting watching the game would be of such choice seats as mine. But still, duty calls. So I bid my colleagues a good evening and head home.

8:00 p.m.   *Arrive Home*

Thankfully, traffic was light and I made it home in record time. Our house is in a suburban area that is further from my office than I'd like, but it has amazing schools and parks and the area is ideal for families. As soon as I step in the door, I hear my son clamoring down the hall from his playroom. He rushes into my arms and buries his head in my neck. After a quick hug, he begins to recount everything that happened to him during the day— evidence of another lawyer in the making?

8:05 p.m.   *Bedtime Routine with Son*

After the usual routine (bath, pajamas, books), I settle my son into bed.

9:00 p.m.   *E-Mail Friends/Spend Time with Husband/Google "damper recipe"*

With my son now fast asleep, I settle onto the sofa with my computer and my husband. I'm grateful that my husband is able to come home early on evenings like this when I have work commitments. Although I sometimes miss the fast pace (and huge salary!) of my previous law firm job, one of the perks of my current position is that life is much less complicated now that my schedule is more predictable. It's in a sense a trade-off between quality of life and income.

I chat with my husband about his day, catch up on e-mail to friends, and research how to make damper—Australian campfire bread—for my son's upcoming International Day festival at school. I then flip through a potential seller's latest markup of the PPA we are negotiating and make some notes for tomorrow's call. I try to watch a sitcom that I recorded earlier, but I'm too tired to really focus and enjoy it after a long day.

10:30 p.m.   *Check BlackBerry (again)*

My previous job primarily involved cross-border transactions. So I would wake several times a night to check my BlackBerry and often have conference calls to close international deals in the middle of the night to accommodate for the schedules of the various other parties involved in the deal. Old habits die hard, as I check my BlackBerry (again).

10:40 p.m.   *Go to Sleep*

Although the pay scale is a lot lower in-house, a good night's sleep is priceless! I set my BlackBerry to silent mode and go to sleep.

6:55 a.m. *Wake-Up (for another 24 hours!)*

I wake-up to a kiss from my son and a demand for toast with peanut butter – another day in my life as an energy attorney!

Final Thoughts

Law school has been a great foundation for my career and for my life. The rigorous academic environment and the terrific alumni connections have been enormously helpful to me throughout my career. Overall, I am very pleased with my decision to attend law school and happy with my life as a lawyer.

17

Profile 17
Mike: Technology and Banking Lawyer

Executive Summary

Name:	Mike
Profile:	Technology and Banking Lawyer (In-House)
Location:	Milwaukee, Wisconsin

As an in-house lawyer for a large technology and banking firm, Mike tries to successfully juggle his work and family. Liaising with fellow colleagues (who are his internal "clients") and facilitating negotiations in conference calls with outside legal counsel is a regular part of what Mike does on a daily basis as a technology and banking lawyer. He is also responsible for drafting IT software agreements, in-house policies as well as sorting out related legal company matters. Mike also tries to keep up with his outside research to use as a benchmark for future corporate policy. Overall, compared to working at a law firm, the relatively flexible schedule—in the form of less e-mail and more alone time—fits more into Mike's work style than with a large law firm. If you see yourself having similar traits with Mike's working style preferences, being an in-house attorney working on various IT issues may be an interesting line of work, as the next twenty-four-hour profile will show.

Profile

Career Field:	Technology/Banking
Current Position:	In-House Legal Counsel
Institution:	US-Based Bank Holding Company
Location:	Milwaukee
Previous Position(s):	Large Chicago Law Firm, In-House Legal Counsel, Large Atlanta Law Firm
Education:	JD, Rutgers University, School of Law
	MIA, Columbia University
	BA, University of Georgia
Licensed (Y/N):	Yes
Jurisdictions:	Illinois/Georgia

Schedule

6:30 a.m.	Wake-Up (when my three-year old wakes me up)
6:35 a.m.	Take Shower and Get Ready
7:00 a.m.	Get Kid Ready for Preschool
7:15 a.m.	Skim First Section of *The Wall Street Journal*/Eat Breakfast
7:40 a.m.	Get in the Car/Drop off Kid at Preschool/Head to the Office
8:00 a.m.	Arrive at Work
8:05 a.m.	Check E-Mails and Voicemails
8:20 a.m.	Make a Coffee Run to Starbucks
8:30 a.m.	Make List of To-Do's for the Day
8:40 a.m.	Return Phone Calls
9:00 a.m.	Law Department Meeting
10:00 a.m.	Legal Research (re: drafting the company's social media policy)
12:00 p.m.	Go to Lunch/Finish Reading the Paper
12:45 p.m.	Review and Provide Comments to Inbound Software Licensing Agreement
2:15 p.m.	Conference Call with IT Department (re: to discuss roll out of new software platform)
3:00 p.m.	Read Client Alert and Internal Privacy Policy
4:00 p.m.	Research Check Fraud Issue
5:30 p.m.	Conference Call with Outside Counsel

6:00 p.m.	Review Regulatory Updates
6:30 p.m.	Go Home
7:05 p.m.	Prepare to Eat Dinner
10:00 p.m.	Read Various Literature on Current Work Matters/Watch some TV
11:30 p.m.	Go to Bed
6:30 a.m.	Wake-Up to Three-year Old (repeat)

24-Hour Schedule

6:30 a.m.   *Wake-Up (when my three-year old wakes me up)*

I abruptly wake-up in disbelief when my three-year-old daughter climbs into my bed to wake me up—as if today is the first time this has ever happened. I turn on the TV and let her catch up on some cartoons while I slowly make my way over to the bathroom and brush my teeth. With the sound of the various TV cartoon characters in the background, I turn on my electric toothbrush.

6:35 a.m.   *Take Shower and Get Ready*

I jump into the shower's piping hot water. This is one of the few rare down times for me, being both a working professional, a loving husband to my beautiful wife, and most recently, a proud father of a young beautiful daughter. So I take this relatively precious time to soak in the water and steam while also trying to relax—this is because I know that once I get out of the shower, the day is going to be non-stop.

7:00 a.m.   *Get Kid Ready for Preschool*

I chase my daughter around the house for a few minutes before I negotiate with her to put on her school clothes. I know that she won't forget what I promised her for that concession in our father-daughter negotiation session. So I make sure not to over-promise and under-deliver. This rule of mine applies both to personal as well as professional matters.

After my daughter is dressed and ready to go, I have to decide what I should wear. I've always liked the clean and conservative look since I was young. Places like Banana Republic and Zara are my favorite places to shop for my casual clothing. When it comes to professional wear, I also try to follow the clean and conservative approach. Ultimately, for today, I choose a nice gray suit, semi-skinny tie, white shirt, and a pair of my favorite black dress shoes (shined up, of course).

7:15 a.m.   *Skim First Section of The Wall Street Journal / Eat Breakfast*

I prepare a quick breakfast and eat while reading the first section of the paper. Working in the technology industry, there is always some relevant article. Today, I see that there is an article about a case before the US Supreme Court about expectation of privacy by a government employee who uses a government owned mobile phone to text personal messages. I'm particularly interested in the case because I'm working on updating our company's employee privacy policy.

I take a final look in the mirror and then step outside. Like every other weekday, I bring my trusty copy of *The Wall Street Journal* and start reading the headlines. At this moment I have the same thought I do every morning and that is, "How can so much happen in the world in just twenty-four hours?!"

7:40 a.m.   *Get in the Car / Drop off Kid at Preschool / Head to the Office*

I convince my daughter to hop into the car with another promise of a "treat" or a "surprise" (I'm a big believer in using tangible incentives!). I then buckle her into the car seat. After enjoying a split second of relief, I head toward her preschool and drop her off before heading in the opposite direction to my downtown office.

During the final mile or so to the office, I start thinking about all the things I have to do today. As I do this, moderate stress starts to set in—and to think that I haven't even stepped foot into the office yet. I also start to wonder if it'll be a relatively quiet day or one of those days where everyone wants everything yesterday. I hope for the former. And while thinking about work-related things I have to do while driving, I start to slowly feel the start of the transformation from husband and father to serious corporate counsel.

8:00 a.m.   *Arrive at Work*

I park my car and get into the elevator to my office. As usual, I'm one of the last ones to arrive at the office. This is because I'm now in an in-house counsel capacity, rather than at a law firm (as we all know, so-called "lawyer hours" usually start later, but end later—but a business tends to start earlier and end earlier, which presents something of a mismatch). Feeling some moderate guilt, I quickly slide into my office and into my chair. Relief sets in immediately, at least temporarily.

8:05 a.m.   *Check E-Mails and Voicemails*

I power up my computer. This takes quite a few minutes since the computer has to load not only all the various software applications, but also must run the various virus checks. In the meantime, I listen to my voicemail messages. Today, it's five voicemails—not too bad. And after the computer is finally done booting up, I check my e-mails—I have about fifteen messages in my inbox—about average (except for Mondays, which have the most since e-mails accumulate over the weekend). I'm thankful every morning that the volume of e-mails and voicemails are moderate compared to when I was at the law firms.

8:20 a.m.   *Make a Coffee Run to Starbucks*

Just like many others in my position, I need my first cup of coffee to get going. So I grab my Starbucks thermo and head outside and across the street to Starbucks. Once I step in, I notice that I'm not the only person in the area who wants coffee—I see a line of about ten people in front of me. At least the music and environment is nice and relaxing. Once I make it to the counter to order, I decide I should get a regular coffee with room for cream. I have a few sips and already I feel more alive. It's going to be a good day, I tell myself.

8:30 a.m.   *Make List of To-Do's for the Day*

I get back to my office and start jotting down on a post-it the mountain of things that I'd like to accomplish today. I do this knowing full well that I'll be lucky to get to even half of it. Nobody ever accused me of not being too ambitious, and I refuse to let them down now. I number the tasks by priority and tackle them in that order.

8:40 a.m.   *Return Phone Calls*

By the time I do all this, I now have time to return some phone calls. I get voicemail half the time. I leave messages knowing that I will be playing some phone tag the rest of the day. This will certainly cut into my productivity today. If worse comes to worse, I can contact the people I need to contact through their mobile phone. But I generally try to save these bullets for the most urgent of matters.

9:00 a.m.   *Law Department Meeting*

It's 9:00 a.m. and I head over to the conference room and sit around the table with my colleagues. We exchange some cordial small talk before the meeting starts. Once the meeting gets underway, I start to jot down some notes of things that I want to raise during the meeting. After about an hour, the meeting is concluded. Some people say that a meeting is what happens when people aren't working. I disagree. I actually find meetings like this to be a good way to hear what the business units are thinking and what they are or will be up to. For an in-house counsel, it's generally better to be more informed than less so. And as part of this, I try my best to get along with my fellow colleagues. After all, if they like you as a person and a professional, chances are greater they will open up the communication line more often and easily. This is a good thing.

10:00 a.m.   *Legal Research (re: drafting the company's social media policy)*

After the meeting, I review my notes from a prior meeting where we discussed the need for a social media policy for the firm. This is in light of the surge in popularity of social media applications over the past few years and the reality that they are used by employees in almost every workplace. To prepare, I also read outside materials on how other companies have dealt with this issue (as industry policy benchmarks) and what legal advisors have suggested companies consider in implementing such a social media policy. I consider our company's position and perspective about what it would be like to address the issue. I then analyze the legal issues and potential risks for the company as it relates to employees' use of social media.

12:00 p.m.   *Go to Lunch/Finish Reading the Paper*

It's amazing how time flies sometimes. Today is one of those days—noon already! So I run over to the nearby deli and have a nice, quiet lunch by myself, which gives me time to finish reading the paper. Afterwards, I slowly stroll back to the office so I can prepare for what's next.

12:45 p.m.   *Review and Provide Comments to Inbound Software Licensing Agreement*

Next on my list is to review a draft inbound software licensing agreement for one of the firm's business lines. Starting on page one, I slowly start reviewing and providing comments in the margins (known as a "mark up"). I also begin noting questions for our internal business people about security and confidentiality issues. I do a thorough mark up and e-mail it out to the business line with instructions to review it. I then set up a time to have a conference call internally to discuss the relevant issues further.

2:15 p.m.   *Conference Call with IT Department (re: to discuss roll out of new software platform)*

After sending out the e-mail, I'm suddenly asked to participate in a conference call with the IT department to discuss the actual roll out of a new software platform (based on a contract that I had previously worked on). It's been a few weeks since I reviewed the contract. So prior to the call, I look at the contract again to refresh my memory about the project details. During the call, I field various questions about specific terms and conditions embedded in the contract such as milestones, timing, obligations of the parties, etc. This is done so that the business line can see if the software provider is living up to its obligations under the contract. Fortunately, everything seems to be on track and we agree to schedule another call as the roll out gets underway.

3:00 p.m.   *Read Client Alert and Internal Privacy Policy*

The next order of business is to print out and read the slew of client alerts that I get from outside law firms and trade organizations on topics of interest to my practice areas. I am constantly reminded that it is difficult to stay on top of everything, especially since I work in the technology field. I could literally spend weeks upon weeks reading this type of work-related literature.

At any rate, I do my best to keep up-to-date, given the fast-paced changing industry that I am in.

4:00 p.m.   *Research Check Fraud Issue*

I read my notes from a prior meeting about a check fraud scheme that caused our company a large loss. I spend some time researching regulatory advisories and the Uniform Commercial Code (UCC) to get my arms around the legal issues involved. By doing this, I can craft the best legal solution to address the loss situation. After my initial review, I put my preliminary findings in a brief memo, and write a note to myself that I should revisit and follow-up on the memo again fairly soon.

5:30 p.m.   *Conference Call with Outside Counsel*

It's 5:30 p.m., and I participate in a conference call with one of our outside legal counsel to discuss updating some of our basic agreements governing our technology products. After I dial in and we each say cordial greetings, we then exchange some meaningful discussion on the topic. After the substantive matters are covered, I conclude the call on a slight down note by bringing up the issue of their last legal fee invoice, which was higher than I had expected. I inform them that I will go through it again with a fine-tooth comb, but manage their expectation by suggesting that I thought the bill looked quite high. I temper my aggressive approach by reminding myself that I was once in their shoes in my former life as a law firm attorney.

6:00 p.m.   *Review Regulatory Updates*

As the day winds down, I start to slow down too. In fact, by this time, I start to feel a little tired. As if this wasn't enough, I start hearing people shuffling out the door. This only makes me feel the urge to follow. But I know that I need to get one more thing done before the day ends so I can make myself feel like I was my usual productive self today. I go to my stack of regulatory updates that I've been putting off reviewing for weeks and start looking at one. I get through a few pages. But my hunger gets the best of me and I decide it's time to call it a day. Before I go, I begin stuffing my briefcase with a small stack of documents that I know I'll never get to at home. But I put it in there anyway. It's just habit.

6:30 p.m.   *Go Home*

I get up and go to the elevator area, which will take me to the basement level of the building where the garage is, and I get in my car and stick the key into the ignition. The sound of the car's engine is sweet music to my ears, I think to myself, as I shift the car into drive mode. A quick ten-minute ride later, I'm home. I say to myself, "Another day, another dollar."

7:05 p.m.   *Prepare to Eat Dinner*

I park my car into my garage at home. And I take my suitcase and jacket with me into the front door. My wife and daughter are there to greet me at the door—what a beautiful sight to behold! I greet them with a big "Hi, I'm home!" and I ask how their day went. I put down my things, change clothes, and then prepare dinner with my wife. Today, it's lasagna and salad. And since it's near the end of the week, I'll also have some cabernet sauvignon. During dinner, they ask how my day is, but I try not to talk too much about work while at home. Mostly, I just want to enjoy my time with the family, which to me, is so precious.

10:00 p.m.   *Read Various Literature on Current Work Matters/Watch Some TV*

After dinner and attending to the needs of my wife and daughter, I head into the study room and turn on some sports or evening news. If I'm lucky, I'll get in one of those many documents that I brought home from work. What I brought home today is mostly light reading. So it's not too bad. But more than anything, I'm really enjoying this quiet time.

11:30 p.m.   *Go to Bed*

I look at the clock—11:30 p.m. already! I end the day as I began it—by taking out my electric toothbrush while looking for the toothpaste. I then change into my sleep clothes and then slide into bed. Ahhh, what a nice feeling!

6:30 a.m.   *Wake-Up to Three-Year Old (repeat)*

Here we go again—another twenty-four hours!

Final Thoughts

The pros and cons of attending law school or not should be something that should be considered *before*, not during, law school. Many students simply choose law school as a default. In other words, they know that they don't want to go to business school or medical school, so the thinking then becomes, "Well, why not law school then?"

Although attending law school teaches some invaluable skills that are helpful in the legal, business, and tech industries—as my "24" profile reflects—it is not always the guaranteed ticket to riches and a glamorous lifestyle as portrayed by TV shows like *Boston Legal* or *Ally McBeal*. Although I do enjoy many aspects of my job and being a lawyer, I recommend that you really search inside you to see what your true passions are—is it reading and writing, is it making contacts and socializing, is it creating ideas? Although the practice of law combines all these things, and is many things to many people, I would say that more than anything, you must be extremely interested (and quite skilled at) researching, reading, and writing. This is the essence of what a lawyer does. If you're just going into law school or the legal profession for the nice office, fancy business card, and fairly decent pay, then these things tend to lose their luster sooner than you would think, in which case, you may end up being at square one all over again.

18

Profile 18
Jason: DUI Defense Attorney

Executive Summary

Name: Jason
Profile: DUI Defense Attorney
Location: Salt Lake City, Utah

Jason's job as a DUI defense attorney is defending people who have been charged with DUI (driving under the influence). As a lawyer who has to show up frequently in the courtroom, Jason's twenty-four-hour day shows that knowing the judges well and being comfortable with the setting is an enormous advantage, which can only be acquired through years of experience. He also zooms in on what it is like to be a private attorney, such as managing staff and being a marketer apart from doing the best legal work possible on behalf of his clients. Among other things mentioned in his extremely colorful twenty-four-hour profile, Jason stresses the importance of hiring good paralegals to secure a good business. Being an incredibly busy DUI defense counsel who needs clients to keep seeking his services to sustain his business, some might incorrectly consider his moral compass as slightly tilted. On the contrary, Jason always tries to find time to personally "help" his clients who are struggling with alcohol or drug abuse problems, which he claims is also a way to gain more lifelong clients in the long run. You can tell Jason really loves his job and does it gladly, even with hardly any spare time for himself.

Profile

Career Field:	DUI Defense Attorney (as well as Private Criminal Attorney)
Current Position:	Managing Partner
Institution:	Boutique Law Firm
Location:	Salt Lake City, Utah
Previous Position(s):	Paralegal
Education:	JD, University of Utah, S.J. Quinney School of Law
	BA, University of Utah
Licensed (Y/N):	Yes
Jurisdictions:	Utah/North Dakota

Schedule

5:30 a.m.	Early Morning Wake-Up Call
6:15 a.m.	Checking E-Mails (Busy Cops Means Busy DUI Attorneys)
6:30 a.m.	Reviewing Files/Getting Ready for My Day
7:30 a.m.	Getting Son Ready for School
7:55 a.m.	Getting Myself Ready for the Day
8:05 a.m.	Out the Door and on the Run
8:20 a.m.	Off to School/Off to Work
8:33 a.m.	Driver License Administrative Hearing (The Slam Dunk)
8:40 a.m.	Fueling the Legal Machine
9:05 a.m.	The Parking Problem
9:10 a.m.	First Court Appearance of the Day/Pre-Trial Conferences
9:45 a.m.	Hurry Up and Wait for the Judge
10:15 a.m.	Driving to the Next Court (My Car as My Mobile Office)
10:45 a.m.	Court Appearance # 2 (Jury Pre-trials): Are We Going to Trial or Not?
11:30 a.m.	Driving from Court to Court (Being a Lawyer versus the "Business" of Being a Lawyer)
12:00 p.m.	New Client Appointment (Clients Make the World Go Round)
1:15 p.m.	More Driving, Another Canceled Dinner
1:35 p.m.	Motion Hearing (You Gotta Love Video)

2:30 p.m.	Lunch on the Run with a Side Order of Legal Advice
3:30 p.m.	Sentencing: Setting a Good Example
5:00 p.m.	Client Meeting to Review Discovery (The Reality Check)
6:00 p.m.	Potential Client Appointment: How Can I Be Arrested for Following My Doctor's Orders?
7:00 p.m.	Potential Client Appointment (If I Can't Drive I'll Lose my Business!)
8:15 p.m.	Gathering My Files (The Day End Shuffle)
8:30 p.m.	Gas N' Go
8:45 p.m.	Dinner Time But No Dinner
10:00 p.m.	Drafting Motion to Suppress (The Evening Shift)
1:00 a.m.	Time for Bed (So I Can Do It All Again Tomorrow)
5:30 a.m.	Here We Go Again!

24-Hour Schedule

5:30 a.m.   *Early Morning Wake-Up Call*

The alarm clock goes off. My wife has to work today and the next two days. Twelve hour shifts as an ICU (intensive care unit) nurse means early mornings and long days. We hardly see each other when she's working a three-day stretch. I try to go back to sleep, but all I can hear is the blow dryer. Five minutes of that and lo and behold, I'm awake for the day. I figure I might as well get up, make some coffee, and get some work done.

6:15 a.m.   *Checking E-Mails (Busy Cops Means Busy DUI Attorneys)*

Just finished my first cup of coffee. I can't believe I received twenty-six e-mails just in the few hours I slept last night—whatever happened to those good old days in school when e-mails were fun both to read and reply to?! I suppose this is one thing that we, as lawyers, get paid to do—provide good legal advice for clients—which means reading their e-mails.

As a member of several different defense lawyer groups, I participate in two different attorney listserves. So as a result, I receive anywhere between 150 and 300 e-mails a day from colleagues, clients, and my staff. Just to give you a sense of the importance of e-mail communication these days, I can tell you that my paralegals and I communicate more by e-mail than we do by phone or in person.

Looks like four of the overnight/early morning e-mails are from potential clients. Since my particular line of work is related to DUI (drinking under the influence) incidents, I can say that such queries are typical for a few days after a good old-fashioned drinking holiday like St. Patrick's Day. I'll let my paralegals contact these potential clients when they arrive at the office and set appointments for them to meet with one of my partners. It's March 20 and for the past two days, our office phone has been ringing off the hook. Looks like the local law enforcement agencies had a big night. To a DUI defense attorney, DUI saturation patrols are bad news for my clients, but good news for my business.

6:30 a.m.   *Reviewing Files/Getting Ready for My Day*

I finish sorting through my barrage of e-mails. Now it's time to start reviewing my calendar for the day. I have eight court hearings and three in-office appointments scheduled already for today, so I need to be prepared for all of them.

My first hearing at 8:30 a.m. is an administrative hearing and I still need to watch the video of my client's arrest. I hope it's not too long. Luckily, this one is only a half hour long. I watch the video and do a quick review of the other seven files.

7:30 a.m.   *Getting Son Ready for School*

I need to get my son up and ready for school. I'm already running fifteen minutes behind schedule. I wake my son, herd him downstairs, and get him some breakfast. I quickly jump in the shower while I watch the news on our bathroom TV. I have split custody with my ex-wife, so my son is with me every Monday and Tuesday, and every other weekend from Friday to Sunday. He hates getting up early, and when he stays at my house he has to get up earlier because it's a fifteen to twenty minute drive from our house to his school (rather than a two block walk from his mom's house).

This type of juggling act of work and family is all part of the art and science of balancing work with family demands—something not really covered in law school or most graduate professional schools for that matter—but both can definitely have their influences on each other.

7:55 a.m.   *Getting Myself Ready for the Day*

My son is now showered up. But he still has to get dressed and brush his teeth. "Hurry up, dude!" I yell from the kitchen as I pack my two briefcases for the day. Yes, that's right, not just one, but two briefcases is what I need to do my job in a typical day. It makes me wish those notions of how the PC computer would make the office paperless really were true!

8:05 a.m.   *Out the Door and on the Run*

I'm so late! I can only hope that there's no traffic to clog up my schedule. I check my voicemails while I drive—one of my ways to clear e-mails during any given moment during my time-compressed day.

One of the messages is from my client who has a court appearance in less than an hour from now, at 9:00 a.m. today. His message is that he's having car trouble and may not be able to make it. I can only speculate that his "car trouble" may have something to do with the fact that he was placed on probation six months ago. As part of this, he was ordered to participate in counseling and community service, but has yet to do either thing as ordered by the court. He is facing an "Order to Show Cause" today, which is likely to result in him going to jail for a few days as punishment for his failure to comply. I call him back on his cell phone and, surprise surprise, it immediately goes to voicemail. I leave a message instructing him that it's in his best interest to appear in court this morning as scheduled, and that he has about an hour to find a ride and needs to call me back to let me know he has done so.

The second message is from another client, Kevin. He was arrested again last night—his third DUI in the past three years— "frequent fliers" we call them. Luckily for him, we were successful in having the first one dismissed on a "Motion to Suppress." Had this not been the case, he would be facing a third offense felony DUI with a possible maximum five-year prison sentence. Thanks to my efforts, his first offense will "only" result in a misdemeanor with a minimum ten-day jail sentence. Not too shabby considering the alternative.

I say this because, unlike in the lecture halls of law schools where theories were judged on an absolute basis, in the "real world" of legal practitioners, things are more based on a relative basis. So in situations where there sometimes is not a clear "best" option, sometimes in my field of work, and I would guess for other fields as well, the best course of action is sometimes the "least worst" one.

8:20 a.m.   *Off to School/Off to Work*

Fortunately, it's clear sailing this morning and it only takes fifteen minutes to get my son to school halfway across town. I drop my son off and immediately head to the driver license division (DLD) of the courthouse. I only have ten minutes, so it's going to be a close call to make it on time. Good thing the DLD hearings have a twenty-minute wait time. So if I'm a few minutes late it's usually no big deal. This, for better or for worse, is often a hallmark of my work in terms of speed and tempo as a DUI defense attorney—rush to wait.

8:33 a.m.   *Driver License Administrative Hearing (The Slam Dunk)*

I arrive at the DLD office. My client is already there and is looking nervous. "Relax," I tell him, "this one's a dead bang winner." Fortunately for this client (a traveling salesman), the arresting officer failed to check the proper box on the DUI "Summons and Citation" form giving him "Notice of Intent to Suspend." So despite the fact that he blew a 0.13 on the breath test (way above the legal limit), the DLD will not be suspending his license due to this technicality.

Some people think getting off on this type of technicality is a faulty loophole in the system where guilty people somehow squirm through the legal system and are left free. In my view, this type of process is a needed "check and balance" on all actors in the system to make sure everyone's doing their job properly.

In terms of the case in hand, I wish they were all this easy. Seems like we used to get freebies like this all the time in the past. But lately the cops are getting smarter and are making fewer mistakes.

8:40 a.m.   *Fueling the Legal Machine*

That was quick! I'll actually be able to swing through the Starbucks drive thru and still make it to my first courthouse on time at 9:00 a.m. for my first three hearings. My order: "One Venti White Chocolate Mocha, skim milk, no whip cream, please!" One of these caffeine-filled delights each morning helps keep me going through the day. Sometimes one of these isn't enough to carry me through the entire day, and I sneak by again for an afternoon boost. But admittedly, the calories wreak havoc on my waistline. I have gained thirty pounds in just the past six years. Looks like my added hemline has contributed to the Starbucks bottom line.

Running your own law office is an eighty to ninety hour a week job. Seldom does a day go by, including Saturday and Sunday, that I don't take and make phone calls to clients or do some work. Being responsible for every aspect of a boutique law firm such as mine from advertising, meeting new clients, managing a staff, going to court, and doing legal work, means there is little time for exercise. Add to that an irregular eating pattern, stress, late nights, lack of sleep and spending the greater part of your day sitting in one chair or another, and you grow out of your suits every couple of years. So it's not always glamour and fun, but everything considered, I still find it worthwhile.

9:05 a.m.   *The Parking Problem*

I find a parking spot across the street from the courthouse with a parking meter. But as luck would have it, I don't have any change left but pennies! Oh well, I don't have time to look for another spot without a meter, so it looks like the possibility of another parking ticket.

I think that I have single-handedly paid for the little three-wheeled traffic cart driven by the parking patrol authorities who were gracious enough to issue all these unwanted parking tickets to me. As I walk toward the courthouse, I use my empty hand without my files to quickly type out a poorly spelled e-mail to my office manager asking her to get a couple rolls of quarters for me the next time she goes to the bank. Makes me think back to my childhood days when the only time I needed quarters was to play video games! Well, at least I'm getting paid for my efforts in exchange for those quarters at this stage in my life, so I guess you can consider this progress.

9:10 a.m.   *First Court Appearance of the Day/Pre-Trial Conferences*

I'm in the door, and say a jubilant "Hi!" to the bailiff working the metal detector at the front door (it's always good to be on their good side, and the next sentence tells you why). He waives me through with a nod of his head sparing me from having to empty my pockets and half undress like all the other poor folks waiting in line to get into the courthouse who waited in line before me. I make it to the top of the steps and two of the three clients are waiting for me. My paralegals do a great job of packing all my hearings in the same court at the same time so I can kill many birds with one stone. Right off the bat, the two clients start to compete for my legal attention and advice—so I tell both of them that I need to talk to the prosecutor first and ask them both to wait outside and I'll come back and speak to them individually afterwards.

I walk into the courtroom and am pleasantly surprised to find that there is a different prosecutor in court that day, one that I like much more than the one I was expecting. The substitute prosecutor and I went to law school together and he's much more reasonable than the newbie prosecutor who is normally assigned to this judge's courtroom. Maybe I can take advantage of this opportunity to work out a good deal on both cases. I tease the prosecutor, who is normally assigned to the district court, about getting demoted back to the justice court. I asked if he got demoted because he can't win a trial and he laughs and says its only a temporary assignment while they attempt to fill a couple of prosecutor positions that opened up when two former prosecutors decided to open their own private practice doing criminal defense work.

I don't understand why these prosecutors think that they can just flip sides and start doing defense work. In order to be good, you have to have passion for what you do. How can you stand up in court one day and defend lying cops and ask for a drunk driver to be sent to jail, and the next day come to court call the cops liars and argue for the judge not to put a similar drunk driver in jail, but instead grant them the privilege of probation? I could never be a prosecutor. The way I see it, it would be like Luke Skywalker joining the dark side (a *Star Wars* movie reference). I could never be a judge for that matter either—yes it may be interesting presiding over trials and seeing the different attorneys argue cases—but other than that it seems like a rather boring job dealing with the same mundane tasks day in and day out. But that's just my take on things.

The prosecutor sees the light on one case and offers my client a plea deal that he is happy to take. It will save his license and his job. The other client isn't so lucky. Despite my best pitch as to the problems with the case and the poor job the cop did in administering the field sobriety tests to my client before arresting him, it's a second offense and the city prosecutor's office has an "office policy" that they don't plea bargain second offenses and they don't plea bargain refusals (the client refused to submit to a breath test). First, I break the bad news to the second client and we decide to set the case for trial. Much like the prosecutors, I have an "office policy" that I don't advise my clients to plead "guilty" to DUI, and maybe as part of this, I've earned a reputation for taking not-so-easy cases to trial if the prosecutor won't strike a deal. Clients hire me to "defend" their case, not hold their hands and have them plead guilty. So there are no freebies in our business and we win our fair share of trials. You can't win a trial without doing one, I always say. I take a few minutes to review the rights waiver with the other client, and we go back into the courtroom to enter his plea. He is very pleased with the outcome. Another satisfied customer!

9:45 a.m.   Hurry Up and Wait for the Judge

The judge finally takes the bench and I'm first in line. I quickly jump up and ask the judge to call the first case and advise her that I need a trial date. Her response is, "Mr. Schatz, why does that not surprise me? Get a trial date from my clerk before you leave." I call the second case and carefully explain to the judge why the prosecutor was agreeing to reduce the DUI charge against my client despite the fact that my client was involved in an accident and had a BAC (blood alcohol content) nearly two times the legal limit at the time of his arrest. This judge knows me well and I have had many motion hearings and trials with her, so she knows that we would fight every point if the deal is not approved. She advises my client that he is very lucky to have me as his attorney and gives him fair warning that she will approve the deal for the reasons stated, but that if he fails to comply with the terms of probation, he will be facing a lengthy jail sentence. Last, but not least, is my client who is having car trouble. He is not in court and I have not heard back from him since his voicemail earlier this morning. I don't have time to wait any longer, so I call his case—and with as straight as face as possible— I explain to the judge why that on this very day when he was to appear in court, he has failed to comply since his car broke down and he could not find another person to drive him to court. With a raise of her eyebrows and a tilt of her head, the judge reluctantly grants my request to continue the hearing for two weeks without issuing a warrant for his arrest. And I assure her my client would be here next time to provide his explanation. "He better be here next time or he may be doing the whole six months," she replies. Crisis avoided, at least for now.

10:15 a.m.   *Driving to the Next Court (my car as my mobile office)*

My last court appearance took longer than I expected, so I am once again running behind schedule. It seems the word "early" is just not in my vocabulary. I have another hearing at 10:30 a.m. today and it's at least a thirty-minute drive to the next courthouse. I quickly call my paralegal and ask her to notify the next court that I'm running a bit late and to call my two clients to let them know as well.

I can't believe it: I have five voicemails and twelve e-mails in just the last hour while I was in court! If it were not for my smartphone, I would not be able to get half of my work done each day. I think back to the days without smartphones and e-mail and wonder how anyone ever got any work done.

I quickly scroll through the e-mails, deleting them as I go. Only two require a response, so I wonder if I can bang out a reply with my right hand while I steer with the left, looking up at the road ahead of me about every five seconds in between words. Sometimes I arrive at my destination and think to myself how did I just get here? I was so busy responding to the e-mails on my phone that I paid little attention to where I was going. It's as if my car is on autopilot. Knock on wood, I have never had an accident. Maybe I need to get a driver, that way I could get even more work done while I drive from court to court each day. How about some young kid who graduated from high school, but isn't sure what he wants to do? Too unreliable. Or maybe a retiree looking for a no brainer part-time job? No, that won't work either—he'll drive way too slow. Looks like I'm pulling double duty as racecar driver and lawyer for now.

I listen to the voicemails: two more potential clients, a prosecutor needing a continuance, and two current clients who have questions. They will have to wait until later. I am just pulling up to the next court.

10:45 a.m.   *Court Appearance #2 (jury pre-trials): Are We Going to Trial or Not?*

At my next court appearance, I have two clients, both set for a "jury pre-trial hearing" today and a jury trial next week. Like many other courts, this court sets ten to twelve jury trials on any given trial day, knowing that only one of those cases will actually go to trial. This creates a scheduling nightmare for me. Each month I have to block out a half dozen or so days in my calendar to do jury trials knowing fair well that of the seven cases I have set for trial this month alone, only one or two of them are likely to proceed. Sometimes none of them proceed to trial. But I have to block out the entire days nonetheless, meaning less time for all the other hearings and things I have to do. Then, only a few days before trial or sometimes even the day of trial, I find out that my client's case is being bumped due to a witness problem or because another older case is being given priority. However, often times the immanency of the pending trial date finally brings a prosecutor to their senses and they offer my client the deal we've been looking for since day one and the case settles. I guess that's the way the game is played. But it would make a lot more sense to me if the prosecutors would just take the time to thoroughly review the case in the beginning. If this was done, they'd realize they have problems earlier on, work out a deal quickly and save us all the six to nine months worth of needless gamesmanship before they finally give us a deal, which would have resolved the case two months after it started instead of dragging it on for a year.

Anyway, no such luck today. My cases are in priority one and six, and both sides are ready to proceed and no new deals are being offered. In the first case, my client has a great case since the arresting officer's certification to operate the breath-testing machine had expired, while my client performed very well on the field sobriety tests. The prosecutor offered a reduced charge of "impaired driving," but my client has indicated that he trusts me and wants to take his case to the jury. I thoroughly enjoy doing motion hearings and trials. I became a lawyer because I love to argue and I love the thrill of being in trial and thinking on your feet. In fact, I wish I could have someone else do all my other work except for motion hearings and trials. But life doesn't work that way, so most days I simply carry out all the usual day-to-day tasks of running a law firm and doing the routine things to represent my clients and wait for those opportunities to get in to court and mix it up with the cops and prosecutors.

I reconfirm with my client that we are willing to accept nothing less than a dismissal and we are ready to do battle to get it. I call the cases and announce to the court that I have spoken to the prosecutor about the first case, that we are unable to reach a resolution, and we are therefore ready to proceed with trial next week. For the other client, this just means that his trial date will be reset again two months later, this being the third time her case has had to be reset. It has also been thirteen months since her arrest, but I assure her that we will get our turn and she too will have her day in court.

11:30 a.m.   *Driving from Court to Court (being a lawyer versus the "business" of being a lawyer)*

I'm on the road again. And as usual, I'm also checking my inbox to find two more voicemails and another dozen or so e-mails. One is from my office manager, payroll is due tomorrow and two rather large retainer payment checks bounced, and our malpractice and liability insurance premiums for the year are due. She asks if it's okay to transfer money from our reserve account to our operating account to cover the costs. I can't be late for the new client appointment, so I kick it into high gear as I race back to the office, all the way continue to make calls and respond to e-mails. I have just enough time to get back to my office for my 12:00 p.m. new client appointment.

As a private attorney, I spend about half of my time being a lawyer and doing actual legal work: going to court, meeting with clients and witnesses, as well as researching and writing motions. The other half of my time is spent on the "business" of being a lawyer. Things such as advertising, managing your staff, office supplies and equipment, drumming up business, worrying about making payroll and other financial obligations. And most importantly meeting with potential clients. You may be the greatest attorney in the world, a regular Clarence Darrow, but if you don't know how to market and sell yourself to potential clients, you could end up sitting in your office twiddling your thumbs all day and eventually going broke. On the other hand, some very inadequate lawyers are great at marketing and make lots of money, but have many clients who are not happy with their results. This may eventually lead to the demise of their practice once word gets around town that they are a dump truck lawyer (only interested in getting money from the client, but not doing good legal work). In order to be successful in private practice, you have to do both sides very well.

12:00 p.m.   *New Client Appointment (clients make the world go round)*

It's only lunchtime and I feel as though I've already put in a full day's worth of work. I buzz into the parking ramp nearly taking out the arm of the gate leading into the ramp. Thankfully, I have a reserved parking spot and don't have to waste a bunch of time driving around finding a spot. I grab my morning briefcase from the back of my car and hop on the elevator to go upstairs. I rush in the front door to the office and introduce myself to the potential client. "Hi. I'm Jason, I'm glad you're here. Can I have just five minutes to get situated before we meet?" Sure thing, he says.

I quickly stop off at each of my three paralegals' desks to give them the files from the morning hearings with instructions on what to do. It's taken a few years, but I have put together a trio of paralegals who are fairly adept at reading my mind. Without them, I couldn't do what I do. In a prior life, I too was a paralegal. Prior to entering law school, I worked as a paralegal for seven years. Having had that experience, I know how important a good paralegal or secretary can be to a busy attorney and I can relate to the dilemma a paralegal faces every day. As a paralegal, it is your job to be proactive and to do as many things as possible for the attorney without having to be told. On the other hand, since you are not the attorney, you can't do too much without input from the attorney to make sure that you are doing things the exact way the attorney wants them done depending on the needs of the client and the attorney's strategy for the case. Paralegals can be vital to having happy clients by providing answers and attention to clients when the attorney cannot. My best advice to any new attorney seeking to set up their own practice, after purchasing malpractice insurance, is to find an intelligent and hardworking paralegal and spend the time and effort to work with the paralegal closely to train that person to think the way you think and to understand the importance of having happy clients.

Back to the potential client. I quickly organize my desk from the previous day's chaos and go back out to invite the potential client into my office. My five minutes has turned into fifteen. I start with a little small talk about the person who referred this potential client to me, a former client who I represented on a similar charge last year. Every private attorney strives for word of mouth advertising. Treat your clients well and do good work and over time your referral base will grow, hopefully to the point that you will no longer need to advertise. A referred client is like money in the bank. They already know someone who has had a good experience with you at the helm of their case and they know how much your fee is. With those things in mind, they have decided that it is worth it to meet with you. During the interview with a referred client, you have to spend less time selling yourself and can spend more time learning about their case.

In this particular case, the potential client is a truck driver who is facing his second DUI and a potential lifetime suspension of his commercial driver's license. As an attorney, you have a tremendous responsibility to your clients. Often they come to you at their darkest hour and they look to you for a ray of hope. When they hire you, they put their trust in you to do everything you can to help them out of the mess they've created. I first explain to the client the process that his case will follow and the different actions that arise both at the DLD and with the criminal charge in court. I then discuss the potential consequences to his driver's license as well as the criminal penalties he will be facing in court. "Just save my license and I will do anything. I will gladly go to jail for ten days if you can save my driver's license and my job." I tell him the same thing I tell every client. "I can't guarantee you a particular outcome to your case, but I can look you in the eye and guarantee you that I will do everything I can to win your case." In response, the client asks, "So how do I get started?" I introduce him to the paralegal who will be his case manager to get him started and he writes us a check. In order to cover my operating expenses, payroll, and my salary, I have to sign up between fifteen to twenty clients per month.

1:15 p.m.   *More Driving/ Another Canceled Dinner*

I have fifteen minutes to get to my next court appearance at 1:30 p.m. and the courthouse is twenty minutes away. I grab my suit coat and bolt for the door. While I drive, I get a call from one of my paralegals and she has another potential client on the phone who says he needs to meet with an attorney today. He was referred to me specifically. She has explained to the potential client that I am already booked solid for the rest of the day with court appearances and other appointments, but he insists that he doesn't want to speak to any of the other attorneys in my office except for me. It's another referral, so the chances of the client hiring me is very high. So I tell the paralegal to schedule him for an appointment at 7:00 p.m. in my office later this evening and I will rearrange my schedule tonight to make time for him. I was supposed to be meeting my wife after work at 7:30 p.m. to have dinner at our favorite Mexican restaurant so that we can actually have some time to be together this week—so much for our dinner plans tonight. I can't even count the number of times I have canceled plans or been extremely late for personal activities due to work commitments. She is not going to be very happy about this, but she has come to tolerate my job and the affect that it has on our personal life. She knows how important my work is to me and that my job provides us with a very good living. I call my wife, and as I expected, she isn't very happy that once again my work is getting in the way of our plans.

1:35 p.m.   *Motion Hearing (you gotta love video)*

I arrive at court to find the arresting officer and the prosecutor huddled in the hallway plotting my client's demise. I have had this officer many times before, and over the years, I have been greatly responsible for his training on how to conduct a proper DUI investigation. I have cross-examined him so many times that he can readily anticipate my questions even before I ask them. And usually, he has a textbook answer for each of them. But it's always hard to teach an old dog new tricks—once again he has made a big mistake and we are set to capitalize on it.

Today I have him in my sights—and I have him dead in my sights—because today I have the power of video. In this case, the video I have is a video of my client's traffic stop. The new digital video cameras being used by the highway patrol actually captures twenty to thirty seconds of video before the overhead lights are turned on—this means the alleged traffic violation was caught on tape. The video provides me with a 100 percent accurate and reliable way of showing that the alleged traffic violation of failing to signal prior to a lane change for which the officer stopped my client was nothing more than a figment of the police officer's imagination. I politely say a big "Hi!" to both of them and stroll into the courtroom with a little smirk on my face. Little do they know that, in just a few minutes, I will have the cop at my mercy just wishing that he had never heard the word "videotape" before.

The judge takes the bench and we get started. I inform the court that we have only one motion before the court today, "Judge, the only issue we are here to address today is whether Trooper Smith's traffic stop of my client was legally justified." "Thank you counsel, let's proceed." The prosecutor goes first. And just as I hoped, the trooper's testimony is that my client failed to signal for "at least two seconds before switching lanes." I feel a tap on my shoulder—my client leans over and blurts out, "He's lying!" "I know, I know," I say, "Just wait and we'll get our chance."

The prosecutor finishes and I ask only one question of the trooper, "Did you submit a videotape of the traffic stop in this case to your evidence department?" "Yes, I did," he says. I ask that the judge allow me to play the video and the prosecutor does not object. I play the video and it takes only about thirty seconds. While the video plays, I count out loud, "One, two, three, four, five, six, seven blinks." I stop the tape and sit down at the counsel table. The look on the judge's face is almost as priceless as the look on the trooper's face. The judge looks at me, then the cop, finally the prosecutor and states simply "Counsel, I'm not seeing a violation here." The prosecutor is caught like a deer in the headlights. These are the moments I live for! This is why I do what I do. I can't believe he didn't watch the video even though I sent it to him along with my motion to suppress. "The motion *is granted* and this case is *dismissed*." My client gasps and I quietly gather my things and shake his hand congratulating him on having his case dismissed. He shakes my hand for what seemed like a minute or more. I was his warrior and today we won. I wish I could stick around and chat, but my day is far from over. I still have two more court appearances and I have to be back to the office by 5:00 p.m. for two more appointments.

2:30 p.m.   *Lunch on the Run with a Side Order of Legal Advice*

I make my way to the next court appearance. And since I'm not having Mexican food for dinner, I have a few minutes to spare, so I swing through the drive thru of Alberto's and grab a steak burrito to go. There is a Starbucks only a few blocks away, so I also swing in for another coffee. Since it's my second coffee drink of the day, I only order a grande this time. And because the day's getting warmer, I have it served over ice.

My phone rings as I'm sitting in the drive thru waiting to pick up my iced coffee. My caller ID says it's a client of mine who is currently on probation for a drug-related DUI charge. I answer and he quickly says in a very panicked voice, "I need your advice. I don't know what to do." Calmly, I respond, "Well, what's the problem?" "My probation officer called me today and left me a message telling me I needed to come in and provide a urine sample for a random UA (urinalysis) by the end of the day." "Okay," I reply, "So, what is the problem?" "Well, it's gonna be dirty." "Why?" I ask. "I went out with some friends this weekend and I smoked some pot." "Your right, that is going to be a problem." "Well what should I do?" "Well, for starters, you should not have smoked pot." "I know, I know. It was stupid, but what should I do? Should I go and do the UA or not?" "Yes, you should, and before you go, you need to call your probation officer back and tell him it is going to be dirty, so he is not surprised when he gets the results. It's better that he hear it directly from you then from the results when he gets them back from the lab." "But I'll go to jail." "Yes, you might, but if you are up front and honest about it, there is a chance you may not." "Are you sure? What if I just ignore the message and tell my probation officer that I never received it?" "Well then you may go to jail just for missing the UA regardless of the result." "Okay. I'll do what you say." "Okay, call me back after you do the UA." "Bye."

It used to cause me great stress when I knew a client was likely to go to jail. But over time, I've come to realize that my clients make their own decision and I'm not in twenty-four-hour control of what they do. They make their choices, and if they make the wrong choice, then they alone will suffer the consequences. Many of the people I represent have drug or alcohol problems. And many of them will violate their probation or re-offend. So no matter how hard I try, and no matter great of a lawyer I become, some of my clients will nonetheless end up going to jail. It's all part of the game. But as an attorney, I feel that I have two duties to my clients. One duty is to help their legal situation and the other duty is to help their personal situation. In virtually every case, I refer clients to some form of education, counseling or drug and alcohol treatment, so that they can correct their behavior to avoid future trouble with the law. This may seem somewhat counterproductive if I'm encouraging clients to get help and decrease the likelihood of committing future offenses for which I could again get paid. But by helping these clients beat their drug and alcohol problems, I develop lifelong clients and a source of referrals for years to come.

3:30 p.m.   *Sentencing: Setting a Good Example*

I'm now at my last court appearance of the day! I gobble down the burrito while I sit in my car in the parking lot of the courthouse—in three minutes flat—a new record! A quick rinse with mouthwash to cover my burrito breath, and I grab my last two files and head inside. I have two cases: one set for sentencing and a second for a review hearing. I'll do the review hearing first. My client's probation is set to expire and she's complied with all of her probation terms successfully. The judge will be happy. So hopefully I can use this case to put the judge in a good mood. I ask for permission to approach and I hand the judge and prosecutor copies of my clients proof of community service, completion certificate for counseling, and most recent paycheck stub. "Well done!" states the judge, "I knew you could do it. I hope this has been a learning experience and I hope to never see you again. At least in my courtroom." My client laughs and thanks the judge for his support and happily shuffles out of the courtroom with proof that she has successfully completed her probation and her case is now closed.

Now for the sentencing. I explain to the judge that my client is a single mother and feels horrible for making such a poor choice to drive after drinking. She is thirty-five years old and has never had anything more than a speeding ticket prior to this offense. She has already completed a drug and alcohol assessment and hopes that the court will give her the option of probation and community service so that her job and treatment will not be interrupted. I point to my previous client as a perfect example of the fact that sometimes good people just made bad choices. And if given an opportunity, they can learn from their mistakes and become a better person. The judge gives my client an opportunity to speak. She begins to cry. I grab her a tissue and she wipes away her tears. The only words she manages to say are "I'm sorry." The judge agrees with our recommendations and places her on probation for twelve months, encouraging her to follow my other client's example.

A perfect way to end a good day. No one went to jail today. I saved the driver's licenses of two clients, got another case completely dismissed, another case was closed and a probationary sentence after that to top it off. I've already signed up one new client and I have two more to go before the day ends. So far, so good!

5:00 p.m.   Client Meeting to Review Discovery (the reality check)

After returning several more calls, accomplishing little because all I could reach was everyone's voicemail, I am back at the office for three more appointments. The first is with a current client to review his police reports and watch the video of his arrest. From what I've seen in the report, I don't expect the video to look very good, but we'll wait and see. I talk the client into my office and we scan over the police report. "This does not paint a very good picture, but we'll watch the tape and see what we have," I state. "I really don't think I was that drunk and I don't remember telling the officer that I had twelve beers that night. I think he is full of it," retorts my client.

Forty-five minutes later after reviewing the video, "Wow! That wasn't very good was it? I had no idea I was that drunk. I really *did* tell him I had twelve beers. Now what do we do?" I have seen many clients who swear up and down they were not drunk, but come to the cold realization of their actual behavior after watching the videotape of their arrest. However, I've also seen many cases that looked hopeless before the video, that eventually turn into very good cases. I discuss with the client our options for trying to plea bargain the case and do damage control. So I send the client off with information on how to schedule a drug and alcohol assessment and begin community service.

6:00 p.m.   *Potential Client Appointment: How Can I Be Arrested for Following My Doctor's Orders?*

My next appointment is a prescription drug DUI. Sometimes these are the most difficult cases to explain to the client because the clients are often charged after doing nothing more than taking the prescription medication given to them by their doctor for legitimate medical reasons. The client has had severe back problem requiring surgery six months ago and was arrested after he was called in as an erratic driver and admitted to taking lortab and soma two hours before driving. I explain the nuances of a prescription drug DUI and the potential consequences if convicted. The client just can't see how he can be guilty of DUI just for taking his prescriptions. He cannot have a DUI on his record or he could lose his job with a major freight carrier because he has to drive a forklift every day at work. He agrees I'm the man for the job and I turn him over to my paralegal for his down payment and signature for the retainer.

7:00 p.m.   *Potential Client Appointment (if I can't drive I'll lose my business!)*

At long last, I now gear up for my last appointment of the day. This potential client is a referral from another attorney who represents the man in regard to his business. The man runs his own construction company and he is concerned about losing his license. If so, he won't be able to drive from site to site to bid jobs and supervise his crews. For me, I know I have an uphill battle because after he was arrested he refused to submit to the breath test. So instead of facing a 120 day suspension, he is facing an eighteen-month suspension. I explain the consequence of the refusal and the fact that under Utah state law, there is no option for a work permit. "How am I supposed to work then?" he replies. "The legislature doesn't really care," I say. "They want the offense to hurt," I continue, "and this will even be more so, if you refuse to take the test."

We review the facts and it sounds like he may have a shot. If what he tells me is accurate, the officer may have failed to follow proper procedure when requesting the chemical test and that may be our chance to save his license from the eighteen-month suspension. He decides to hire me—and since my paralegals have all gone home—I prepare the retainer and release forms myself (it takes me about twice as long as my paralegals) and he makes his payment and we are on the case.

Three for three with new clients today! That will fill the bank account again, so I won't have to transfer money from the reserve account after all. Talk about just-in-time income!

8:15 p.m.   *Gathering My Files (the day end shuffle)*

Time to gather up my files for tomorrow so I can get home and have something to eat. Afterwards, I'll spend a few hours catching up on the dozen or so e-mails that I didn't have time to respond to today and write a "motion to suppress evidence" that is due tomorrow. I never made it to the dry cleaner today to drop off my suits for cleaning. So I'll have to try again tomorrow. I also forgot to call and make the dentist appointment that my wife has been reminding me to make for the past two weeks. She finds it ironic that I seem to remember everything that has to do with work, but I can't remember to do even the most simple tasks for myself.

8:30 p.m.   *Gas N' Go*

I stop for gas on my way home and while I'm at the pump, I realize I forgot one of the files I need for tomorrow (lying on my paralegals desk). This means I'll have to get up twenty minutes earlier than usual tomorrow morning since I'll have to stop into the office before I go to court—I'd do it now, but I'm just too tired to go back to the office at this hour to get it now. I go inside to pay for the gas. At least there's one thing that perks me up—chocolate iced cake donuts—I can't resist, so I grab one for the road.

8:45 p.m.   *Dinner Time but No Dinner*

I finally make it home. My wife is downstairs on the treadmill, so I open the fridge to find something to eat. I'm starving but nothing in the fridge looks good. My final analysis of what to eat leads me to none other than…Frosted Flakes cereal. I'm a cereal junky, so I eat two bowls while watching the last fifteen minutes of *Deadliest Catch* on the Discovery Channel. "You really need to work out," my wife says as she enters the kitchen. Despite her own busy schedule, she seldom misses a day to workout. "Just three times a week would be good for you. You're going to die from a heart attack at forty if you don't take care of yourself." I know she's right, but there's just not enough time in my twenty-four hour day.

10:00 p.m.   Drafting Motion to Suppress (the evening shift)

My wife yells down from our bedroom, "Are you coming to bed anytime soon?" "No. I still have this motion to write." I've spent the last hour catching up on e-mails and reviewing our bank account and deposits for the day to see how my law firm is doing. Now it's finally time to start researching and drafting this motion. I have basic motions outlined for most of the issues we deal with, but this one is different. It involves a very unique search and seizure issue, which requires a more extensive research. I never have any uninterrupted time at the office during the day to sit down and write. So I usually end up doing major research and writing projects at home on nights or weekends. Looks like this is going to be another late night!

1:00 a.m.   Time for Bed (so I can do it all again tomorrow)

I've been working on the motion for three hours and I'm not quite done, but I can't keep my eyes open anymore. I'll wake up early tomorrow and put the finishing touches on the motion before I leave for the office. 5:30 a.m. the next day is going to come way too soon.

5:30 a.m.   Here We Go Again!

Can't believe it's *that* time already. Well, here we go again!

Final Thoughts

Some days are busier than others are, but being a DUI defense attorney is what I've always wanted to do. And I can't imagine doing anything else. Running your own law firm or practice is not for everyone. As the owner, the buck stops with you. But with all that responsibility comes a lot of opportunity. If you work hard and strive to take good care of your clients, the rewards will come in the form of the respect and admiration of your colleagues, financial success, and most importantly the "thank you's" from your clients. If I have any advice, based on my experience, it is this: find what you love to do and good things will happen.

19

Profile 19
Christopher: Legal Guardian (State Appointed)

Executive Summary

Name: Christopher
Profile: Legal Guardian (State Appointed)
Location: Trenton, New Jersey

Christopher is a state-appointed legal guardian of one of the most vulnerable classes of people, young children. As a legal guardian, Chris represents a beacon of hope for many. Rightfully so, Christopher is proud of what this position enables him to do: seeking justice on behalf of those children who need it most. Being a legal guardian comes with heavy responsibility and many challenges that require long hours and possible fatigue, which may possibly put severe strain on your personal life. But if your heart lies in a stable government job with designated responsibilities, this may be the right field for you. With diligence, care, and thoughtfulness, to even the seemingly insignificant details, Christopher's twenty-four-hour profile representing underprivileged children on behalf of the state is both eye-opening and inspiring.

Profile

Career Field:	Government/State Attorney
Current Position:	State-Appointed Legal Guardian
Institution:	State of New Jersey
Location:	Trenton, New Jersey
Previous Position(s):	Legal Advisory
Education:	JD, Rutgers University, School of Law
	BA, Rutgers College
Licenses (Y/N):	Yes
Jurisdiction(s):	New Jersey/Federal Third Circuit/US Supreme Court

Schedule

12:01 a.m.	Receive Emergency E-Mail (re: reply brief)
5:35 a.m.	Wake-Up to the Chorus of Three-Year Old Twins (as a twenty-first century version of Mr. Mom)
6:30 a.m.	Negotiate with My Son
7:30 a.m.	Get Dressed/Breakfast Feeding Frenzy
8:00 a.m.	Work on Reply Brief (while managing the kids)
8:40 a.m.	Take Children to School
9:25 a.m.	Finish Reply Brief (while waiting for my wife to return)
10:10 a.m.	Attend Marriage Counseling Session
11:35 a.m.	Finish the Counseling Session/Grab an Early Lunch with My Wife
12:35 p.m.	Phone Conference Call (re: child abuse case)
2:43 p.m.	Work on Administrative Payment for Expert Witness Testimony (used in a recent case)
3:10 p.m.	Write Letter-Brief Opposing Visitation Rights
4:25 p.m.	Drive Secretary to Train Station/Go Home
5:11 p.m.	Arrive Home/Get Ready to Eat Dinner (with the family)
6:00 p.m.	Finish Eating Dinner/Play with the Kids
7:30 p.m.	Watch TV Show/Put Kids in Bed
8:20 p.m.	Work on Transcripts and Rough Draft
11:11 p.m.	Get Ready to Sleep
12:01 a.m.	Lights Out/Go to Bed

24-Hour Schedule

12:01 a.m.   *Receive Emergency E-Mail (re: reply brief)*

I've been helping the supervisor in my office with a high-profile case, which is on appeal. We lost at the trial level and we are in process of appealing the judge's decision. The supervisor wrote the statement of facts and procedural history and I authored the legal argument sections of the merit's brief. Earlier in the week, we received our adversary's response. Procedurally, we must have a reply brief filed by this coming Monday.

At approximately 9:27 p.m. a few hours earlier, I received an e-mail from the supervisor asking me when I can have a rough draft reply brief prepared. In my reply e-mail, I responded that I could have a rough draft finished by this Friday. She then sent me another e-mail informing me that she wants a rough draft sooner than that. While reading this, from my vantage point, it's important to remember that I work for the government and do not bill hours or get paid overtime. As a result, the extra work was on my own dime.

At approximately 12:01 a.m., I start working on the reply brief. This particular case has three novel issues that New Jersey courts have never decided. It's quite rare for a case to have one legal issue never decided before. Usually one novel issue requires hours of research. So the level of work needed to be dedicated to the brief is about triple of what would normally be required. Nonetheless, from midnight to 2:00 a.m., I conduct research in all fifty states and various federal courts on two of the three novel issues. At 2:15 a.m., I end up going to sleep without my rough draft finished, despite my best efforts.

5:35 a.m.   *Wake-Up to the Chorus of Three-Year Old Twins (as a twenty-first century version of Mr. Mom)*

Sometime in the middle of the night, my three-year-old twins crawled into bed with my wife and me. They woke me up at 5:35 a.m. and want to have cups of warm milk and watch cartoons. I didn't wake my wife to help me— I felt like being generous this morning—and instead, I let her sleep until 8:00 a.m. Between 5:30 a.m. and 6:30 a.m., the twins kept me busy. I prepare their milk, took the pull-ups off them that they wore to bed, and got them dressed.

Truth be told, my wife and I have had some marital issues that have recently led us to both contemplate filing for a divorce. But before taking this step, we jointly decided that we would pursue marriage counseling to explore whether our marriage should continue or not. Our first marriage counseling session is scheduled for 10 a.m. later today. So I'm taking the first half of the day off from work.

6:30 a.m.   *Negotiate with My Son*

At 6:30 a.m., my son Matthew woke up. He was a bit grumpy and claimed his legs hurt, which is why he could not get off the couch—or so he claims. Instead, he preferred that I let him sit there idly watching cartoons. I give him some leeway and allow him to drink his cup of milk.

7:30 a.m.   *Get Dressed/Breakfast Feeding Frenzy*

By 7:30 a.m., Matthew was showered and dressed. From this point, the breakfast feeding frenzy begins. And it's not a minute too soon—all three kids, in unison, complain about being hungry. I make them waffles and hide from the carnage left behind. Pancake syrup overflows onto the table and scraps of waffles fall on the floor around the kitchen table. My kids are messy eaters (who raised these kids, oh wait, never mind!). I clean up the mess the kids left behind and let them all watch cartoons (again).

8:00 a.m.   *Work on Reply Brief (while managing the kids)*

At 8:00 a.m., I began to work on the rough draft of my reply brief. Kimberly wakes up and takes a shower. I look over and see that my son Matthew is still hypnotized by the TV. But my other two kids, Kyle and Mallory, take turns opening the refrigerator and freezer doors. When I attempt to intercede into this early morning chaos, I discover that they were hiding their toys in the refrigerator and freezer (my role as father in my household is often half spent working on such Sherlock Holmes-type detective work). Once that's straightened out, I go back to work on my reply brief.

8:40 a.m.   *Take Children to School*

Kim gets out of the shower and is dressed by 8:40 a.m. She walks Matthew to school, which is a block from our home. Although Matthew's class starts at 8:45 a.m., Kimberly hasn't returned home just after that time, which is what she normally does. By 9:15 a.m., I text her three times, but with no response each time. The twins were very whiney and wanted to be held. I was having a difficult time writing my brief and was getting frustrated that Kimberly hadn't yet returned to help me with the kids so that I can finish my work.

9:25 a.m.   *Finish Reply Brief (while waiting for my wife to return)*

Finally, after what seems like a small eternity to me, my wife returns back home at 9:25 a.m. When I asked her what took her so long to get back home, she tells me that her phone was on vibrate mode and that she didn't get any of my text messages. Kimberly continued by telling me that she was talking to another mother at the school and had lost track of time. By 9:45 a.m., I finish the rough draft of my reply brief and e-mail a copy of it to my boss. I quickly shower, and my wife and I get ready to go to our first marriage counseling session. We argue a bit while we get in the car, which makes for a fairly quiet and uncomfortable ride to the counseling session (what a perfect beginning, I say to myself).

10:10 a.m.   *Attend Marriage Counseling Session*

After a short (but uncomfortable) drive, my wife and I arrive at the marriage counseling location—since it's our first session, we're both a little anxious since we don't know exactly what to expect. The main reception area is fairly quiet and what you would expect to see—pretty minimal in terms of furniture, with a few magazines on a table and several replicas of famous paintings hanging on the wall.

When we walk in to see our therapist, I'm a bit relieved since the therapist appears, at least from my first impression, to be a relatively nice and intelligent woman. During the next forty-five minutes, we explain the details of our marital problems (I'm surprised that's all the time it took, to tell you the truth!). And at the end of the hour, she advises us that we would need to come back for more therapy, so we schedule an appointment for a week later. All in all, the session wasn't as bad as I imagined.

11:35 a.m.   *Finish the Counseling Session/Grab an Early Lunch with My Wife*

My wife and I exit the marriage counselor's office at 11:35 am. Afterwards, we get in the car and find a local diner—New Jersey is famous for its plethora of street side diners—to grab an early lunch (marriage counseling sessions have a way of working up an appetite in me!). So we look at the menu and both choose to eat a light lunch. While doing so, we discuss the issues that have been causing all the strain in our marriage. I'm not sure but I think the waitress, who has a nose ring and her lip pierced, was flirting with my wife.

After lunch, I remember that I have a phone conference scheduled for 12:30 p.m. with a professor of a local law school and the supervisor from my office's appellate section at my office. I drop off my wife back at home and rush to work at 12:17 p.m.

12:35 p.m.   *Phone Conference Call (re: child abuse case)*

After rushing to find a parking spot and run into my office for my scheduled conference call, I quickly dial into the designated conference call number, type in the conference call pin number, and enter into the conversation. I find out that—much to my relief—I only missed the introduction of the people present for the conference call.

The professor represents two of the children in our high-profile child abuse case. She wants to appeal the ruling of the judge from a previous hearing. Although we did not oppose the filing of the appeal, all persons who participated in the conference call disagreed on the best way to effectuate the appeal as well as how to stay the trial court's order. During the course of the conversation, honestly, I felt incredibly frustrated. Despite my years of experience doing appellate work—and despite the fact that the managing attorney from my appellate section agreed with my suggested course of action—the supervisor from my office did not support us, and instead, agreed with and adopted the professor's approach. We decided to file the appeals both ways as alternative pleadings. Twenty-one days later, we learned that the Appellate Court disagreed with the professor's approach and granted the motion based on my pleadings. It's nice to be right.

2:43 p.m.	*Work on Administrative Payment for Expert Witness Testimony (used in a recent case)*

I open up a letter I received from a psychiatrist who I used as an expert in a recent trial. Although I primarily do appellate work, I volunteered to handle this trial to break up the monotony of my appellate practice. The psychiatrist's letter was a bill for his services and a request for immediate payment. I mailed the psychiatrist a blank voucher form and instructed him to fill out the form and submit it with his itemization of services.

3:10 p.m.	*Write Letter-Brief Opposing Visitation Rights*

In addition to filing appellate briefs, I'm responsible for replying to all motions, no matter whether they are frivolous or meritorious, for each of the cases assigned to me. Between 3:10 p.m. and 4:20 p.m., I write a letter-brief opposing visitation rights between the biological parents and their child because the termination of their parental rights have been affirmed by the appellate division. In my opinion, it was a meritless motion, but one that had to be responded to. I submit the brief to my boss for review before I file it with the court.

4:25 p.m.	*Drive Secretary to Train Station/Go Home*

At 4:25 p.m., I leave work to drive my secretary to the train station so she wouldn't miss her scheduled train. This small courtesy is worth a positive relationship with my secretary (if only marriage was so easy, I think to myself). At 4:35 p.m., I depart from the train station and then drive home. While driving, I receive a phone call from my wife letting me know that she was getting hungry and was thinking about what to eat for dinner tonight.

5:11 p.m.	*Arrive Home/Get Ready to Eat Dinner (with the family)*

I drive into my driveway and get out of the car. My home isn't extravagant, but it's enough for my needs (I was never the materialistic type, which is in part what allows me to do the work that I do, at a government pay rate). I walk through my front door. The kids are glad to see me (wait until they're teenagers though) and in unison rush toward me to give their father a big hug. My daughter Mallory gives me a hug and a kiss, and the boys wrestle me to the ground and bear hug me again.

I really do enjoy coming home from work. Matthew told me that he finished his homework and that he received a certificate in school for being good all week. We usually try to eat dinner together as a family and today is no exception. Dinner is filled with mostly the kids clowning around and avoiding eating their dinner (my story of how there's starving children in other parts of the world has yet to wield the persuasive response that I had hoped for). Luckily, the dinner menu tonight of chicken and rice goes over well with the kids.

6:00 p.m.   *Finish Eating Dinner/Play with the Kids*

By approximately 6:00 p.m., we finish eating dinner. While my wife works on cleaning up after the meal, I give the twins a bath and dress them in their pajamas. Yes, it's a bit early for pajamas, but I figure it's better to do this sooner than later, so I can frontload my responsibilities to leave some time for me to do some work later in the evening. My son Matthew showers and dresses for bed without incident. And between 6:45 p.m. and 7:30 p.m., I play with the kids. The boys want to pretend they are good guy characters with me as the bad guy. At the same time, Mallory pretends to be making meals and snacks for me to eat.

7:30 p.m.   *Watch TV Show/Put Kids in Bed*

At 7:30 p.m., play time ends and I end up spending half an hour just trying to calm down the kids by watching an episode of a popular kids TV show. After the show ends thirty minutes later, the kids brush their teeth and they are all in bed for the night by 8:15 p.m.—mission accomplished!

8:20 p.m.   *Work on Transcripts and Rough Draft*

My wife Kimberly sits at the kitchen table to study for an upcoming microbiology exam. The course is a perquisite for the nursing school she will be entering in the fall. I settle down with a box of transcripts and the laptop trying to refine a "rough draft." We take turns doing the laundry, folding the clothes, and putting the clothes away.

11:11 p.m.   *Get Ready to Sleep*

Kimberly announces she's done studying for the night and is going to bed. I let the dog outside, lock the doors and windows, check up on the kids, and join my wife in bed at approximately 11:30 p.m.

12:01 a.m.   *Lights Out/Go to Bed*

While crawling into bed, my wife wakes up, despite the fact that I tried to be as quiet as possible. She asks me whether I'm happy with our married life as well as with my career. It's late at night. So as a good lawyer, I try to delay the issue as much as possible by saying, "I really want both to work out in the best way possible. And with continuous effort, I'm sure everything will work out fine." After saying this, I reach over to turn the lights off—to await another twenty-four hours in my life as a state-appointed law guardian (as well as a father and husband).

Final Thoughts

To explain a little bit about what I do, I am a law guardian. A law guardian provides legal representation to children who have been the victim of their parent or parents' physical, emotional, or psychological abuse. Often the goal is to provide the family with support and to reunify the child with their biological family. When those efforts fail, I represent the child in actions brought by the state to terminate their biological parents' parental rights. I do not do the trial work, but am assigned to the appellate section of the law guardian's office and represent children in the state of New Jersey's Appellate Division, the state's Supreme Court, and the United States Supreme Court. One of my career highlights, in fact, has been arguing a case in front of the esteemed judges of the New Jersey State Supreme Court. So, attending law school definitely helped me to pursue and attain the career that I am in now. It may not be glorious work in terms of money. But more than money is the overwhelming feeling of accomplishment I get from knowing that I am helping to fight for justice for the ones who need it the most—the innocent and disadvantaged children of our community.

20

Profile 20
Jonathan: Media and Entertainment Laywer

Executive Summary

Name: Jonathan
Profile: Media and Entertainment Lawyer
Location: Los Angeles, California

Did you ever wonder what it would be like to work for an extremely prominent magazine and media entity centered around the glitz and glamour of Hollywood and Beverly Hills? Well, you need to look no further. Jonathan's twenty-four-hour profile provides a rare glimpse into the high-flying lifestyle of a media and entertainment lawyer. But as you'll see, his life is not always filled with cocktail parties and celebrities—although sometimes it is. The sense you'll probably get is that media and entertainment is largely about the creation and protection of ideas, which links in part, to copyright protection. Jonathan's role also involves trying to expand his firm's global media and entertainment presence to other parts of the world outside the US, which is becoming an increasingly common trend. Read more about the conquests and pitfalls that someone in Jonathan's shoes may face in his or her typical day as a media and entertainment lawyer based in the heart of the entertainment industry— Los Angeles, California.

Profile

Career Field:	Media/Entertainment
Current Position:	In-House Legal Counsel
Institution:	Major International Media Company (focusing on Entertainment)
Location:	Los Angeles, California
Previous Position(s):	General Counsel, Media and Technology Company/Associate Major Law Firm
Education:	JD, Duke Law School
	MA, Duke University
	BA, University of Colorado, Boulder
Licensed (Y/N):	Yes
Jurisdictions:	California

Schedule

5:45 a.m.	The Grand Entrance: Child Enters Room to Start the Day
6:00 a.m.	Check E-Mails from Australia/Asia/Europe/East Coast/Respond to E-Mails
6:45 a.m.	Make Breakfast and Lunch for Kids/Continue to Respond to E-Mails
7:05 a.m.	Receive Emergency E-Mail from Cable Company
7:15 a.m.	Make Calls to Address Emergency While Getting Kids Dressed
7:45 a.m.	Get a Shower/Get Dressed/Get in Car
8:20 a.m.	Make Calls in Car
8:55 a.m.	Arrive at Office
9:00 a.m.	Make Calls Internally to Ensure Emergency Response is Fulfilled
9:30 a.m.	Legal Staff Meeting
10:15 a.m.	Quickly Review E-Mails before Senior Staff Meeting
10:30 a.m.	Senior Executive Meeting
11:30 a.m.	Review Major Distribution Deal with US Content Distributor
12:25 p.m.	Go to Lunch with Content Distributor
1:45 p.m.	Call with Europe to Finalize Agreement Along with Staff Attorney

2:00 p.m.	Meeting with International Partner on Internet Expansion in South America
3:30 p.m.	Peruse Company Content Delivered to Office
3:45 p.m.	Meeting with Staff Attorney to Review Key Issues in Small Transactions
4:30 p.m.	Call from President of Company Asking for Update on M&A Transaction
5:00 p.m.	Review Letter Claiming Copyright Violations
5:30 p.m.	Meeting with Talent Regarding Proposed Joint Venture
6:45 p.m.	Leave for Drinks with Talent
8:30 p.m.	Get Home and Help Put Kids to Bed
9:25 p.m.	Review Latest Drafts of M&A Transaction Documents
11:30 p.m.	Call with Australia Regarding Programming Delivery Issues
12:15 a.m.	Go to Bed to the Sound of My BlackBerry Buzzing with More E-Mails
5:45 a.m.	Another Grand Entrance Awaits for a New Day

24-Hour Schedule

5:45 a.m.   *The Grand Entrance: Child Enters Room to Start the Day*

You never know which one of my children will make their grand entrance first. But it's usually my two-year old who enters my room first. You can hear him from the time that he crawls out of bed. His door always makes a loud "crack" when opened. Then the footsteps. Bump, bump, bump, bump. Then he's standing right next to the bed saying "uppy" so that he can climb in bed, sit on my chest, and ask to watch TV. Occasionally it will be the five-year old boy informing me that he has wet himself, although he is usually already in our bed cuddled up to my wife. I seldom remember him coming into the room. On rare occasions, it will be my five-year old daughter, wondering where everyone is. It doesn't matter. This is how the day starts. Every day. Time to get going.

6:00 a.m.   *Check E-Mails from Australia/Asia/Europe/East Coast/Respond to E-Mails*

Time to grab my son, plop him in front of *Phineas and Ferb* (a TV cartoon comedy series), and check the BlackBerry. Hmm, only twelve new e-mails overnight. Not too bad. A sample of my in-box e-mail issues include the following: a request from Australia on when next draft of the contract will be sent; a question from Korea (as to whether we have content that edits out the more explicit scenes of a show or if the Korean company will need to edit it themselves); the fiber link between England and Spain went down for twenty minutes; a Middle Eastern government is trying to shut down our channel in that country; and the business development executive in New York is wondering where his term sheet is to buy another media company.

Time to start answering some of my e-mails. I start by pushing off the Australia-related query for later, forwarding the Korea-related question to the programming department, and adding to my task list that I need to check service level agreement provisions of the contract to see if there is anything due to us. As for the issue related to the Middle East, that's a problem. I'm going to have to find local legal counsel there to let us know what is going on. There's not a ton of revenue there. But there's enough to hurt the guy's chances of hitting their number (target quota) for this fiscal year. I also remind the business development executive that the term sheet was sent to him two weeks ago.

6:45 a.m.   *Make Breakfast and Lunch for Kids/Continue to Respond to E-Mails*

I take a quick break to get back to the kids. What should I make for breakfast? I made pancakes yesterday and the day before. I guess it's going to be instant French toast for today. Should I make bacon? Not today, too much to do. And lunch, what's for lunch? I don't know. Did I make them chicken nuggets yesterday? I don't think so. Okay, chicken nuggets it is! Oh, there's that buzzing sound coming from my BlackBerry. This means more e-mails are coming in. After reviewing the e-mail, I notice that it's from a client in New York asking for another copy of the term sheet. Also, I notice another e-mail that just came in—my office is writing to demand immediate attention to the fiber issue. What do they want me to do? I need to see the contract.

In between checking my e-mails, I try to focus on the other issue at hand—breakfast for my children. I say to them, "What's that munchkin? Juice? Sorry. Apple or grape?" When I look at my BlackBerry again, I see yet another e-mail from Germany—they're asking me if I'll be coming to Berlin this year. I don't think so, not at this rate.

7:05 a.m.   Receive Emergency E-Mail from Cable Company

After a quick break, I hear another buzz indicating an e-mail coming in. Uh oh, this is a problem. Some tech worker doing maintenance put one of our more adult-themed channels up on a kids channel for almost two minutes this morning. The cable company wants to get a copy of what was playing on Channel XX from 5:32 to 5:34 a.m. this morning. It's almost too much, so I ask for some assistance from my wife with the kids, "Honey, can you watch the kids for a second. What? Oh, you're in the shower?" Ugh. I need to call the cable executive right away about this. I think to myself, "What happened? Oh Lord. Any complaints yet? Okay, let me call the operations department to get a copy of the tape showing what exactly was aired."

Among this storm of e-mails and thoughts, I turn my attention to my daughter, "What's that sweetheart? You don't want French toast? You love French toast. Okay, just eat your fruit and I'll get you some cinnamon toast."

I return to my work e-mails. I type a quick message, "I'll have the content FTP'd (file transfer protocol, a standard protocol to copy one file type to another) to you ASAP." I also call the operations department and make sure that they have the playback duplicated and sent out to the cable company ASAP.

7:15 a.m.   Make Calls to Address Emergency While Getting Kids Dressed

I then call out to my wife again while I go into the various bedrooms to pick out clothes for my kids, "Honey, can you watch the kids? I need to call Mike (the company president) and George (the company general counsel.)." I dial up the company general counsel first, "Hey, George. We had a problem last night. 'Cable Company X' switched feeds and put 'Channel XX' onto a kids feed for two minutes on the East Coast. George replies by asking me if I've relayed this information to Mike, the company president, "No, I haven't called Mike yet. But I will. And I'll notify the programming department to make sure that any calls get rerouted to the cable company."

I then call the company president, "Hello, Mike? This is Jonathan. One of the cable companies had a problem…." After several minutes discussing the relevant details with him, I hang up. I then get the kids dressed while making sure everyone in the firm that needs to know there was a problem knows.

7:45 a.m.   Get a Shower/ Get Dressed/ Get in Car

I try to get my wife's attention yet again, "Hey honey. Can you watch the kids? Thanks." Finally, I can now use the bathroom! I know full well that this time is precious yet short. So I use this time to for a quick shave and then jump in the shower and pick out some clothes for the day. After this, I head to the kitchen where I see my wife. Despite my best efforts to be fashionably smart, much to my dismay, the first thing she tells me is that my clothes don't match. What to do? I can't exactly embarrass myself by not meeting my full fashion potential and/or run the risk of some comments by my fellow coworkers about it (in good humor, of course). So I go back and change my shirt. That will do, I figure. I then corral the kids into the car, jump in, put the keys into the ignition, and drive to work.

8:20 a.m.   Make Calls in Car

Coffee is essential. I grab a mug and fill it to the brim. It's now time to make some calls. Whom should I call first? I quickly decide that I better follow-up with the operations department and make sure they are doing what they need to be doing. I place the call, "Steve, yeah, is it out yet? No? What are you doing? Well, stop working on that and get the stuff out. Sure, call Mike or George. I don't care, just get it done as soon as possible."

One of the problems of being a lawyer is that everyone is always in CYA ("Cover Your [A--]") mode when you call. I guess it's just the nature of the defensively postured legal profession to always try to minimize legal risk. I then think whom I should call next. I decide to call Peter. "Hey, Peter, what's up? Are we still on for lunch? Great. See you then." I then make a mental note to myself: start using your assistant to confirm appointments! And then what's next after that. Wait, it doesn't matter, at least not this very moment—there's a good short piece on NPR (National Public Radio) that I tune into for a few preciously brief minutes while driving to the office.

8:55 a.m.   *Arrive At Office*

When I walk into the office, it's always the same obligatory salutations in the morning, "Good morning," "Good morning." "Good morning." "How about that game last night?" "Good morning." Yes, there's a ton to do and getting into my office and getting started is important. But it's important that people feel that you care enough to go through the pleasantries. I ask these people to go well beyond the norm for me when necessary. So I figure that the least I can do is to greet them each day.

9:00 a.m.   *Make Calls Internally to Ensure Emergency Response is Fulfilled*

Now that I'm settled, it's time to make sure that the critical matters on my plate are addressed. "Steve, did you FTP the footage out yet? Yes? Please copy me on the e-mail then when you send it out. And make sure that your team isn't talking to anyone about what happened." Now I call the customer. "Hey, did you get the tape? Great. We're going to re-direct any calls we receive to you. Where do you want the calls sent? If I were you, I'd set up a dedicated line with a couple of customer service reps (representatives) ready with an answer as to what occurred. I can't imagine you'll get more than a few calls. If needed, give them (disgruntled customers) a couple of months free cable service. Sure, I'm available if any of your execs (executives) want to talk. Let me know what I can do." Now I check in with our own customer service reps to see if any calls have come in up to this point. My guess is probably not since people probably didn't know the footage was ours. I confirm this, and good, no calls so far. Time to move on.

9:30 a.m.   *Legal Staff Meeting*

Time for our legal staff meeting. These meetings are funny. They are important because they keep everyone in the loop and on the same page. But, and I stress this point, if not conducted correctly, these meetings start to become redundant. The secret is to keep the meeting organized and brief. And always have an agenda.

For me, I have a master task list for my entire legal team that is updated at these meetings. Then specific questions can be asked. For the meetings, I try to mix it up a bit, and try to bring coffee and donuts every so often (it's amazing how caffeine and sugar do wonders to get the legal mind going!).

I start the meeting with domestic deals. "No, you can't give MFN provisions (short for 'most favored nations provisions that provide that the entity you are contracting with will get the best deal you offer any other party for a similar deal) to that small of a system. Just tell them that we won't do it. Period." Now onto international legal issues. One issue relates to a Scandinavian transaction, "Doesn't the TV deal in Norway conflict with granting those rights online in the territory? Check out the chart and pull the contract. I seem to remember that cable television is defined broadly enough to include online distribution. We need to make sure that doesn't happen in future contracts." Done.

10:15 a.m.   Quickly Review E-Mails before Senior Staff Meeting

After about forty-five minutes, the legal staff meeting finishes. I take a quick look at my watch—wouldn't you know it, I have another meeting—this time it's a senior executive staff meeting that's set to begin just a few short minutes from now at 10:30 a.m. Almost instinctually, I wonder how many e-mails have come in since the start of the legal staff meeting? I check—whew, only five. One is from my wife. She wrote, "Do you know where the keys are?" I respond by writing, "No, I don't know where the keys are." On a separate note, the cable company is now saying that so far no calls to complain about the incident have gone to the call center. That's great news. I also get an e-mail reminder from a business development executive to send along the promised term sheet. I quickly find the file in my computer and then click the "Send" button—done. As I prepare to head off to the senior executive staff meeting, I grab another cup of coffee.

10:30 a.m.   Senior Executive Meeting

The senior executive meeting has the same purpose as the legal staff meeting, but at a higher level. I have to provide a quick update on "material" issues that I'm working on. First, the company president talks about how we need to focus on getting more revenue from Europe. Then he mentions that the CEO of our South American partner called him to complain that we're not being cooperative enough. Next, the corporate financial officer (CFO) talks about the need to keep travel and entertainment expenses in line with budgets.

Now it's my turn. I give a brief update on deals that are big enough for anyone to matter. That's when the president tosses in, "Did you hear what happened at the party last night?" "No." "One of the guests grabbed one of the female workers. She didn't seem very upset initially, but she called this morning saying that she's traumatized. Do I hand this to you?" This is when it's nice *not* being the boss. "No, that has to go to George. Make sure nobody deletes any e-mails or text messages. George will want to see a guest list and he'll want to know why security didn't tell him about it yet." "I was hoping it was going to blow over." "Okay, well, it hasn't blown over yet, so let's get George the info and see where it plays from here." The rest of the meeting is filled with updates on each of the departments. I have to resist checking my BlackBerry during the meeting since I hear it buzzing all the while.

11:30 a.m.   *Review Major Distribution Deal with US Content Distributor*

It's almost noon and it's only now that I finally have a chance to get some of the work on my desk done. A major US-based platform has been waiting for comments to the contract for almost a week now. And the sales guy is calling every couple of hours to find out when the document will be ready. The main focus is on the business terms. Let's get to work. Business terms seem to match the term sheet. Wait, I think to myself, what's this change to the MFN provision. No, no, no. Any MFN must require matching all terms and conditions for getting the terms. MFNs are tricky since they can create a major headache if it's not complied with properly. I also notice that this proposed representation goes too far—there's no way we can confirm that a girl who will appear in one of our upcoming magazine publications hasn't been published in this particular way before. That's a crazy thing to ask for from my view on things. We also need to work on the indemnification language. I keep reading. Ugh.

12:25 p.m.   *Go to Lunch with Content Distributor*

I look at the time—is it really already past noon? I need to get out of here. I'm meeting Jerry over in Hollywood at the sushi place he loves. We've been trying to get Jerry's boss to license a bunch more content from us for a while now. I run out the door and make it to the restaurant with no time to spare. Jerry is already sitting at the sushi bar. We chat about sports and how good the tuna looks. We order oyster shooters and a bunch of sliced fish. Toward the end, I ask what it's going to take to get more content licensed. I'm not happy with Jerry's response: "Well, a little bit of money under the table would probably help move things along a bit." "We don't do that." "That's too bad, because your competitor has some great new content that it's trying to get sold in right now." This is not a productive lunch—except for the decent sushi.

1:45 p.m.   *Call with Europe to Finalize Agreement Along with Staff Attorney*

I'm upset now. I hate being shaken down, as I felt I was during the lunch I just had with Jerry. I call the sales guy on the drive back to the office and let him know about my discussion with Jerry. The sales guy is pissed also. Oh well. After a few more seconds, I say, "Hey, I got to go. I have a call." I reach out to my lawyer in London to jump on a call with an English (UK-based) mobile company. It's almost 9:00 p.m. at night over there, but everyone is going strong. I ask, "What's left on the contract?" I'm told about three open issues. "Okay, we can give you a bit more time to pay at the end of each quarter. We can't move at all on the indemnification language or the MFN. Sorry, but those are things we have to have." A lot of hemming and hawing occurs during the call. But the deal closes. To which I say, "Great. We'll get revisions to you by tomorrow." I try to always have my side make revisions. I prefer having the control over this part of the process to make sure everything is done as I believe it needs to be done.

2:00 p.m.   *Meeting with International Partner on Internet Expansion in South America*

Our Mexican partner's CEO is in the office today to attend a big meeting to discuss how we can permit the partner to expand further into South America. I've prepared a chart that shows what territories are available on what media platforms, and who owns the platforms that are not available. Of course, the discussion starts with the insistence that all of South America must be in the deal. Executives then start to come up with "innovative" (complex) solutions. I am an advocate of making things as simple as possible, but I'm in the minority. So I provide advice on why certain strategies don't work, but at the same time, also provide some ideas on what might work. A fundamental rule I have for lawyers is; if you raise a problem, you must propose a solution. People hate lawyers because they are always pointing out why things can't be done. I want lawyers around me that find ways to get things done. Of course, this meeting is testing my own ability to comply with my own rules.

3:30 p.m.   *Peruse Company Content Delivered to Office*

I return to my office. There is a package of materials that my company will be offering to the public in the next month. I flip through some articles as well as admiring some of the pictures (it's always strange having it be a legitimate business activity and legal career to look at, shall I say, artistic memorialized images of models). I also watch some of the video (as part of my job). While not a critical element of my job, I do believe that all employees should be up-to-date on what the company is doing, and know the latest. This way, if a comment arises in a conversation with a customer, you don't sound too distant from the company's business.

3:45 p.m.   *Meeting with Staff Attorney to Review Key Issues in Small Transactions*

One of my team stops by my office and knocks on the door, wondering if I have a few seconds to talk. It turns out there is a major problem with a small customer who is insisting on a MFN provision. The attorney recommends a few work-around recommendations. I am happy that he is meeting my expectations in presenting a solution. Yet, in this case, I hold firm. No MFN's for small customers. Period. I tell him the important thing is to make sure that our business executive knows that I will not budge on this issue. I don't want any back-channel communication with the customer that we will provide some wiggle room on this issue. The company's position with this customer is firm. We will walk away from the deal over this point. My gut feeling is that the customer is not going to kill the deal over this point, and that it is important that the company maintain as firm a stance on this topic as possible.

4:30 p.m.   *Call from President of Company Asking for Update on M&A Transaction*

The company has been in a long and arduous negotiation to acquire another media company, and there is mounting frustration with the process. The company president has taken to calling both me and outside counsel on a regular basis to obtain status reports and to push hard to get the deal done. There are a myriad of problems, including a lack of quality due diligence on the (media) library we may be acquiring. The data dump from the target with respect to the library listed all of the individual scenes shot that will be acquired. I explain to the company president that I need the content guys to go through the library very carefully so that we have a good understanding of what we're buying, and that we need to spot check the footage to ensure that it is of the quality we need. This will take some time. But I'm advising against the company shelling out this much money without a substantial understanding of what we're getting our hands on. Mike understands, but it is clear he is getting frustrated. I'm below the rank of the top content executive. So I ask Mike if it makes sense for him or I to call and push on moving the process forward. We both agree that Mike should do it.

5:00 p.m.   *Review Letter Claiming Copyright Violations*

I get very few important letters nowadays almost all my written correspondence is by e-mail. That's why it piques my interest when I see a letter from a law firm I don't recognize. I open it and take a look. It's a cease and desist and settlement demand based on our use of a photograph taken by a school photographer twelve years ago. It's always nice when an issue falls onto someone else's lap. While I understand the company's position with respect to fair use (which, in certain specified circumstances, allows for the limited use of copyrighted materials without consent from the copyright holder) in this circumstance, I joyfully have my assistant scan the letter and send it off to the general counsel's office, where it will be dealt as we have dealt with the numerous similar claims we get each year.

5:30 p.m.   *Meeting with Talent Regarding Proposed Joint Venture*

After spending some time going through e-mails and answering questions, I notice that it's time for the meeting set up by our business development department for a proposed joint venture with some talent that we regularly work with. It's always fun to get to meet talent. This particular talent has done a number of pictorials for us before. Thus, when she comes into the room with a big smile, it's hard not to think of some of those pictures. That said, this is about business. Her husband is there as well. As is usual with people who are not experienced in the business aspect of our business, the understanding of how deals work and the actual dollar amounts involved is low.

These meetings usually go the same way. The other side presents what they believe to be a great idea. Then they lay out the proposed business proposition. Then we say that we'll either think about it (with no intent of thinking about it) or spend some time educating the other side on what a deal might look at. This proposition is actually interesting. So we start the process of the reality of the economics on a deal like this. There just might be something here.

6:45 p.m.   *Leave for Drinks with Talent*

It's the end of the day. So we decide to continue the discussion regarding the joint venture over drinks. I, of course, try to find a place to grab drinks that is closer toward my home. But we end up heading the other way to a nice spot that is an up and coming hot spot. It's always fun to see people turn to look at a beautiful woman and then have that woman make room for you to sit down. Of course, if I mention where I work, a few women will work their way over to speak with me, hoping for an opportunity to work with my company. Economists like to call this a "positive externality" of the job—I just see it as one of the unsolicited fringe benefits of working where I do.

8:30 p.m.   *Get Home and Help Put Kids to Bed*

I look at my BlackBerry and notice that it's getting late. I tell the talent that we should work on a business plan and talk next week. I then excuse myself and head for my car. I like to be home to help put the kids to bed, and it's going to be close tonight. You hate to get home right as they're getting into bed since then they get up for hugs and kisses and don't go to bed for another half hour. But sometimes that is inevitable.

I get home and the kids' bedrooms are dark. So I enter quietly and whisper a quiet "hello" to my wife. Then you hear the crack of the door open to my youngest son's bedroom followed by the word, "Daddy!!!" This creates a domino effect—then all the kids come out and give me hugs and jump around. Now I get to spend the next forty minutes reading, telling stories, and getting them back to bed.

9:25 p.m.   Review Latest Drafts of M&A Transaction Documents

Finally, the kids are asleep. I decide to use this time to catch up on some work and pull out the latest drafts of the M&A (merger and acquisition) documents we've been working on. We have outside counsel for a deal this big. But I still need to review these documents carefully to pick up company specific issues that outside lawyers might miss. I force myself to read every word of every document. Of course, this is going on with the peppering of conversation and questions from my wife. I draft an e-mail with my comments to outside counsel with a note that we should speak first thing in the morning.

11:30 p.m.   Call with Australia Regarding Programming Delivery Issues

We've been having some problems with a network in Australia claiming that our content delivery is not in compliance with the contract. So I've scheduled a call to go over the issue. On the call, I remind everyone that the goal is for us to be working together and not fly specking the contract looking for breaches.

The network is a long-term partner. I don't want to get into a fight over contractual interpretation. Let's work on a solution, I say. The network feels that we should be encoding the content into multiple formats for them (instead of the network having to pay for it). Multiple formats were not contemplated in the initial contract. This is a tough one because when costs are involved, no one wants to eat them. We go through the language of the contract and what the costs we're talking about amount to. I have an idea of doing the encoding for the network as a rate that covers our costs since we have the capacity. But I can't make the offer until I run it by the facility guys. I let the network know that we will send them a note tomorrow our time with a couple of ideas.

12:15 a.m.   *Go to Bed to the Sound of My BlackBerry Buzzing with More E-Mails*

I look at the clock—wow, past midnight already?! I decide that's enough work for today (well, technically, it's another day) and I jump into bed to get what few precious hours of sleep I can.

5:45 a.m.   *Another Grand Entrance awaits for a New Day*

It's a twenty-four-hour world. I get up and take my BlackBerry into the kitchen. I need some sleep!!

Final Thoughts

What is the practice of law? My career has taken me down so many paths, I don't know how to answer that question anymore. For law firm attorneys, the practice of law is better defined. For those of us in an in-house legal counsel position, the practice of law takes on many aspects of legal analysis and guidance, while also taking on the role of a business executive.

From my perspective, the most important thing for in-house lawyers to remember is why we are there in the first place. Lawyers are often the only people to be reading every word of a document. And we are trained to understand the legal consequences of each provision of a contract. That is critical, given how long and complex many documents have become, and how many people try to sneak things into agreements. Just as important, in-house lawyers should serve as a moral compass to the company they serve. If lawyers start to dance on the line of ethics, every other executive will take that lead. And soon, the entire company is crossing that line. Finally, in-house lawyers need to make sure that the workflow continues. The legal department is where all deals travel through. So a backlog starts to affect the entire company. We all get overwhelmed and backed up. But it is important for the legal department to roll up its sleeves and get the work done (or at least beg for more lawyers!).

I often say that the reason that lawyers get paid better than other executives is that we do the work that nobody else wants to do. No matter how fun the job seems to others, being a lawyer is tough work.

21

Profile 21
Kem: Musician

Executive Summary

Name: Kem
Profile: Musician
Location: Bangkok, Thailand

If you have already secured a comfortable position and professional status in your legal career—enough to be able to balance work with your "other passion" and try new things—then Kem's simultaneous career as a musician (songwriter/producer) and legal consultant could be a great inspiration to those interested. As a musician, specifically, Kem miraculously organizes his day so that he can work on his music most of the time (including the wee hours of the early morning) while acting as a legal consultant for a private Thai real estate company leveraging his legal background. However, this life may not be for everyone. As Kem acknowledges, some of the challenges can be the probable scenario of relatively less income or perceived success in both careers, compared to being focused on just one career. To maintain his career lifestyle, Kem shows a great deal of commitment and ability to take risks even if it is a big life-altering decision. His career might be portrayed as a lucky and unique case in a unique setting. But he sets a good example that his passion was his biggest asset that guided him. As you will see from reading Kem's twenty-four-hour career profile, it is such innate passion for music that has allowed him to remain true to himself, which is, in and of itself, a truly noble virtue.

Profile

Career Field(s):	Music Production (and Law)
Current Position(s):	Songwriter/Producer/Lawyer
Institution:	Independent
Location:	Bangkok, Thailand
Previous Position(s):	Vice President, Lehman Brothers
	Training Officer, Siam Commercial Bank
Education:	JD, Suffolk University, School of Law
	MA, Indiana University of Pennsylvania
	BA, Thammasat University
Licensed:	Yes
Jurisdictions:	New York

Schedule

5:20 a.m.	Wake-Up (with a flash of inspiration)/Summarize and Write Ideas
5:50 a.m.	Experiment and Practice the Ideas on Guitar
7:30 a.m.	Review the To-Do List for Today
8:00 a.m.	Revise Arrangement/Prepare for a Recording Session
8:45 a.m.	Record "Punch-Ins" for Various Songs in Home Studio
10:20 a.m.	Check E-Mails/Check the Thai Stock Market/Read Newspaper
10:45 a.m.	Review a Lease and Service Agreement/Draft a New Section
11:30 a.m.	Walk My Dog/Make Phone Calls
12:30 p.m.	Meeting with a Potential Distributor
1: 45 p.m.	Arrive at the Mixing Studio/Audition Mixed Songs with ` Engineers
3:10 p.m.	Go Back Home/Have Lunch/Work on Lease Agreement
3:30 p.m.	Magazine Interview
4:40 p.m.	Check the Markets (again)/Call Stockbroker
5:00 p.m.	Call My Mother/Walk My Dog
6:10 p.m.	Attend a National Jazz Competition/Confirm Session Dates with Musicians
7:30 p.m.	Eat Dinner/Review Reports (sent by equity analysts)
8:15 p.m.	Finalize the Proposed Section for the Lease Agreement

8:45 p.m.	Discuss Album Cover Concept with Photographer
10:15 p.m.	Attend a "Reality Party" (sponsored by a mobile phone brand)
11:20 p.m.	Go Back Home/Confirm Mastering Session Details (over e-mail)
11:40 p.m.	Hop In Bed/Watch Dorama (Japanese TV show)/Read a Book
2:00 a.m.	In Bed/Can't Sleep (so I get up to play piano)
3:30 a.m.	Finally Sleep (somewhere around this time)
5:20 a.m.	Wake-Up to the Sound of the Alarm Clock

24-Hour Schedule

5:20 a.m.   *Wake-Up (with a flash of inspiration)/Summarize and Write Ideas*

It has to sound "Fierce and Free." "Laser Shrieks" and "Jet Engines." This is what you may call a flash of inspiration—and I don't know how it came. I only know that I have to record it before I forget it. On a notepad at my bedside table, I hurriedly write down the words that just dawned on me, perfectly describing the guitar solo part of a song that I'm working on. The song is called "Endgame," with lyrics about the need to stay focused in a hostile environment. Or so I thought. I already e-mailed the song demo to some principal musicians. The demo has a complete, but rudimentary, harmony and time signature arrangement in the song. But still there's no guitar solo, since I had no idea how to approach my role for that part yet. I'm in the process of completing the recording sessions for my third album. So it seems inevitable that I'll have to record that solo. But I wasn't sure how—until this morning. Jet engine? Laser shrieks? If I was lucky, a musical idea would come with such clarity that I could almost hear it in its finished form. That's not the case here. But I get up, very excited to find out more about it.

5:50 a.m.   *Experiment and Practice the Ideas on Guitar*

Whenever a musical idea arrives as it did this morning, I try to articulate it in my head as much as possible before reaching for a musical instrument. Like many musicians, I find that instruments tend to carry you away from the idea, and land you where you're most physically comfortable (e.g., where your fingers usually move when you practice, etc.). This may result in something that sounds fine, but not original enough. After settling with some concrete ideas in my head, I experiment playing the Jet Engine squeals with various approaches. Finally, I hear something I like: a combination of picking the notes while simultaneously manipulating the tremolo bar and a Whammy Pedal. The melodies I had in mind for the solo are then executed with this approach, constituting a passage. After practicing the passage against a metronome until I can play it comfortably, I record a take of it on my cell phone.

7:30 a.m.   *Review the To-Do List for Today*

Whatever I do for a living is largely a means to produce music. To arrive at that means, I have two main tools: a long-term investment plan and a set of short-term goals that keep me focused on a daily basis. I usually set my alarm for early in the morning. Looking at my to-do list is the first thing I do. Today the priorities are: (1) finish the recording of certain items by 10 a.m. today; (2) sign-off on mixing directions for three songs with a mixing engineer; (3) confirm my recording schedule with certain musicians who have agreed to play on my next album; and (4) get more information on whether there is an opportunity in the Thai equity market as a result of intensifying political protests. I also notice a distributor meeting. So I "write" a demo CD for them. A magazine interview around 3 p.m. (if they confirm) is another item on the list.

8:00 a.m.   *Revise Arrangement/Prepare for a Recording Session*

To me, musicians and lawyers are alike: you share logical connections between abstract ideas with the world. As a musician or lawyer may tell you, there's a fun part and there's a grind part in extracting such logic. For me, a good example of this in musical works is the arranging process, where all sounds are prioritized based on how the musician would like the audience to perceive his or her logic. As of today, seven songs for the album are "finished" —all the arrangements and recordings were finalized, ready for mixing. Three songs are not finalized, "Endgame" being one of them. So arranging today means that I audition a few keyboard sounds, prepare their tracks at my home studio, record their MIDI signals, and decide which sounds to use. By process of elimination, I arrive at what would be my recording items.

8:45 a.m.   *Record "Punch-Ins" for Various Songs in Home Studio*

Using my recording items as a guide, I punch in several keyboard parts into Pro Tools (software used for music production). Punching in and out in recording means you add to, or improve on, an existing recorded material by recording a short passage at certain areas on the material. When I finish with the keyboards, I "warm" the guitar amplifier by turning it on standby mode for a few minutes. The amp (amplifier) sounds better hot. While waiting, I listen to the guitar solo that I recorded earlier on my cell phone. I practice that solo passage again a couple times and start recording just that passage. As I usually do, I just keep on recording until there's about three takes that I like. Time is one benefit of home studio recording. Today I get them well before 10 a.m. But I decide to keep on going (in case there's a better take). I stop at about 10 a.m., review the takes, and choose the one I like best.

10:20 a.m.   *Check E-Mails/Check the Thai Stock Market/Read Newspaper*

I usually reconnect with the world at around 10 a.m. If I didn't record today, I would have been practicing musical instruments, writing, or arranging my compositions from 7 to 10 a.m. This is so I can have my music life with some room for my other life, which needs to reflect "office hours." So I switch my iPhone out of airplane mode and check missed calls, e-mails, etc. I scan a newspaper and the Internet for news of the ongoing political protest (in Thailand) as well as read various reactions to the protest from government officials and some prominent analysts. I check how the Stock Exchange of Thailand (SET) opens—it looks rather gloomy today. In my e-mail inbox, I also see a request to address an issue related to a lease and service agreement.

10:45 a.m.   *Review a Lease and Service Agreement/Draft a New Section*

After I left my previous job in banking (to pursue my current career in music), a Thai private real estate company retained me as a legal consultant on a monthly basis. Their business includes renting spaces in mostly commercial buildings and some residential buildings. Sometimes I spend the day working exclusively on their legal issues. But today the issue is fairly simple. A lessee asks whether the company could offer a right of first refusal (ROFR) in a lease agreement. I call the company's manager and she explains that the lessee is a foreign company, and that she was not sure what they meant. I discuss the right of first refusal and find out she's already familiar with the concept, if not the terminology. After consulting with her colleagues, she decides they like the lessee enough to add a section reflecting the concept in their standard lease agreement. After discussing the business terms, we agree that by this evening I will e-mail her the draft section and incorporate it into their existing English translation version of the agreement. After reviewing the company's standard lease agreement and my inventories of ROFRs, I start drafting the proposed section.

11:30 a.m.   Walk My Dog/Make Phone Calls

My wife and I also have an agreement of our own—she agrees to walk our dog in the morning and I walk him around noon and in the evening. This became a reliable routine for us since our veterinarian prescribed that our dog—a bull terrier named "T" —needs to get out and do his things as much as possible. As I walk T, I often make phone calls. After chatting with a close friend, I call the sound engineer who agreed to mix my third album. We then confirm our plan to meet this afternoon at a professional studio to go over three songs. After bringing T back home, I board the BTS— Bangkok's sky train service—to attend the distributor meeting.

12:30 p.m.   Meeting with a Potential Distributor

In my view, artists are okay as long as there's a label or distributor willing to return their calls. Although my previous two albums received favorable reviews and won some major awards, I am far from a household name. Thus, I am very grateful to meet with a distributor. I worked with this distributor before on my debut album. On my second album, I signed on a per-album basis with a label, so all costs were covered up front.

Maybe it's just me, but I sensed that the label is not that enthusiastic with my current work. Maybe this is due to disappointing sales from my second album. This is understandable. But it means I have to have a Plan B in case the label "goes silent" on me. So my manager and I meet with a marketing director of the distributor and his assistant. The director says, "We may have a deal with Apple and your downloads may be on iTunes!" At the time, I thought he was being overly positive, but later he actually delivered on this promise.

The focus of this meeting is arriving at the projected sales volume for my third CD that is feasible for us to manufacture and for them to distribute. I thought the meeting would be brief since this is mainly comparing numbers. I was wrong—due to the depressed CD market (in part to mp3 downloads) —the marketing director requests to hear my materials *before* we discuss other things. He said he could only distribute a few artists per month. We hand him the demo CD that I prepared earlier today. Luckily, he likes it. We then compare numbers and agree to touch base again in a couple months when I'm finished mastering the CD.

1:45 p.m.   *Arrive at the Mixing Studio/Audition Mixed Songs with Engineers*

To keep costs low, I do the recording process for my albums "in-house" to my home studio as much as possible. But by this album, I'm better at deciding which instruments and/or process will benefit from professional facilities and which will not. Mixing is one such area: You need a mixing engineer who has access to good studios, knows your style, and has good ears for "the current sounds." The mixing engineer I meet today has worked with me on my previous album and is one of the most respected engineers in the industry.

About two months before we met today, we first discussed his schedule and picked the recording studios together (where we would be working on my next album), and I then contacted the studios, each of which having its own separate payment arrangement with him. This allows us to be more flexible than sticking with one specific studio or one specific set of in-house engineers. Today we meet in a control room at one of the studios and "audition" mixes together. This means I'm taking notes of parts I like or dislike as I'm hearing different versions of a song that he mixed during the past week. The sound engineer who recorded parts of my album also joins us. Afterward we go over my notes, marvel at certain parts, and hatch out our sonic differences.

The engineers are very candid and are not afraid to challenge or introduce me to directions that they think would be more interesting than what I have in mind. We discuss whether the drums have enough reverb, which keyboard tracks should have volume priority over guitars, what are the reasons for certain song to sound "live and urgent," or "fictional and well-produced," etc. We audition two to three mixes of three songs and agree to meet again next week for more definitive versions of these songs as well as to audition two more new songs.

3:10 p.m.   *Go Back Home/Have Lunch/Work on Lease Agreement*

Bangkok traffic being what it is (heavily congested most times), I take the BTS back to my home/office/studio in the midtown area. If I didn't have the two meetings earlier, I would usually have lunch around 1 p.m. But with today's schedule, I'm eating lunch more than two hours later than usual. With bagel and cream cheese on one side—courtesy of my wife before she left for work this morning—I open my laptop and fiddle with the wording of the ROFR section in the lease agreement. It's not long before someone from a local music magazine calls me to confirm the direction to my place—for an interview I agreed to earlier—and he tells me he and his crew will be at my place in about fifteen minutes. I eat the rest of my bagel, clean up my place a little bit, and wait for them to show up.

3:30 p.m.   *Magazine Interview*

As a non-celebrity musician, magazines rarely interview me, unless it's "launching season" (i.e., a couple months after I release something). So today is a surprise. Last week, an editor of a Thai magazine (in the genre of *GQ, Esquire*, etc.) called my label and said the music page editor suggested that I might be a good subject for their upcoming "Double Lives" issue. In that issue, they will profile six people who pursue two or more "seemingly incompatible" careers.

I was grateful and didn't know what to expect, until the crew shows up and the photographer tells me to go change into a suit! He helpfully describes his shot: me in a suit, holding a type of guitar with one hand, and a different type with another. While he's explaining how this shot would reflect both symbols of balance and justice, I express my doubt that anyone would look good in such a shot. But we agree it'd be fun. So in the end we do it.

The interview covers my background as a musician, investor, and lawyer. The interviewer finds out that I have the lowest income expectation for my music career (compared to my investment and lawyer-related work), but am most passionate about it. We also discuss how I manage my investment, and how that my legal career has fueled my music career. We conclude with a discussion of what a "well-balanced" life means to people. I have no idea what that is. And I tell him that much. But I also suggest that many people are like me in that they want to keep looking. For me, it's a mix of three areas now. I guess the negotiation of what one wants to do and what society values can be an ongoing process.

4:40 p.m.   *Check the Markets (again) / Call Stockbroker*

After the magazine crew leaves, I look at my to-do list. I need to do something with the SET: determining whether there's an opportunity to buy stocks cheaply, given the current political situation (i.e., the anti-government protests). Although most of my investments are in the debt market (various bonds, directly or through mutual funds), I have a sum that I often move in and out of the equity market, depending on the opportunity. Thai politics in the past five years often offer disruptive waves to Thai equity growth.

The SET is dominated by foreign and institutional investors, and as such, is highly sensitive to domestic news. This may present an opportunity to buy certain "blue-chip" stocks whose prices are driven down due generally to the global recession, and due particularly to foreign investors' perception of Thai politics (i.e., news about Thailand on their Bloomberg terminals). Currently, a political protest group has threatened to close the Bangkok international airport and the market has been down for several days. Should I bet on the Thai government's ability to deal with protestors and restore confidence to the SET or not? First, I need to know more about the fundamentals of those blue chip companies. I call my stockbroker and she agrees to fax me the latest analyst reports on those stocks.

5:00 p.m.   *Call My Mother / Walk My Dog*

I'm walking with T again, and on the phone with my mother. We discuss how I wish she would move out of our family house—since it's a maintenance burden for her—to a midtown condo that she bought years earlier, which is closer to my place and requires substantially less maintenance. We discuss how she wishes I would stay in a proper job as well as how my father is doing. We see each other every weekend and my mother always cooks a delicious meal. So we agree on what she will cook this upcoming weekend.

6:10 p.m.   *Attend a National Jazz Competition/Confirm Session Dates with Musicians*

My wife had just returned from work when she came to the door and found I was back with T. We trade stories of the day. She reminds me that I need to meet with a group of musicians at a jazz competition very soon from now. I thank her for reminding me and say I'll be back by 8 p.m. With that, I arrive at the competition, about five BTS stops from my place.

It's an outdoor event at a beautiful park, and today is the semi-final round. Backstage, I meet many friends, including a young bassist who played with me on my past albums and concerts. Since he's in the competition this year, we discuss how he plans to perform his numbers. At the judging panel table, I make my rounds with journalists and musicians I know, including the group that may come to my recording session tomorrow. These guys are for real: they are tenured college professors, perform regularly, and often organize events like this with big corporate sponsors to promote music education. Frankly, it's a challenge imagining myself working with them. Maybe they're also a bit curious about me. One of the awards I received is the year's best instrumental recording. Unlike many artists, most of them singers, maybe this award helps my credibility as a musician? So I gather my courage and chirp to them that they have a session date with me tomorrow. We confirm the time to meet and the professional studio that would be best for our recording session (this is not home studio stuff). So far, so good! I watch my friend the bassist perform. Later, we have a beer backstage, while another good friend—a drummer who just finished backing up some musicians in the competition—kindly offers me a lift back home. After I bid farewell to my bassist friend, I help my drummer friend carry his gear back to his car.

7:30 p.m.   *Eat Dinner/Review Reports (sent by equity analysts)*

I arrive back home and look forward to having dinner with my wife. While we have dinner, we page through the analysts reports on the blue-chip stocks that the broker faxed over earlier. I look at the analysts' current takes on target prices, scanning for potentially bad news, changes in dividend policy or material debt undertakings. Compared with similar reports several months earlier on these companies and my previous notes on them, I don't see substantial change. It sure looks like they're solid companies and that their current prices are more a result of general lack of confidence in the SET than anything specific to these firms. My wife discusses these numbers with me extensively—as the CFO of a company, she's much better than I am at looking at balance sheets. We both wonder, however, whether the companies' prices could go much lower given the continuing global recession. And domestically, we are not sure how the government will deal with the ongoing political protests—if the situation is resolved fairly quickly and peacefully, the markets will settle down and then hopefully pick up afterwards—else, there could be more volatility in the horizon. I decide to wait another week before doing anything further about these companies.

8:15 p.m. *Finalize the Proposed Section for the Lease Agreement*

After dinner, I sit down at my desk to review the lease agreement again. This ROFR section is a good example of something that you can spend less time on if you go through it in one sitting! I'm frustrated that I'm still looking at it. By this time, the section is 90 percent there. I compare it with the language of the existing lease agreement and make some minor adjustments (so the section doesn't look out of place with correct cross references to other sections, etc.). After some more tweaking, I e-mail my thoughts and attach the lease agreement with the incorporated ROFR section to the manager of my client.

8:45 p.m. *Discuss Album Cover Concept with Photographer*

One of my best friends is an architect, who also kindly designed every one of my album packagings thus far. We hoped that he could drop by tonight to go over the template for my third album that he had created earlier. But he calls to tell me that he's still in his office. So we decide to postpone our meeting. But we did bounce some ideas with each other.

So after we hang up, I call the photographer who will be responsible for all the pictures in our cover materials. After I relay the ideas to her—the album would be titled "Space Station" about a person locked in a time loop, lonely and confused in vast space—she suggests many interesting locations and promises to scout them next week. This is an example of the pleasant surprises you get when you relate a concept to other people, and they sort of know what you're talking about and help you shape that concept. We agree she will send the scouting photos toward the end of next week.

10:15 p.m.   *Attend a "Reality Party" (sponsored by a mobile phone brand)*

Most of the time, I prefer staying home to going to parties. But tonight the plan to meet my friend the architect was canceled. And a friend who's a prominent producer personally called earlier to summon me to a particular party going on tonight. I promise to drop by if I can, so now I have to go. Besides, parties are good for checking out the music scene, and for networking.

Upon arriving, I realize this one is sponsored by a mobile phone company at a hip joint: a cafe that has a lawn area and a sizeable recording studio inside complete with a control room and fancy studio gear. After negotiating my way through the bustling crowd to the counter, I meet the friend. He gets me a drink and gives me a tour of the place.

The party works like this: one by one, six up-and-coming rock bands are performing live in the studio; the video crew feeds the footage live to the mobile phone online site; engineers in the control room mixes sounds in real time, much like they would do in live concerts (but with fancier studio gear); and with live performances throughout, in which people in the music industry are partying and offering their takes on the performances. After watching some bands, I have this thought: maybe music wasn't meant to be complicated after all. Duh. I mean, these kids play furious music that exudes such palpable energy. Guns N' Roses members were in their early twenties when they released *Appetite for Destruction*, which is good music, right? Then why do I beat myself up so much over intricate arrangements in my music? Well, there surely are different kinds of good music, I guess. After an hour, I head back home.

11:20 p.m.   Go Back Home/ Confirm Mastering Session Details (over e-mail)

I get home and take a shower, in part, to get rid of all the smoke and other odors from the party. After a shower, I check my e-mail inbox. One of the items is from a famous mastering studio in New York. It confirms the availability dates of the mastering engineer that I had worked with on my second album. I'm happy he's available to work with me again. Mastering is the final process in shaping the ultimate sonic character of an album. While I like to participate in the mastering session to learn about sounds, it's a highly technical area and I would rather trust a veteran engineer like him to adjust the knobs.

The e-mail has two attached forms that I need to fill—one for details about the session files and the other a form for New York sales tax purposes. I already prepared these forms in advance based on how we did them last time. So I attach the completed forms and confirm the date with them. I make a note in my to-do list to book the flight to New York early next week. Prior to mastering, I'll have to have completed recording and mixing all the songs for the album. I'll also need to backup the session files into several mediums: laptop, iPod, portable drive, DVD-R, etc. If you get to the mastering session, you are about to cross a finish line. At this point things are progressing along to the point that I'm fairly positive they will gather enough momentum to cross the finish line.

11:40 p.m.   Hop In Bed/ Watch Dorama (Japanese TV show)/Read a Book

After about twenty minutes of e-mail, I look over and notice that my wife is asleep with the TV on. By now, I'm also ready for some passive entertainment. During the years I spent with Lehman Brothers in Tokyo, I became a fan of Japanese television dramas (or "Dorama" as they are called locally). They are well made, and have a uniquely brief quality—the whole show lasts about three months, with each episode airing once a week. Tonight I watch an episode of "Iryu" about a talented surgeon dealing with hospital politics. Afterward I read "The Black Swan" by Nassim Nicholas Taleb. I'm sure I don't understand everything in it. But it seems to tell an engaging story about uncertainty. Like many musicians I know, books and films play very inspiring roles in my life.

2:00 a.m.   In Bed/Can't Sleep (so I get up to play piano)

After about two hours, I turn off the light at my bedside. But like most nights in my life, I find it very difficult to fall asleep for some reason. So I get up and decide to play the piano in the living room.

That's not as bad as it sounds. Although I'm most fluent on guitar, piano is my first instrument. As a kid, I took piano lessons for a couple months. While I may not be a good pianist, I do find the piano relaxing to play—the notes are visually easier to identify than on the guitar, very symmetrically laid out on the instrument. The piano is also practical—no electricity needed, just step on the mute pedal, and you can play at low volume. Although I find mornings to be the best time for practicing and arranging music, I wrote most songs after midnight, at this piano. There's something inspiring about late night and music, I guess.

3:30 a.m.   Finally Sleep (somewhere around this time)

After playing off a stream of consciousness for more than an hour, I ultimately decide, "Well, I guess there's going to be no song to be had for tonight." I feel spent, grab my notepad and go to bed. Maybe the playing has a meditating effect on me. At any rate, I now feel peaceful enough to fall asleep.

5:20 a.m.   Wake-Up to the Sound of the Alarm Clock

It's that time already!?! Not quite, so I reset the alarm for 7:00 a.m., at which time, I will grab my notepad at the bedside table. And when this time arrives, I'll need to do the following for my next twenty-four-hour day: (1) prepare the Pro Tools session file for the external recording studio; (2) finalize the charts containing chord symbols and notes for the musicians; and (3) call them to confirm the session before noon. Okay!

Final Thoughts

Asked if he has a philosophy or some way of looking at life, the jazz musician Pat Metheny said this line sums it up for him: "It is always worth the trouble." I often doubted the "always" part, but came to accept the line as a good attitude. I have two major "troubles": guilt and regret. I need to be responsible to my family financially and I need to be able to express myself musically. This is not a new dilemma for musicians. But the past decade presents a new set of challenges.

The first challenge is how technology affects the "album sales" marketing model. At the beginning of 2000, when Napster was all the rage, the music industry experienced the beginning of a global decline. According to *Billboard* magazine, year-on-year album sales have increasingly dropped from 6.5 percent in 2001 to almost 20 percent in 2009. If you look at the Billboard Top 10 Albums of the Decade (2000-2009), you will find that most albums were released during the first half of that decade. Because of music migrating from a physical medium to digital downloads, giant retailers such as Tower Records and Virgin Megastores were forced to close down many of their major store branches. Thailand followed the same trend. When I released my debut album in 2005, an industry survey revealed Thai artists releasing about 500 titles in album format that year. In 2009, only about 200 in album format were released by Thai artists. While the Internet presented new distribution channels, it also produced new challenges—specifically, too many artists alongside the increasing problems of digital piracy. Technologies like videogames and social networking have also advanced to attract more of our spare time (rather than being spent on music).

The second challenge is more personal. I'm thirty-eight-years old. When I left my full-time job and debuted as a thirty-four-year-old artist in 2005, the teen-pop/*American Idol*-based marketing idea was already the most popular. Thailand has two shows similar to *American Idol*, and they produce about a dozen artists each year. Thai magazines that feature music review sections may dedicate a space for three to five album reviews for Thai artists each month. There are bands with members around my age or older that are still popular, but they started out years earlier than I did. With this, it's reasonable to assume that my chance of making it in the music industry is much smaller. Just to be heard is difficult. This is true even if you broaden a definition of "making it" to include qualities beyond sales like cult status, favorable reviews, media awards, and other types of recognition.

In short, I knew that I would be in for a hard time in the music industry, and I decided to jump in anyway. But I took the jump only after I did some planning on providing a sufficient, even if modest, income stream for my family. Thus, while I am not as passionate about practicing law and investing as I am about producing music, I have to find a lifestyle to combine them to "make it work." In such lifestyle, I may not sell as many albums as other artists, and I may not make as much money as being employed by firms. I may also not have a typical day, and in fact, many days for me are less interesting than the day that you just read about. But this is a lifestyle that I feel lucky to be able to maintain. For this reason, whenever I receive an e-mail complimenting me on the brave choice I made to pursue the music career, I feel like a fraud. I don't know if I was brave, but I do know certain things will happen if I'm not lucky. It could have been much worse. But with luck and some planning, I have found it is "always worth the trouble."

22

Profile 22
Colin: Music Industry Consultant

Executive Summary

Name: Colin
Profile: Music Industry Consultant
Location: Sydney, Australia

A law degree can take you to many places, including the ever-increasing and important market of intellectual property (IP) and patents related to the music industry, which is an area that is more important now than ever before. In Colin's case, his prior experience as an entertainment lawyer in Australia—home to such bands as Men at Work and AC/DC—helped him structure his life so he could work as a music industry intellectual property consultant at home. This gives him more flexibility to teach in colleges and meet with clients to assist them in organizing music-related performances or in business ventures. For those lawyers who have already gained a certain amount of law firm or other related experience, and are planning a possible exit strategy, Colin's flexible schedule is maybe just what some people may be looking for and more. It is not easy to afford the relatively relaxed, balanced schedule while working as a music industry consultant (and being invited to performances!). But, as you will see from his twenty-four-hour schedule, Colin also recommends having enough prior experience before getting out of the industry to do what he does as a music industry consultant.

Profile

Career Field:	Music Industry/Intellectual Property
Current Position:	Consultancy
Institution:	Consultant Abilong Pty Ltd (Galvanising Ideas)
Location:	Sydney, Australia
Previous Position(s):	Media Legal Practice
Education:	LLB, Monash University
Licensed (Y/N):	No

Schedule

6:45 a.m.	Wake-Up to a Mental Alarm Clock
7:00 a.m.	Check Schedule/Begin Walking the Dog
7:15 a.m.	Organize Day of Events
7:30 a.m.	Check E-Mails
7:45 a.m.	What to Wear/Make a Call via Skype
8:20 a.m.	Take Public Transportation to Nearby College
9:00 a.m.	Teach a Music and Law Course
11:00 a.m.	Finish Music and Law Course/Take Train to Next Appointment
11:20 a.m.	Settle Terms of a Co-Venture Deal at a Local Coffee Shop
12:00 p.m.	Meeting to Commercialize a Business Venture Idea
3:15 p.m.	Speak with Event Producer for Upcoming Performance
4:00 p.m.	Lecture on the Law of the Internet
6:00 p.m.	Eat Dinner at a Thai Restaurant
8:00 p.m.	Meet Client/Grab a Beer
9:10 p.m.	Listen to Band Performance
9:45 p.m.	Talk with Band Backstage (after concert)
10:30 p.m.	Arrive Home/Receive Call from Client (re: urgent matter)
12:30 a.m.	Write E-Mails (for various client issues)
1:20 a.m.	Finish E-Mails/Chat with Son over Cups of Tea
2:20 a.m.	Go to Bed
2:21 a.m.	Fall Asleep
6:45 a.m.	Wake-Up

24-Hour Schedule

6:45 a.m.   *Wake-Up to a Mental Alarm Clock*

It's 6:45 a.m. and the alarm goes off. But it's not a physical alarm clock sitting next to my bed—it's the one in my head that's gone off more or less at the same time for years. I'm not one of nature's natural morning people—I much prefer working until late at night—but some things just have to be done, like walk my wonderfully well-preserved twenty-year old Blue Heeler dog (who is, incidentally, the reason I now wake-up automatically at this time instead of 9.30 a.m.).

7:00 a.m.   *Check Schedule/Begin Walking the Dog*

I climb out of bed, lose my balance, and crash against the wall. No harm done. I just shrug it off as an after effect from the night before. I throw on some temporary clothes—the real stuff will go on later once I've read my diary and decide with whom, when, where I am meeting people and, most importantly, why I've meeting the people I'm supposed to meet.

My dog is next to me. I put the leash on him, and walk out the front door for the usual morning ritual of walking my dog.

7:15 a.m.   *Organize Day of Events*

Today is a gorgeous day in Sydney, Australia. It's right next to the beach with the famous Sydney Opera House a stone's throw away. And everyone is so laid back here in the "Land Down Under." Maybe it's the weather. At any rate, it's these quiet peaceful times in the day when I really appreciate what I'm doing and where I'm doing it.

I always find that walking the dog does just as much good for me as my good canine buddy of twenty years. Like other days, this morning my brain is whirring with all sorts of thoughts—what's on, who to call, where to be, what to follow up on. As I'm walking the dog, I check my mobile phone's calendar to get a quick feel for the types of overnight messages that might await me in my e-mail inbox. I use up to four different e-mail accounts to do the various types of business that I do. And all four e-mail addresses can be accessed from my phone. I just can't imagine how work got done before the mobile phone, Internet, and computers. Maybe that's why we're all so jam packed with things to do. But don't get me wrong, I think technology is very helpful. But it comes at the cost of being accessible to work at all hours of the day.

I make notes of things that occur to me as having to be done—whether it's today or sometime in the future.

My role is often to be the air-traffic control for projects I take on—much of my working day is spent reminding people of what they are meant to do and by when they should do it. I need my smartphone, a diary, and a notebook. Each has its place. The trick is to have a definitive list of all the meetings in one place. The others are back-ups and cross-references. There are at least 400 entries in my smartphone's address book: some are people I call regularly, and some are colleagues whose conversation and skills I value and to whom I can refer people when they ask for a recommended supplier of some arcane service or product.

7:30 a.m.   Check E-Mails

I always start my day with coffee—how does anyone get things done without coffee? After two cups, I believe I'm now ready to check the office computer.

I work from home, which I've been doing for the last fifteen years. Working from home suits me just fine. I've acquired enough discipline while in my old law firm practice days to know how to run multiple deals and how to get the nose to the grindstone. For some people, working from home has too many distractions. But for me, it's an ideal way to work long hours and still spend time with the family. The lack of balance was one of the reasons I sold my half of my past practice to become an intellectual property (IP) consultant—not that there was a big name or buzz for it back then—only a handful of people anywhere spoke about intellectual property as if it mattered in those days.

7:45 a.m.   *What to Wear/Make a Call via Skype*

The big order of the moment is what to wear. I'll be teaching a music and law college course today followed by meetings with co-venturers in the afternoon. So nothing too casual. I'd been getting rather relaxed in my clothing as of late. And I suspect it was skewing the way I came across to clients. So now I'm making a conscious effort of appearing more professional and less casual.

I next log onto Skype and lob a phone call to a client in Florida (who is the one person who keeps worse hours than I do). He wants me to do an audit of the royalty fees he should be receiving (i.e., a royalty audit) —this involves taking on two of the world's biggest publishers that appear to have been collecting his royalties for the past fifteen years. So one thing I need to find out is why it's taken him this long to take action. He's a delightful person and I give him a battle plan to get the documents in order as well as an MP3 recording of him talking me through the documents.

8:20 a.m.   *Take Public Transportation to Nearby College*

I catch the bus (Sydney has a wonderful public transportation system, which many people use) into the city to do two hours of teaching at a nearby college. While waiting at the bus stop, I chat to two of the locals who also happen to be waiting at the same bus stop. It's not that I am or am not an excessively friendly person. It's just that, here in Sydney, talking with other people you don't know in this context isn't unheard of—it's part of Sydney's charm.

9:00 a.m.   *Teach a Music and Law Course*

I get off the bus and walk into the college campus grounds. It's quite a different environment with so many young kids with their future dreams and aspirations. It always rejuvenates me. I take a right to the building where I'm lecturing, go up a couple flights of stairs, find my lecture hall, and then bounce into teaching mode. The room is full of eager soon-to-be music business moguls, mixed in with some who seem at the very least, definitely interested in what I may have to say. Today's lecture is about the origins of law. But it ends up as a quick tour of British constitutional history

(Australia is based on British common law) with a dash of Politics 101 with Max Weber and the like making guest appearances by reference.

11:00 a.m.   *Finish Music and Law Course/Take Train to Next Appointment*

After I finish my lecture, I answer a couple questions from students. After a little while, I look at my watch and notice I have to get to a meeting across town with some co-venturers in a new software-based business fairly soon. So I call it a day in terms of lecturing and head back to the bus to then take the train to my next destination. The train-bus journey gives me time to make three calls on my mobile phone while jotting down some notes in my diary. A US lawyer is coming to town next week and wants to meet. Thank the gods for a mobile plan that gives me relatively cheap calls to the United States (again the virtues of modern technology!).

11:20 a.m.   *Settle Terms of a Co-Venture Deal at a Local Coffee Shop*

I'm walking down one of the main roads in Sydney—Darling Street Balmain—and look inside one of my favorite coffee shops in the area. Big surprise—sitting there with a mobile phone literally clamped to his ear is a colleague who I've been trying to catch for the past three weeks—fortune is on my side today! We catch a java and settle the terms of a co-venture deal we have been trying to settle on the past few weeks.

12:00 p.m.   *Meeting to Commercialize a Business Venture Idea*

We part company and I continue my way, dragging my bag-on-wheels behind me. Five minutes and two calls on my mobile phone later, I arrive. The meeting is a team meeting to commercialize a business venture idea a client had a year ago. She spotted a gap in the market for a particular process. But she had no idea how to make it happen. She was recommended to me by someone who had attended a lecture I gave months ago about innovation and patents. At that time, I saw the market potential for her idea. But I was stymied as to how to make it work. I then had lunch a few weeks later with another colleague I'd not seen for about two years. And it turned out, he was consulting a software developer that was "The Answer" to making the client's idea work—I didn't hit upon this epiphany until about a week after meeting the software developer consultant, while walking down the street on my way to an appointment.

Fast forward two months later and I've created a co-venture to create the product, found highly skilled team members (including a marketer and a guy who's built billion dollar ventures), found a funder, found software developers and web-masters, helped write the business plan, and prepared a provisional patent for filing in the United States. The meeting runs for three hours and ends well, though the "elephant in the room" is the issue of each team member's share of the proceeds and how to deal with the proceeds of a sale of the venture.

3:15 p.m.   *Speak with Event Producer for Upcoming Performance*

After the meeting, I'm back on the bus when my mobile phone rings. It's a call from an event producer who does light shows and staging for international acts such as Crusty Demons and Andre Rieu. He's a very funny guy. I then call colleagues in Adelaide (Sydney) regarding a tour we're working on for next February by a major international act. This requires organizing orchestras, a rock band inside a light show, and smoke machines. We're at the planning and budgeting stage right now for the tour. At the same time, funders are in the wings waiting for spreadsheet calculations and estimates of earnings relating to possible returns on investment (ROI). In conjunction, a different team is hard at work getting raw data related to tour costs. Other teams conceptualize the event so we know exactly what expenses are needed to make this event happen.

4:00 p.m.   *Lecture on the Law of the Internet*

Coming up is my second lecture of the day. This time the course title is *The Law of the Internet*. This class is also a two-hour course. The class is attentive and interested with several questions from students along the way. Students may not realize it, but this type of two-way active participation and interest always makes for a better lecture.

6:00 p.m.   *Eat Dinner at a Thai Restaurant*

I step outside the building where my lecture just ended and notice that it's starting to rain quite heavily. By virtue of being located next to the ocean,

Sydney's weather can change quickly and frequently. Today is no exception since just this morning the weather seemed fine and beautiful.

Although it's raining, I promised to see a new band with a client. So since there's some time before the show starts, I look for a bit to eat. I end up finding a fairly good Thai meal—it's a de facto vegetarian dish as the restaurant apparently ran out of chicken for the dish I originally ordered. Oh well, these things happen. While eating, I try to read bits from a text on commercial law to while away the time since Wi-Fi connection isn't available in this eatery. Otherwise, I'd definitely be on my smartphone reading and replying to my e-mail.

8:00 p.m.   *Meet Client/Grab a Beer*

The client with whom I'll be seeing the show arrives. As we chat while we wait for the band to arrive, I also bump into a friend and his wife who also happen to be here to see the same band. We all decide that a beer or coffee is needed before the main band shows up on stage. So we leave the opening act to deafen the punters and go to a nearby renovated hotel, which serves cold beer and so-so coffee. We chat and swap gossip about some mutual friends. They tell me about some of the exploits of some industry colleagues and we feel noble for not being involved with them.

9:10 p.m.   *Listen to Band Performance*

After the drink and talk session, we go back to the venue to watch the main act. After a few minutes, they appear and start to perform. It turns out they are very talented and gave an outright terrific performance. It's a bit hard to explain their sound. But imagine Led Zeppelin fronted by vocals with a fantastic falsetto voice. Overall, they were great musicians.

9:45 p.m.   *Talk with Band Backstage (after concert)*

After the concert, I meet the band out at the back of the venue as they are packing up. I chat with them a bit and give out some encouragement, promising to get to their next gig (I mean to try, but it's two weeks out and anything could happen by then—there's a good chance I will be in Hong Kong with clients sorting out business structures for them in China).

10:30 p.m.   *Arrive Home/Receive Call from Client (re: urgent matter)*

It's 10:30 p.m. and I arrive home. The family is still awake. My client was very nice in giving me a lift home and he and my son start a discussion about management and new breaking bands. Meanwhile the phone rings and it's another client—he wants to talk urgently. An hour later (the other client, by the way, has since left) and he is still talking and making baseless accusations against the whole world including me (though I know it is a tempest in a teapot and will dissipate in a few days). But it means I have to write a couple of e-mails at midnight in order to clear things up.

12:30 a.m.   *Write E-Mails (for various client issues)*

Just as I suspected, it's 12:30 p.m. and I'm at the computer composing an e-mail for the client who called me a couple hours earlier. Writing the e-mails, along with its technical details, takes about half an hour.

1:20 a.m.   *Finish E-Mails/Chat with Son over Cups of Tea*

I finish the e-mails and my son starts his usual commercial interrogation about all the projects (who knows, maybe I have a future entertainment lawyer in the making). He's both interested in them as money-makers and as a learning experience. We chat for an hour over fresh cups of tea. And I explain to him where we are on various deals. Doing this with my son is actually useful for me too—it's a form of review, revision, and consolidation.

2:20 a.m.   *Go to Bed*

I sneak into bed so as not to wake my darling other half. She can't function on the hours I keep. And I suspect neither should I. But this is the life of a consultant in this business.

2:21 a.m.   *Fall Asleep*

Exactly one minute after my head hits the pillow, I am sound asleep. I don't have any dreams, at least as far as I can recall. I just sleep really, really well as usual. It's a knack, really—I could sleep sitting on a rock if I had to. And sleeping on planes is easy for me. I suppose I'm lucky in this sense too.

6:45 a.m.   Wake-Up

My dog is licking my face. It's a sure sign that it's the start of another twenty-four-hour day of this music consultant!

Final Thoughts

The thought processes and skills one acquires while studying and practicing law are universal. Just reading cases is enough to engender caution in most people. A law degree is portable, life-long and frankly, gives you bragging rights at dinner parties. It has a certain cachet regardless of whether one practices or not.

I recommend every graduate at least try working in a small firm. And I recommend always having an exit plan (out of the industry or firm you entered). Law is not a simple profession now. But boutique practices with a small number of loyal clients have a definite place in the world. As a lawyer, you will also often be one of the first to see interesting commercial opportunities.

23

Profile 23
Lizzle: Sports Broadcaster

Executive Summary

Name: Lizzle
Profile: Sports Broadcaster
Location: Los Angeles, California

Is law school student turned sports broadcaster a vast career change? Not in Lizzle's case. For her, it all came naturally. It isn't hard to see law school graduates in the field of broadcasting, journalism, or media these days. The reason is because lawyers also have to be good writers. Lizzle took another step along the career and became a broadcaster. After working as a business litigator in entertainment law and partly working as a journalist for a magazine, she now works for the same magazine as a broadcaster reporting on the USC Trojans college football games for the local area (having graduated from USC herself). To a sports fan, Lizzle's job might seem more like play than work. She gets to watch sports games all day and celebrate after winning the game with other fans. A slightly inconvenient factor would be that she can't relax on weekends. Instead, she has free time during weekdays when other people are normally busy working. Lizzle makes it clear that she would never want to switch her working hours with anyone else's, as you will see from her twenty-four-hour career profile.

Profile

Career Field:	Sports Broadcast Media
Current Position:	On-Camera Sideline Reporter
Institution:	ESPN Affiliate WeAreSC
Location:	Los Angeles, California
Previous Position(s):	Business Litigator
Education:	JD, University of Southern California
	BA, University of Southern California
Licensed (Y/N):	Yes
Jurisdictions:	California

Schedule

8:00 a.m.	Alarm Clock Rings
8:30 a.m.	Wake-Up/Shower / Pick Outfit for Day
8:45 a.m.	Read *San Francisco Chronicle* and Other Online Sports Media News
9:15 a.m.	Turn on TV/Channel Surf (ESPN, Fox Sports, NFL Network)
10:30 a.m.	Change into Clothes for Day/Do Hair and Makeup
11:30 a.m.	Head to BART Station to Go to Berkeley
1:00 p.m.	Arrive at Berkeley
1:35 p.m.	Meet Up with Law School Friend
2:15 p.m.	Head to Meet Publisher
3:10 p.m.	Meet with Publisher
3:30 p.m.	Go to Memorial Stadium
4:15 p.m.	Arrive at Memorial Stadium
4:30 p.m.	Check out Press Box and Pre-Game Events
5:00 p.m.	Game Kick-Off
5:45 p.m.	Review First Quarter Stats in Press Box
6:35 p.m.	Halftime at Press Box
7:30 p.m.	Review Third Quarter Stats in Press Box
8:15 p.m.	Return to Field/Prepare Post-Game Questions
9:05 p.m.	Postgame Interviews
10:45 p.m.	Join Colleagues for Drinks at Local Popular Pizza Parlor
1:15 a.m.	Catch a Taxi Back to Hotel/Check E-mails/Go to Sleep
8:00 a.m.	Alarm Clock Rings

24-Hour Schedule

8:00 a.m.   *Alarm Clock Rings*

The alarm on my cell phone goes off. I prefer to use my cell phone alarm for familiarity, rather than figuring out a different alarm clock each hotel I go to. During the college football season, I can travel a decent amount, depending on where the USC (University of Southern California) football team is playing. The sports magazine I work for, WeAreSC.com, provides localized coverage of the USC Trojans for ESPN.com. This includes print articles, audio podcasts, and video features, including post-game interviews. In the past, on-camera reporters would often have to go to a news station in the middle of nowhere to get experience in front of the camera. But the growth of the Internet has affected the media industry. As a result, sports media sites like WeAreSC.com, among others, are popping up allowing for increased opportunities in the much-desired Los Angeles area (which is market level two, second only to New York City).

8:30 a.m.   *Wake-Up/Shower/Pick Outfit for Day*

After hitting the snooze button a few times, I finally get up at 8:30 a.m. It's a Saturday in October. And while most people would be sleeping in right now, after perhaps a late night out, today is a workday for me. Around early January, after the college football season ends, I should have my Friday nights back. I quickly check my e-mails before jumping in the shower.

8:45 a.m.   *Read San Francisco Chronicle and Other Online Sports Media News*

I have a full day ahead of me, so it's time to do the "research" for the game. This means scouring the sports pages of *The Los Angeles Times, San Francisco Chronicle*, ESPN.com and Foxsports.com, to see what people are saying about the game. Cal's (aka, U.C. Berkeley's) coach, Jeff Tedford, is seen as one of the coaches who can hang with Pete Carroll. Every year the media seems to be doing something to build up the game. This year, the Trojans are 4-1 (four wins to one loss) heading into the game, coming off a decisive victory at the Coliseum against the Washington State Cougars. They were most likely taking revenge after suffering their first loss to the Washington

Huskies the week before. The Huskies were at the bottom of the Pac-10 Conference just last year, but have filled their coaching staff up with former USC staffers Steve Sarkisian, Nick Holt, Dennis Slutak, Jared Blank, and Ivan Lewis. I'm glad they seem to be turning the program around.

9:15 a.m.   *Turn on TV / Channel Surf (ESPN, Fox Sports, NFL Network)*

Having read what the beat writers have to say, it's time to turn on the tube and see what the main stories are. Not surprisingly, everyone is talking about the injury suffered by Stafon Johnson in what has been described as a "freak accident" while weight lifting, earlier in the week. The star tailback was rushed to the hospital and had to undergo an emergency tracheotomy. I remember Johnson was the only athlete who showed up at a fundraising event a couple of years back. He's a real good kid, and I hope he will be able to heal 100 percent. I can't even imagine what he must be going through. I also wonder how the Trojan offense will adjust, since they do have a stable of running backs to turn to.

10:30 a.m.   *Change into Clothes for Day / Do Hair and Makeup*

Time to change for the day. First I have to curl my hair. I have naturally straight hair, so I like to curl it to give it a little body for the camera. Then it's time to apply makeup. I normally like to wear very little makeup, mostly natural looking. But again, on camera, makeup needs to be stronger. So I have to dab on some extra blush powder. Finally, time for the outfit. It's much cooler up here in Berkeley (located in the San Francisco Bay Area) than it is in sunny Southern California. Jeans, boots, and a jacket it is. And by boots, I mean wedge boots. This is because shoes with the traditional heel (as opposed to the continuous wedge) can get caught in the field, which is never a good thing.

11:30 a.m.   *Head to BART Station to Go to Berkeley*

The one thing that I envy about the San Francisco/Berkeley area is its public train system, known as BART (Bay Area Rapid Transit). It's too bad Los Angeles is so spread out that it can't do subways or trains as they do out here. I just realized that I haven't had anything to eat or drink yet. Luckily, Starbucks is everywhere. While I would normally get an iced chai latte around this time, it's fairly chilly here. So I opt for a hot chocolate instead. At the BART station, the waiting area is packed, mostly with people wearing blue and yellow Cal jerseys. But there are a good number of people in the cardinal and gold USC colors. It takes a while to get into a train because of the lines. Thank goodness I was able to maneuver my way into a seat!

1:00 p.m.   *Arrive at Berkeley*

Ahhh, the college football atmosphere, something I don't think I could ever tire of. It's hard to not get into the sport, having spent both my undergraduate and law school years at USC. It's a nice college town in Berkeley though.

1:35 p.m.   *Meet Up with Law School Friend*

I meet up with Ray, a friend of mine from law school. Ray is originally from up north (Northern California). After law school, he moved back home and is now doing tax law work in the area. He is decked out in USC gear. If I wasn't working, I'd be wearing a USC shirt as well. It's called "media neutral," and the policy is that if you are a member of the media, you want to avoid wearing the colors of either of the teams that is playing. It makes sense. At any rate, Ray is very chipper and excited to see the game. To him, it's weekend fun. To me, it's weekend work. But I still wouldn't trade schedules. We end up grabbing a quick bite to eat at a popular local hot dog stand recommended by media personality Petros Papadakis, who actually played football for both the Cal Bears and USC Trojans.

2:15 p.m.   *Head to Meet Publisher*

With nourishment now out of the way, I start heading toward the USC pep rally where I will meet up with the boss, Garry Paskwietz, the publisher of WeAreSC. Berkeley is a pretty decent-sized college town. On my way to the pep rally, I run into various people I know from college and law school, as well as subscribers of WeAreSC. The buzz is all the same, with people asking if there is any more word on Stafon Johnson and his health condition.

3:10 p.m.   *Meet with Publisher*

A few songs into the pep rally, Garry (WeAreSC's publisher) shows up. I meet with him briefly to talk about how we're going to cover the game. In between, lots of people come up to ask us questions. There's always lots of hand shaking whenever Garry is around. It's hard not to know Garry if you are a USC fan. Garry took what was once a small website that covered USC football, and turned it into one of the largest and most highest trafficked website on the Internet devoted to USC athletics. His site got so much traffic that ESPN took notice and took WeAreSC in as one of its affiliates. I'm just happy that I got involved with WeAreSC when I did. I used to just write articles for the magazine, years ago in my spare time while I litigated entertainment and fashion apparel cases involving breach of contract and intellectual property disputes. When WeAreSC became affiliated with ESPN, they needed increased content. So my role increased, including me ultimately doing on-camera sideline reporting at the games.

3:30 p.m.   *Go to Memorial Stadium*

One and a half hours before game time, it's time to head in. Lots of uphill walking to the stadium. It'll be good exercise for the standing and walking I'll be doing for pretty much most of the game. Heading closer to the stadium, I pass by a row of fraternity and sorority houses. I've heard that this walk to the stadium can be pretty daunting if you are wearing an opposing team's colors (fortunately, I'm still in media neutral mode). From what I can tell so far, when I see USC fans walk by, the Cal fans seem pretty tame. The closer I get to the stadium, the slower the line is. It's a little harder to access the media entrance at Cal's Memorial Stadium than it is at the Coliseum (where USC plays its games).

4:15 p.m.   *Arrive at Memorial Stadium*

I finally get to the media check in. I get my media pass and head into the stadium. As I walk in, I feel a sudden chill and realize I left my jacket in Ray's book bag. I quickly text him to find out where he is so I can meet up with him. Luckily, he is already in the stadium watching pre-game workouts.

4:30 p.m.   *Check out Press Box and Pre-Game Events*

Before I get my jacket, I head up to the press box. While I will spend a majority of the game on the sidelines, because I like to be right near the action, it is always good to know what media members are around. The press box also has the food and drink, which is also very important. I notice they are serving soup as well, which is different from the traditional hot dogs and popcorn (the standard concession items at the Coliseum press box). I walk down the row of media, say "Hello" to the WeAreSC beat writer, Greg Katz, as well as the other familiar media that cover USC. The press box is outdoors. I was hoping it would be indoors so I could take shelter there if the weather got too cold to handle. Oh well.

5:00 p.m.   *Game Kick-Off*

The game kicks off while I am still up in the Press Box. I usually like to wait a few minutes after kickoff before I head to the field. Usually guests and VIPs of both schools are allowed on the field up until a few minutes after the game starts. This can often create a very crowded sideline. I wait for them to be cleared into the stands, and then I head over to where Ray is seated to get my jacket. One of his friends offers to trade my sideline pass for his ticket. After a few more minutes chatting, it's time to get to the field.

The first drive of Cal ends with an interception by USC's Taylor Mays. I pull out my notepad and jot down the interception and quarter. This will serve as a good reference of the post-game interviews later. It's interesting how much louder the USC band is than Cal's band, although I think a lot of it has to do with where the USC band is located in the stadium. USC scores a touchdown in its first possession, with Joe McKnight running the ball in for a touchdown.

5:45 p.m.   *Review First Quarter Stats in Press Box*

I head up to the press box to get the printout of the first quarter stats. It's always good to get that sheet because it details how many yards each player gained and does the play by play. USC's quarterback Matt Barkley has had a decent first quarter. Damian Williams returned a punt 66 yards for a touchdown. Not bad for the Arkansas transfer. I always try to keep information like this in the back of my head, because it is always good to throw information like this into interviews, to make them more personal. The first quarter ends with the score 17-0, USC ahead.

6:35 p.m.   *Halftime at Press Box*

I spend a lot of the second quarter on the field. The second quarter is when I usually do a complete lap of the field. I usually like to stand on the visitor's side of the field, or right at the end zone, at the games. These areas are usually less crowded and give a better view of the game. Because USC is the visiting team, I spend most of the quarter on their side of the field. The second quarter was pretty boring, activity-wise. USC added a field goal toward the end of the quarter. The score is now 20-0, and you can hear angry Cal fans asking when their team is going to score. I head up to the press box since the field gets pretty empty during halftime. It is freezing now, at least by Southern California standards. Time to get some soup. I also meet up with Garry and Greg to get their perspectives on how the game is going so far. Both are loyal USC fans, so they are pretty happy with the 20-0 score.

7:30 p.m.   *Review Third Quarter Stats in Press Box*

The third quarter is also pretty uneventful. The Trojans got another field goal to start the quarter off, but then produced nothing else the remainder of the quarter. That is still more than Cal produced. USC kicker Jordan Congdon has been having a good evening. The score is 23-0 now, with USC still on top, at the end the third quarter. Everyone is beginning to wonder if the Trojans are going to shut out the Bears on their own home field.

8:15 p.m.   *Return to Field/Prepare Post-Game Questions*

After getting the third quarter stats at the press box, I head back to the field to start working on the post game questions and begin figuring out who I'd like to interview. It's usually a mad rush to get to the athletes, as all of the members of the media will be rushing to them. I meet with Garry to find out what he wants to do. It is freezing at this point, and we both decide on two quick interviews—one player from the offense and one from the defense should do it—whomever we can grab on the field. A few minutes into the fourth quarter, Cal scores a field goal. Scratch out that earlier question related to a shutout. The Cal band plays a very familiar fight song to celebrate the field goal. They have the same fight song as UCLA (not surprising given they are both from the same UC system). I talk to other sideline reporters to ask them who they want to get so we don't all run to interview the same athletes. The game ends with the score 30-3, USC on top.

9:05 p.m.   *Post-game Interviews*

After the game ends, the football team, as is its custom, huddles up in front of the Trojan marching band, celebrating the victory in front of the band and the USC contingent at the game. This is a good time to grab the athletes for an interview, before the run into the locker room. If they get into the locker room, the media has to wait a while for the coaches to do their post-game team speeches (which is done without the media). Drew McAllister is standing around and available. So I run to him and get the interview, asking him how it felt to play in front of his family, and to have a great game on defense, holding the Bears to just one field goal. After that, I see that running back Allen Bradford is free. Allen had a solid game against the Bears. In my interview with him, he discusses how inspired his play was by fellow running back Stafon Johnson. After those two back-to-back interviews, we are done with post-game videos, and my work here is over for the evening.

10:45 p.m.   *Join Colleagues for Drinks at Local Popular Pizza Parlor*

I head over to the very popular Zachary's pizza parlor to join some friends who are in the area for some food and drinks. It is a mix of both Cal and USC fans. While it is great to catch up with old friends, I am not able to stay out for too long, since by this time, I am flat-out exhausted from the day's events.

1:15 a.m.   *Catch a Taxi back to Hotel/Check E-Mails/Go to Sleep*

After spending time with my friends, it is time to head back to my hotel. Game days, especially when you have to work them, can be pretty exhausting. I get back to my hotel, wash up, and change into my pajamas. After a quick check of my e-mails, it's off to sleep.

8:00 a.m.   *Alarm Clock Rings*

My cell phone alarm goes off. Arghh! I forgot to turn it off from yesterday. Now it's *my* turn to sleep in!

Final Thoughts

I never imagined while I was in law school that I would one day get paid to cover my favorite sports team. They say law school doesn't teach you much about what it's like to be a practicing lawyer. Well, it teaches even less about being a sports reporter. But I will say that I feel like a better reporter having gone through law school and practiced law. I've never been nervous interviewing high profile athletes when I've already had the experience of arguing before much more intimidating judges. I thoroughly enjoy what I am doing. I am a huge college football fan and a big USC fan. For me, covering USC sports is a dream come true.

24

Profile 24
Chris: Politician

Executive Summary

Name: Chris
Profile: Politician
Location: Denton, Texas

Chris decided to obtain his law degree much later than most people do. Even after building a stable real estate business for fifteen years before his JD degree, Chris now fully appreciates his law degree even more and considers it a huge asset as a politician, specifically an elected public official. In addition to aiding him in many decision-making processes, reviewing legal strategies, and developing city policy, his law degree has also given him a boost of intellectual confidence and training to discover his hidden skills. After seeing Chris in action—as he constantly takes advantage of his law degree to be more productive and weighs the pros and cons when making the right judgments when deciding how best to help the people in his city—we can see why many politicians come from legal backgrounds. No doubt, Chris is more than satisfied with his life at present, as you will see throughout his twenty-four-hour day as a locally elected politician.

Profile

Career Field:	Politician (as well as Real Estate Development/Solo Practitioner)
Current Position:	Elected Public Official (as well as Real Estate Broker/Investor/Developer)
Location:	Denton, Texas
Education:	JD, Texas Wesleyan University, School of Law
	MEd, University of North Texas;
	BS, University of North Texas
Licensed (Y/N):	Yes
Jurisdiction:	Texas

Schedule

6:00 a.m.	Wake-Up/Meditation/Prayer
6:15 a.m.	Feed the Sheep
6:35 a.m.	Shower/Dress for the Day
7:15 a.m.	Drop off Kids/Head to Office
8:15 a.m.	Breakfast/Arrival at Office
9:00 a.m.	Pay the Bills/Miscellaneous Paperwork
10:30 a.m.	Errands/Inspections of Property
12:00 p.m.	Lunch
1:00 p.m.	Negotiate Mineral Lease for Family
2:30 p.m.	Final Review of Back-Up Material (re: upcoming City Council meeting)
3:30 p.m.	Meet with Appropriate City Staff (re: briefing prior to meeting)
4:00 p.m.	Council Work Session
5:00 p.m.	Council Executive Session (Closed Meeting)
6:30 p.m.	Council Meeting
9:00 p.m.	Head Home
9:30 p.m.	Feed Sheep/Unwind
10:30 p.m.	Go to Bed
6:00 a.m.	Wake-Up

24-Hour Schedule

6:00 a.m.   *Wake-Up/Meditation/Prayer*

I never use an alarm clock unless I need to get up for a red-eye flight. For some reason, I just wake up. I got married about six months ago and must admit it was easier getting out of bed when I was single because now I so enjoy being with my wife! I lay in bed for a few minutes reflecting on the events of yesterday, praying for my wife, family, and the day ahead. Usually on mornings like this following a city council meeting, I (as a city council member of the city of Denton, Texas) will go over the information presented and the reasoning for my vote. In doing this, my legal training has been a great tool in assisting me when analyzing the issues and facts before deliberating on issues presented to the city council.

6:15 a.m.   *Feed the Sheep*

Now it's time to feed my sheep. Yes, you read it correctly. Having four step-children who are heavily involved in 4-H and FFA (agriculture-related extracurricular activities), I volunteer to feed the sheep that they take care of—once in the morning as well as in the afternoon. The children compete at livestock shows with their sheep for an opportunity to "make the sale." If the animal makes the sale, it is then auctioned off with the proceeds going to the participants. I experienced my first livestock show at the age of forty-eight—never too late for new experiences!

I crawl out of bed, put on my clothes, strap on some rubber boots, and head to the barn. Make no mistake about it, in doing this, boots are imperative since, to be honest, it gets a little messy in the pens. In the winter, I have to bundle up with a warm winter jacket, gloves, and cap to ward of the frigid Texas winter. Once I get to the barn, the sheep are up and waiting to be fed. While I'm preparing each bucket of feed, the sheep are hurling themselves at the door of each pen to let me know they are starving hungry. It almost sounds like an army of men beating the walls down with sledge hammers—pretty deafening and annoying at this early hour of the morning. While my legal training prepared for many of the decision-making processes needed when I wear my city council hat, it in no way prepared this city boy for the country way of life. Each stall contains two sheep, since during feeding they must be separated so one will not eat the food of the other. This gives me a few minutes to reflect on my schedule for the day: property to show, plans to review, calls to constituent calls, and e-mails to return.

6:35 a.m.   *Shower/Dress for the Day*

Arriving back from the barn, I head to the shower. You can't begin to imagine how the sheer stench of sheep permeates the air and will cling to anything it can find—hair, clothes, shoes, socks and anything else I may be wearing. I have a special place for my coats, gloves, and hat because they seem to attract more of the animal scent than anything else does, oh, except my hair, which my wife promptly points out before attempting our morning wake-up kiss.

Once showered, it's time to choose what to wear. I'm not a suit-wearing kind of guy. Frankly, I only dress up when needed. Jeans and a polo shirt are just fine with me. Walking past my wife once dressed usually solicits a "Hey, didn't you wear that the other day?" type of response (you see, my wife is a beautiful woman who always looks together even when she is not!). Once dressed, I now watch the news to catch up on any late night events or read my e-mails until it's time to take the kids to school at 7:15 a.m.

7:15 a.m.   *Drop off Kids/Head to Office*

I take the kids to school and head to the office. The drive time is spent with the radio morning DJs: George, Craig, and Gordon, 1310 the Ticket, an AM sports radio station in Dallas, Texas. It's my own little private moment to listen to zany moments, sports, and other unrelated antics, as reported by the radio morning show crew. Oftentimes, this is the favorite part of my day because I really don't have to think about anything work-related—I'm just enjoying and having fun.

8:15 a.m.   *Breakfast/Arrival at Office*

I grab a quick bite to eat at the local *Braums Ice Cream Store*. I order my usual of hotcakes with bacon and a strawberry shake. No wonder I have difficulty losing those last ten pounds!

I then arrive at the office. Once there, I pick up the mail and/or rent checks that were placed through the mail slot from the day before. I take a few minutes to sort the mail to determine what, if anything, needs immediate attention. I place the bills and invoices in the "bill basket" —a little straw basket that sits on the credenza behind my desk. I guess if the bills aren't scattered all over the place, it somehow seems there's less of them. I think there's a word for this, and it's called "denial." Having sorted the bills, I check my e-mails for any new developments or information. I usually have several e-mails from constituents and city staff that need attention. I also spend a few minutes reading online news sources for current financial and political stories. Then I meet with my maintenance man to discuss upcoming projects and service requests knowing, from my experience in the property business, that a maintenance emergency can occur at anytime.

9:00 a.m.   Pay the Bills/Miscellaneous Paperwork

I sort through invoices and pay some bills. This is where I decrease the pile in the bill basket. I love to see the stack decrease, but hate to see the balance decrease in the checkbook. I balance my checkbook after each entry. What a revelation it was to me after I got married that there are some out there that never balance their checkbook—wow! Having seven business accounts, I couldn't imagine having to juggle all those balances and outstanding checks in my head. And in terms of paying bills, if it's around the first of the month, much of the time is spent preparing deposits and mortgage payments for my real estate portfolio.

10:30 a.m.   Errands/Inspections of Property

I leave the office to run my daily errands to the banks and post office. To save time, I return phone calls while on the road. Cellular technology has certainly increased my efficiency. I also check on any various real estate projects in progress at the time by making "readies" (getting a rental unit ready for occupancy), remodeling, or new construction projects.

I try to meet with various city staff once or twice a week regarding agenda items for future city council meetings. The meetings are very productive. It allows me time to gather critical information necessary to make an informed choice. I'm pleased to say we have great city staff since they're committed to improving the quality of life for our community. That doesn't mean everyone agrees all the time, but we have the same goal. My legal training has proven critical on several occasions when negotiating contracts, reviewing planning and zoning requests, and developing city policy.

12:00 p.m.   *Lunch*

It's high noon, so I grab a quick bite for lunch. On some days, I choose to workout, but not today. I also always enjoy meeting my wife and friends for lunch when possible. It provides a nice break in the course of the workday to catch up on more important matters. If the workload is unusually heavy, I'll use this time to inspect current real estate projects.

1:00 p.m.   *Negotiate Mineral Lease for Family*

After lunch, I review several mineral lease proposals for family members. We've been involved in bankruptcy litigation for more than two years regarding a defunct oil/gas operator who leased our mineral interest in acreage outside of town. Thankfully, we were able settle the case, thereby terminating the mineral lease allowing us to pursue a new lease agreement with a more reputable operator. My legal training has been paramount in dealing with this particular issue since it allows me to provide my extended family members with important information and negotiation strategies. Many people often have forewarned me that giving family member's advice and direction on such complicated legal issues can be perilous. I agree. That's why before executing any other lease agreement; I'll engage the services of an oil and gas attorney for final approval. We all know the saying, "He who represents himself has a fool for a client!"

I then meet with new and existing tenants for execution of new leases and/or renewals. No lease signing is the same. I'll typically perform a criminal background check while the prospective residents are in the office. I usually tell them that I'm going to run such a check in order to give them a chance to come clean before running the report. It's just amazing to me how many people will tell me they're absolutely sure nothing will show up on the criminal background check, only to be surprised when I print the report and begin to inquire about the some of the more questionable entries printed in it.

2:30 p.m.   *Final Review of Back-Up Material (re: upcoming city council meeting)*

It's time to review the back-up material for the upcoming city council meeting scheduled at 4:00 p.m. today. Tonight we're scheduled to consider a re-zoning request for a new master planned community. The request has encountered strong opposition from the retirement community adjacent to the development because of the density of housing, commercial uses, and inadequate infrastructure to support the project. Upon review of the documents, I discover that the applicant had failed to provide the necessary information pertaining to the requirements for new infrastructure, and who and how such improvements would be funded. The developer was hoping to receive approval tonight because it has taken many months to finalize the application prior to submission to the council. I suspect that they certainly won't be happy about this.

I return as many phone calls as possible during this time because I'll be unavailable for about four to six hours due to the city council work session and regular meeting I'll be attending later today. Most of the calls are from students at the local university wanting to secure housing for the upcoming fall semester. It gets a little crazy in the summer because you have so many tenants moving out that you must get turned around as quickly as possible in order to lease out again for the new school year. If I have vacancies once the semester starts at the university, the units usually stay vacant for the entire semester. So it's imperative to fill up as many units as possible *before* (not after) the first day school's in session.

3:30 p.m.   *Meet with Appropriate City Staff (re: briefing prior to meeting)*

I now arrive at city hall. City council meetings begin with a work session beginning at 4:00 p.m. or earlier, if needed. The work session allows city council members to request clarification of agenda items for the regular session. Additionally, the work session provides an opportunity for city staff to brief the city council and request direction and clarity on various policy issues affecting city governance. During this particular day, I meet with the city attorney and assistant city manager (ACM) of planning to discuss possible options due to the incomplete application for the upcoming zoning request of the master planned community. As I described the situation to the city attorney and assistant city manager, I could tell they were not looking forward to informing the developer of this development. The city staff knew the developer would be upset because of the time it took simply to get the zoning request to the city council for a vote. As a way to help smooth the situation, I suggest we give the developer a heads-up notice that we will not be able to decide the ordinance on this particular meeting later this evening due to an incomplete application. Although we all hoped for a better outcome, we simply had no choice on this one, mostly since we at the council simply didn't have the information necessary to pass the ordinance.

4:00 p.m.   *Council Work Session*

The city council work session begins. During the meeting, I spend about twenty minutes requesting clarification on several agenda items. I ask for certain consent agenda items to be pulled for individual consideration (consent agenda items are those items that are administrative in nature and can be voted upon as a group instead of individually). As reference, a council member may pull a consent agenda item to be considered individually thereby requiring a separate vote on the specific issue.

During the meeting, a member of the city staff reported they had informed the developer of the zoning request of the incomplete application. I'll never forget that conversation. The ACM approached me during a break and said they talked to the developer about the omitted information. All of the city staff expected the developer to be belligerent, hostile, and angry because of the time delay. But much to our surprise, the ACM stated (with a big grin of success and surprise) that the developer was willing to do almost anything to get the request passed tonight. I looked at the ACM and said confidently, "Fred, I knew they would come around. The only reason this has not happened before is because we were unwilling to say 'no' for fear of losing a project or public backlash. However, the position we are taking now is the right one and in the best interest of the city. Let us use this as an example going forward that we do not always have to accept less than what we reasonably require." The work session ended with the city council going into executive session (which occurs in a closed meeting format).

5:00 p.m.   *Council Executive Session (Closed Meeting)*

Having completed the public work session, the council has now adjourned into a closed meeting on any item on its open meeting agenda consistent with the Texas Government Code. Being a closed session, I am not at liberty to discuss specific items. But what I can say is that my legal training has been beneficial when suggesting specific negotiation and legal strategies regarding various issues before the Denton city council. Admittedly, I speak with greater emotion and candor during closed sessions since public dialogue deserves greater restrain and decorum given the open door nature of the occasion.

6:30 p.m.   *Council Meeting*

My attention is next geared toward attending a regular (non-closed) city council meeting. We begin with the pledge of allegiance to both the United States and Texas flag. We then consider each item as they are listed on the agenda. On this particular evening, we're slated to vote on the re-zoning request of the master planned community as discussed above. A large group of residents, numbering around 150 to 200, has assembled to oppose the re-zoning request. The public is allowed to address the council for agenda items listed as public hearings or items for individual consideration. The re-zoning request requires a public hearing pursuant to state law. Approximately seventy-five people had turned in cards requesting to speak during the public hearing. If they all take the four minutes allotted to each speaker, it's going to be a long night. Once the agenda item has been called, the city staff will usually then give a presentation on the merits of the request followed by a recommendation to the council.

Having completed the presentation, I called the staff member's attention to the particular section of the ordinance that was in question. I asked him if the developer had supplied the information prescribed by the ordinance. He replied they had not. I then read aloud the section of the ordinance that stated the council shall "find" that the developer has *not* provided the necessary information in question. I simply stated that since we do not have this needed information before us, we are unable to pass the ordinance. You could hear a collective gasp emanate from the gallery since this effectively meant that either the request would be delayed or denied outright—neither of which was an expected outcome from tonight's session.

During the public hearing, the applicant requesting the zoning change (the developer) is allowed to address the council. The developer asked the council to table the item in order to allow sufficient time to prepare the information required by the ordinance. Fortunately for me, the attendants seemed satisfied and pleased that the council had been thorough in its analysis and deliberation of the zoning request—after all, we are here for the people, and this is who we aim to serve as city council members.

After this, the meeting was adjourned earlier than anticipated because the public hearing on the zoning request did not last as long as anticipated. This also meant that the fifty to seventy opponents who signed up to speak against the re-zoning would wait another day (until the issue was presented to council with the completed application).

9:00 p.m.   *Head Home*

It's finally time to wrap up the evening and head home. I use this time to return the many phone calls that had accumulated during tonight's city council work session and meeting. I noticed that a couple of the calls were from prospective residents inquiring on various apartments I have available for lease. That's good news to me! I then call the wife to see if I need to pick up anything on the way home. This leads me to stop off at *Braums Ice Cream* (one more time) as well as the local dairy store to pick up milk and a little something to satisfy my sweet tooth: frozen yogurt with strawberries and bananas.

9:30 p.m.   *Feed Sheep/Unwind*

I arrive home, feed the sheep, and change clothes to get comfortable. If I had my choice, I'd wear jeans and a nice shirt to the council meeting—if I could get away with it—but the reality so far is that I haven't been quite brave enough to try.

I use this time to catch up with my wife to see how her day went. It's so nice to come home to her after a long, exhausting day. Along with this, I watch the local TV news to unwind before going to bed.

10:30 p.m.   *Go to Bed*

I take a shower and get in bed. I pray and meditate, thanking God for the day and the blessings of life while looking forward to the challenges and opportunities of a new day.

6:00 a.m.   *Wake-Up*

Amazing how time flies—looks like, according to the clock, it's time to feed the sheep and start the day anew again!

Final Thoughts

Having attended law school in my late thirties, my JD degree and law school experience changed my life in a dramatic way. I'd always wanted to be a lawyer since I was an idealist you might say—justice for all, good triumphs over evil, etc. You know the type.

I graduated from college and spent fifteen years building my real estate business and obtaining my graduate degree. Yet the dream of law school never faded. But for some reason, I began to doubt my ability to be accepted and successfully complete my law degree. Honestly, I just questioned whether I was smart enough or not.

One day a friend of mine informed me he was going to law school in Lubbock, Texas. It inspired me to reconsider my dream. So not long after, I invited a trusted friend of mine to breakfast one morning. And at the age of thirty-seven, I told him I was going to apply to law school! That began a personal journey that continues to this day. Honestly, I went to law school simply to prove to myself that I could do it. In the process, it changed me in the sense that it made me realize that I had inherent skills that—with the right training and education—could be used to help others.

My legal education and experience as a practicing lawyer has been an invaluable asset in my real estate business, community service, and as an elected official. My dream was to help people who have a voice or have no voice. That is what I do now. Whether it be in the courtroom, leasing office, or council chambers, my JD degree has allowed me to give back to my community in ways I could have never have imagined without it.

ABOUT THE AUTHOR

Jasper Kim has worked in various traditional and non-traditional careers—as a lawyer, banker, consultant, author, columnist, and academic—since graduating from law school. He is department chair and associate professor at Ewha Womans University, where he was director of the university's Global Career Management Center, and is adjunct faculty at Pepperdine University's School of Law. He was previously a lawyer and investment banker with Lehman Brothers and Barclays Capital, and is now a frequent contributor to *The Wall Street Journal*, CNBC TV, BBC TV and Bloomberg TV. He has been selected as a 2011 Visiting Scholar at Harvard University. His recent books include, *Korean Business Law: The Legal Landscape and Beyond* (Carolina Academic Press, 2010) and *mini Messaging: The Art of Smart Texting* (Ewha Womans University Press, 2010).